Measurement and Evaluation of Musical Experiences

Measurement and Evaluation of Musical Experiences

J. DAVID BOYLE
UNIVERSITY OF MIAMI
CORAL GABLES, FL

RUDOLF E. RADOCY
UNIVERSITY OF KANSAS
LAWRENCE, KS

SCHIRMER BOOKS
A Division of Macmillan, Inc.
NEW YORK

Collier Macmillan Publishers
LONDON

Copyright © 1987 by Schirmer Books
A Division of Macmillan, Inc.

Schirmer Books
A Division of Macmillan, Inc.
866 Third Avenue, New York, N. Y. 10022

Collier Macmillan Canada, Inc.

Library of Congress Catalog Card Number: 86-13044

Printed in the United States of America

printing number
1   2   3   4   5   6   7   8   9   10

Library of Congress Cataloging-in-Publication Data

Boyle, J. David.
  Measurement and evaluation of musical experiences.

  Includes index.
    1. Musical ability—Testing.   2. Music—Psychology.
3. Music—Instruction and study.   I. Radocy, Rudolf E.
II. Title.
ML3838.B697   1986   153.9'478   86-13044
ISBN 0-02-870300-6

CONTENTS

Four TYPES OF MUSIC TEST BEHAVIORS 85

PREFACE

Music teachers, performers, and critics have always made judgments regarding musical behaviors, but the application of systematic testing, measurement, and/or evaluative procedures as bases for educational decision making regarding musical behaviors is a relatively recent phenomenon. The original *Seashore Measures of Musical Talents* (1919) was the first music test battery to gain wide recognition. While a certain number of other tests were published in the 1920s and 1930s, it was not until the 1960s that another surge of interest in formal means of measuring and evaluating musical behaviors appeared. This resurgence coincided with the publication of three books specifically concerned with tests, measurements, and evaluations in music: Whybrew's (1962; 1971) *Measurement and Evaluation in Music,* Lehman's (1968) *Tests and Measurements in Music,* and Colwell's (1970) *The Evaluation of Music Teaching and Learning.* Essentially, these books provided much useful information regarding the purposes of measurement and evaluation, criteria for selecting music tests, interpretation of test and measurement data, reviews of published tests, and principles and procedures for developing and constructing tests. Labuta's (1974) *Guide to Accountability in Music Instruction* has offered much useful information regarding the role and nature of evaluation in providing feedback for music education programs that use a systems approach to instruction.

More recent publications relevant to measurement and evaluation of musical behavior have been in chapters or sections of books related to broader aspects of music psychology or music education, and each appears to have its own particular focus. George (1980) provides reviews of virtually all published music tests, including those presently available and many no longer available. Shuter-Dyson and Gabriel (1981) also provide reviews of selected music aptitude and achievement tests as part of their broader concern for defining musical ability and attributes influencing or related to it. Colwell (1982) focuses primarily on accountability issues and program evaluation. Abeles, Hoffer, and Klotman's (1984) chapter on the measurement and evaluation of musical behaviors provides discussions of various types of tests and evaluative techniques useful in evaluating cognitive, affective, and psychomotor musical behaviors. Tait and Haack (1984) consider evaluation to be one of four basic processes in music education. They advocate a broad evaluation base with emphasis on the *quality* of students' musical experiences and their related growth developments in thinking, feeling, and sharing music.

While each of the above sources provides much useful information, the need for a comprehensive sourcebook specifically devoted to concerns related to the measurement and evaluation of musical behaviors still existed. The present volume is intended to be such a sourcebook. At the suggestion of reviewers, however, the title of the book is *Measurement and Evaluation of Musical Experiences* rather than *Measurement and Evaluation of Musical Behaviors* in order to avoid misleading potential readers. To "behaviorists" the word *behaviors* suggests a primary focus on overt behavioral responses which the book does not have, and to non-"behaviorists" it might suggest that the book is too narrowly focused. In the text, however, the term *musical behavior* still is predominant, but the sense in which it is used should be clear to the reader not only from the definition offered in Chapter 1, but also from the context in which the term is used. Although it is oriented mainly toward music education, this book contains material that is relevant to music therapists and students of aesthetics as well.

In an attempt to cover a broad range of material and to relate the measurement of musical experiences to some fundamental issues in the use of measurement and evaluation tools in contemporary society, the book is purposefully expansive and perhaps goes into more detail in several areas than all readers might desire. Therefore, it is organized so that individual chapters or sequences of chapters may be used variously according to the particular objectives of an individual, class, or instructor.

Prerequisite to the development and application of tests and other evaluative measures in the various levels and aspects of a music program is an understanding of relevant terminology and the functions of the various types of evaluative measures. Chapter 1 discusses basic terminology and the functions of testing and evaluation programs for individuals, groups, and music programs. Chapter 2 then examines some contemporary issues in testing. Particular emphasis is placed on the differing functions of norm- and criterion-referenced measurement. The chapter also examines limitations and potential dangers of testing, as well as some of its moral, social, and political implications. Chapter 2 concludes with discussions of several issues that are particular concerns for measurement and evaluation of *musical* behaviors.

Essential to meaningful interpretation of measurement data is an understanding of statistical concepts underlying test reliability and validity, as well as those underlying basic techniques for analyzing distributions of test scores. Chapter 3 discusses the conceptual psychometric bases of reliability, validity, central tendency, variability, and test norms.

Chapter 4 reviews various types of responses that have been used in music tests. Nine basic response behaviors are identified and examined. Response methodologies used with the various response behaviors are also discussed. Chapter 5 focuses on evaluation of instruction in relation to specific instructional objectives. It discusses the specification of objectives, sampling of objectives in test items, and item construction and analysis.

Chapters 6 through 9 examine issues, techniques, and representative tests for measuring, respectively, (a) aptitude and ability, (b) music achievement, (c) music performance, and (d) attitudes and other affective responses to music. Chapter 10 reviews other useful measurement tools, including behavioral observation techniques, measures of musical background and nonmusical variables, selected electronic measures of response to musical stimuli, and some potential uses of the computer for assessing musical behavior.

Chapter 11 focuses on procedures for administering and scoring tests, both group and individual. Specific problems involved in testing young and handicapped children and using adjudicators are discussed. Chapter 12 examines purposes and problems in reporting systems used in school music programs, emphasizing particularly the need for multidimensional systems that have sufficient flexibility to allow for meaningful reporting in the various types of classes in a school music program.

Chapter 13 discusses program evaluation in schools. Particular

emphasis is placed on the need for a broad-based evaluation plan
that includes both formative and summative evaluations. Selected
evaluation models are reviewed, and the concluding discussion
examines program evaluation as a basis for curricular development.
The final chapter examines reactions to accountability and emerg-
ing trends in competency testing, concerns about humanism and
cultural bias, arguments relevant to goals and measurement of aesthetic response versus skills and knowledge, and continuing philosophical issues relevant to measurement and evaluation of musical
behaviors.

Test, measurement, and evaluation data are not viewed as a panacea for music education, but there is little question that the use of
valid and reliable data from such can provide music teachers,
administrators, counselors, and therapists with both broader and
stronger bases for decision making relevant to music instruction and
learning. Judicious use of these data ultimately will facilitate instructional improvement, increase students' learning, and foster
students' positive affective/aesthetic experiences through music.

JDB
RER

REFERENCES FOR PREFACE

Abeles, H.F., Hoffer, C.R., & Klotman, R.H. *Foundations of music education.* New
    York: Schirmer Books, 1984.
Colwell, R. *The evaluation of music teaching and learning.* Englewood Cliffs, N.J.:
    Prentice-Hall, 1970.
Colwell, R. Evaluation in music education: Perspicacious or peregrine. In R. Colwell
    (Ed.), *Symposium in music education.* Urbana-Champaign: University of Illinois,
    1982.
George, W.E. Measurement and evaluation of musical behaviors. In D.A. Hodges (Ed.),
    Handbook of music psychology. Lawrence, Kans.: National Association for Music
    Therapy, 1980.
Labuta, J.A. *Guide to accountability in music instruction.* West Nyack, N.Y.: Parker
    Publishing Co., 1974.
Lehman, P.R. *Tests and measurements in music.* Englewood Cliffs, N.J.: Prentice-Hall,
    1968.
Seashore, C.E. *Measures of musical talents.* Chicago: C.H. Stoelting, 1919.
Shuter-Dyson, R., & Gabriel, C. *The psychology of musical ability* (2nd ed.). London:
    Methuen & Co., Ltd., 1981.
Tait, M., & Haack, P. *Principles and processes of music education: New perspectives.*
    New York: Teachers College Press, Columbia University, 1984.
Whybrew, W.E. *Measurement and evaluation in music* (2nd ed.). Dubuque, Iowa:
    Wm. C. Brown, 1971. (Originally published, 1962.)

ACKNOWLEDGMENTS

The authors appreciate the important assistance of various individuals and groups in preparing this book. William Hipp, Dean of The University of Miami School of Music, Dale Scannell, former Dean of The University of Kansas School of Education, and George Duerksen, Chairman of The University of Kansas Department of Art and Music Education and Music Therapy facilitated the authors' abilities to devote necessary attention to research and writing. The University of Kansas School of Education Word Processing Center and its staff provided vital secretarial support. A timely sabbatical leave awarded to Rudolf E. Radocy by The University of Kansas was of critical importance.

Much of what the authors have learned about selecting, preparing, and defending tests and measures is attributable to their interactions with numerous students, undergraduate and graduate, at The Pennsylvania State University, The University of Miami, and The University of Kansas, who shared their experiences and thoughts in the authors' classes.

Finally, the authors appreciate the loving support of their wives, Arlene Boyle, Ed.D., and Judith Radocy, RMT-BC, who offered words of encouragement and provided a comfortable and secure environment in which to spend many hours. Judy also encouraged essential discussion of test adaptation for exceptional children. Thomas Radocy inspired particular concern for meeting the evaluation needs of young children.

JDB
RER

Measurement
and Evaluation
of Musical
Experiences

1

Why Measure and Evaluate?

The extent to which music teachers and administrators use formal testing and evaluation for decisions that affect music instruction and curricula is unclear. Nevertheless, it is clear that music teachers, administrators, and others necessarily must make and do make decisions that influence learners' instructional opportunities and experiences. One can only speculate the consequences of such decisions for the learners' musical development, but it is apparent that for many learners some decisions have vital and long-range consequences. Not only do instructional and curricular decisions affect individuals, but they also affect broad school, community, and societal goals for music education. It is therefore imperative that such decisions be made from a strong information base.

An information base usually includes information from two broad realms of knowledge: subjective and objective. Subjective knowledge may include information derived from a broad range of "ways of knowing," but it generally is recognized as including information based on informal, nonsystematic observations and interpretations made in light of the observer's training, experience, knowledge, feelings, intuitions, and even prejudices regarding the behavior, object, event, or phenomenon under consideration. Subjective information is much more apt to vary from observer to observer than objective information. The latitude for interpretation, and hence any resultant decision based on the interpretation of the information, is great.

Objective information, however, is relatively unaffected by personal feelings or prejudices and therefore should be recognized as the same by all observers, regardless of their feelings, prejudices, or experiences regarding the object, event, behavior, or phenomenon under consideration. At least some objective information is essential for adequate evaluation of most musical behaviors. The tests, testing procedures, measurement techniques, and evaluation procedures described here are designed to facilitate the elicitation and interpretation of objective information about musical behaviors and/or music programs.

The need for objective information does not, however, negate the importance of subjective information in the evaluation of musical behaviors and music programs. Music is an art form, the impact of which is recognized by many philosophers, psychologists, and educators to be most potent when response to it involves a strong feeling component. Further, evaluation by definition involves decision making, in itself a subjective process. The thesis of this book is that *evaluative decisions are better when they have a strong information base, that is, a base including both subjective and objective information.* An information base that does not include appropriate objective information is inadequate for most educational decision making.

Whether all evaluation of musical behaviors and music programs is undertaken to strengthen the information base for instructional and programmatic decisions, however, is questionable. Individual teachers and even directors of music programs in schools, including universities and conservatories, occasionally use tests for spurious reasons. Some appear to test for "window dressing" or because it is expected of them. Others may even use tests as punishment.

Traditional evaluations may rely excessively on subjective information bases, many of which are determined haphazardly, ritualistically, and/or are developed with disregard for available objective information. The need for stronger objective bases for evaluative decisions regarding both individual musical behaviors and music curricula is apparent, and central to the development of such bases is an understanding of the tests, measurement techniques, and evaluative procedures available. Even evaluation procedures that are inherently subjective, such as auditions, can be made more valid by making them have a more objective focus. The judicious selection and application of tests, measurement techniques, and evaluation procedures can only improve the quality of information used for decision making in music education.

This chapter reviews some of the functions of testing and evaluation for individuals, groups of individuals, and music programs. Prior to discussion of the functions is a discussion of some basic terms and concepts essential for the ensuing discussion.

EXTENDED DEFINITIONS

Although most readers have general concepts and/or personal definitions of the basic terminology related to the measurement and evaluation of musical behaviors, brief discussions of *musical behavior, test, measurement,* and *evaluation* are included here so that readers may have a common perspective for subsequent discussions.

Musical Behavior

Musical behavior is an integral and important part of human existence. It includes that facet of human psychological behavior through which people, either individually or collectively, interact with musical phenomena. The range of behaviors that may be called musical behavior is great, both in type and complexity. Musical performance (singing or playing an instrument individually or in a group), reading or writing music, improvising or composing music, listening to music, moving to music, reading about music, having a feeling response (affective/aesthetic) to music, or analyzing music are all musical behaviors. That these types of musical behavior are neither discrete nor exhaustive should be apparent. Musical behavior may involve highly complex integration of various levels of cognitive, affective, and psychomotor behaviors related to musical phenomena or may be limited to a single, simple response to a given musical stimulus. *Any* observable human activity that is related to music may be conceived as musical behavior.

Changing musical behavior is the essence of music teaching, and the study of musical behavior is the subject matter of the *psychology of music,* which the authors maintain would be more accurately titled the *psychology of musical behavior.* Describing, defining, measuring, and predicting musical behavior traditionally have comprised a major area of study in the discipline. Virtually every book written on the subject attempts to redefine such terms as talent, capacity, aptitude, ability, and achievement. Yet, the terminology problem persists, partly because identical definitions of abstract terms inevitably have different connotations.

The root of the problem seems to be related to measurement and the extent to which test makers, psychologists, and educators draw inferences from musical behaviors. *Talent, aptitude, musicality, musical intelligence, music ability,* and *music audiation,* to use some of the more prominent terms, reflect *constructs* that are used to differentiate between individuals and groups of individuals who demonstrate different levels of performance on selected musical tasks. Individuals who perform better on given tasks are considered more "talented" or as having higher level "aptitude" or "ability" than individuals who perform the tasks less well. Teachers, musicians, and lay people add to the confusion by applying these labels to individuals on the basis of various informal criteria, many of which appear to lack any systematic observation base.

Many of these constructs, or labels, are highly inferential, rely on different testing procedures, lack consensus with respect to definition, may be highly theoretical, and often are used to reflect certain *functions* relative to the assessment of potential, selection of students, or evaluation of achievement. An understanding of these terms and constructs is important, and they are discussed in subsequent chapters.

The position taken here is that the term *musical behavior* refers to the overt manifestations of a myriad of psychological, physiological, and neurological processes that an individual has in relation to musical sound and/or other music-related events or phenomena. While musical behavior may involve a "response to a musical stimulus," it need not be limited to such a perspective. Human musical behavior includes autonomous activities of individuals that do not have a "stimulus" as defined in the sense of the true *behaviorist.* While this broader definition of musical behavior may not satisfy readers with a strong behaviorist perspective, it is believed necessary, because in recent years the covert processes underlying musical behavior have indeed become the primary focus for many music educators and psychologists concerned with understanding and changing musical behavior, for example, Taylor (1981) and Deutsch (1982).

However, there is need for caution: Attempting to describe or attribute "cause and effect" regarding covert processes is highly inferential, and persons undertaking to describe covert processes or assess covert constructs are obligated to define clearly both the testing procedures and the theoretical basis (bases) from which any covert processes are inferred. Clear specification of testing procedures and the inferential basis will enable educators and psychologists to draw their own conclusions regarding the usefulness of the covert processes and constructs in evaluating, understanding, and developing musical behavior. If the testing procedures and inferential bases are not specified clearly, the descriptions of the covert processes and the inferred constructs will have little meaning or utilitarian value for either music teachers or psychologists.

Test

As used in educational and psychological measurement and evaluation, the term *test* refers to the application of a systematic method for gathering data that indicate the extent to which an individual or group of individuals demonstrate a specific behavior or set of behaviors. Cronbach (1970, p. 26) states, *"A test is a systematic procedure for observing a person's behavior and describing it with the aid of a numerical scale or a category system"* [Emphasis in original]. Usually such tests include a series of questions, exercises, or other tasks designed for a specific function. Some common functions of educational and psychological tests include assessment of knowledge, achievement, skill, ability, aptitude, attitude, and selected psychological traits, states, and abilities. (Specific functions of music tests are discussed later in this chapter.)

Tests are the primary means for obtaining objective information about individuals' behaviors relevant to specific purposes, and a test's real value is dependent upon the extent to which it serves the purposes for which it was administered. (Specific technical criteria for evaluating music tests, including validity and reliability, are discussed in Chapter 3.) In constructing a test, the test designer should systematically include items (questions, exercises, or other tasks) that require the test taker to perform or demonstrate behaviors reflecting the knowledge, skill, ability, attitude, or whatever is being assessed. The form, format, and general characteristics of educational and psychological tests, and particularly music tests, may vary greatly; these characteristics depend on many variables, including the function of the test, the nature of what is being measured, the characteristics of the individuals being tested, as well as many practical considerations, such as individual versus group testing, time and cost factors, and necessary conditions of administration and scoring. Regardless of the function, form, format, and other characteristics of educational and psychological tests, a basic principle of measurement and evaluation is that the testing procedure involve a *systematic method* for assessing the test takers' *behaviors* relevant to the questions, exercises, or tasks specified in the test. Tests that lack a systematic method for assessing test takers' behaviors relevant to specific tasks are of dubious value in providing objective information for use in educational and psychological evaluations.

Measurement

Measurement in education and psychology essentially involves quantification of test data. Just as tests must involve a systematic method for assessing behaviors, procedures for quantifying behavioral responses to tests must also be systematic. *Virtually all definitions of measurement* state that it involves the assignment of numerals to objects, individuals, or events according to specific and systematic rules. However, Payne (1982) notes that measurement is more than counting and sorting. It allows "the comparison of something with a unit or standard or quantity of that same thing, in order to represent the magnitude of the variable being measured" (p. 1182).

As Leonhard (1958) has observed, measurement attempts to achieve improved precision and objectivity of observation. Further, it provides a basis for subsequent objective, statistical treatment of test data.

The quantification of data from the many various types of tests and testing procedures employed in assessments of musical behavior in formal education settings, as well as the many other settings, is a fairly recent phenomenon and one that shows promise of providing a much stronger objective data base for decision making. In the past, the musical world seems to have been overly dependent on excessively subjective information as a basis for evaluation of performance and musical response. Even in situations where professional judgment must remain the final criterion in evaluation of performance, increased specificity regarding evaluative criteria and the quantification of ratings relative to those criteria may greatly enhance the objectivity of the ultimate decision making.

Evaluation

Evaluation is a broader term than either test or measurement. In education, it usually involves or at least implies the use of tests and measurements, but in addition involves making some judgment or decision regarding the worth, quality, or value of experiences, procedures, activities, or individual or group performances as they relate to some educational endeavor. Evaluation should be an ongoing, systematic process that is an integral part of any educational endeavor, whether concerned with the learning of individuals in the applied music studio, rehearsal hall, or classroom, or with improvement of instructional, program, or teacher effectiveness.

The extent to which an evaluation process uses formal tests and measurements obviously varies from one situation to another, and there is little doubt that much excellent instruction and efficient learning occurs with instructional decisions based solely on subjective, yet enlightened and thoughtful, judgments of teachers, curriculum specialists, and administrators. Enlightened, thoughtful judgment is central to any evaluation process, but as Gronlund (1981, p. 4) argues, "instructional decisions are more likely to be sound when they are based on information that is *accurate, relevant,* and *comprehensive.*" Objective information, as available through tests and measurements, is particularly useful in increasing the accuracy of an information base for educational decision making.

Evaluation also should be functional. Too often it is done ritualistically, merely because teachers are expected or required to provide grades or some other type of feedback regarding their students' educational progress. Further, with accountability mandates from school districts, state agencies, and various other government agencies that provide funding, some program evaluation efforts appear to serve more of a "window dressing" or public relations function than true evaluation functions. Only to the extent that evaluation efforts provide information that may help improve the quality of an educational enterprise are they serving true evaluation functions.

Traditional views regarding the evaluation of educational experiences have focused primarily on student achievement relative to educational objectives in the cognitive and psychomotor domains. Tait and Haack (1984), however, maintain that the affective, humanistic qualities of students' educational experiences also are important and should receive strong consideration in educational evaluations, both in the evaluation of individuals' musical behaviors and in the evaluation of school music programs.

The quality of educational endeavors, whether for individuals or groups or at the preschool, elementary, secondary, or collegiate and adult levels, partly depends on the quality of the evaluation decisions relative to these endeavors. It is therefore imperative that evaluation decisions in music education be the best possible. The authors contend that evaluation decisions in music education will approach their best when decision makers (a) have a strong, relevant information base, including both subjective and objective information, (b) consider affective and, where appropriate, aesthetic reactions of (or to) the individual, group, or endeavor being evaluated, and (c) be made with the primary goal of improving the quality of the learners' educational experiences.

FUNCTIONS OF EVALUATION

Although this discussion is concerned with the functions of evaluation, it should be understood that tests and measurement techniques, which involve the systematic gathering and quantification of data relevant to specific purposes, form the base for much educational evaluation, particularly with respect to student aptitude, ability, or achievement. In fact, tests often are classified according to evaluation functions, for example, aptitude tests, diagnostic tests, achievement tests, and so on, but until a test is indeed used as a basis for making some judgments about a student's potential for learning, strengths or weaknesses with respect to given skills, knowledge, or understanding, or achievement relative to instructional objectives, the test really is serving no evaluation function. It is merely being used to gather data.

It must also be understood that while the present discussion of evaluation functions is in terms of functions for either improving the learning experiences of individuals or for increasing the quality of school programs, the evaluation is also serving the needs of the evaluators, that is, the decision makers and other users of tests. With respect to functions for individual learners, the evaluators usually are teachers, counselors, parents, or other individuals who must make decisions relevant to individual learners. The learner may even be considered an evaluator when using evaluative feedback in making decisions that influence his or her own learning experiences. Evaluation decisions for school programs usually involve a number of people, including teachers, supervisors, administrators, school boards, certification agencies, professional evaluators, and funding agencies.

Functions for Individuals

Although the functions of evaluation could be categorized at various levels of specificity, they are considered here as *achievement, diagnostic, aptitude,* and *attitude functions.* Essentially the four functions require the evaluator, respectively, to (a) examine the learner's behavioral changes as a result of *past* experiences, (b) assess the learner's *present* abilities and traits, (c) make decisions relative to the learner's *future* behaviors, and (d) make instructional decisions based on the learner's *feelings, interests,* or *preferences* regarding learning activities, subject matter, events, objects, individuals, and/or other phenomena.

It also should be recognized that, while the evaluation functions are discussed under selected categories, the functions of particular evaluative measures are by no means discrete. A given test may serve more than one function, and Mehrens (1982) notes that there has been much debate regarding whether even aptitude and achievement, perhaps the two best known functions of evaluation, should be thought of as separate concepts. Further, individuals usually have feelings or attitudes about subject matter, tests, or learning tasks. Nevertheless, it is believed that the functions may be understood more easily if discussed separately.

Achievement functions. A learner's achievement may be evaluated in relation to the achievement of others or in relation to specific performance criteria that may be used to define competency or mastery. When a learner's achievement is evaluated in relation to that of others, the evaluation is considered to be *norm-referenced,* that is, it compares the behavior (usually scores) of an individual on a given test to those of some normative group, usually either his or her classmates or a well-defined population of similar age, grade level, or experience. Decisions about an individual's achievement therefore are partially dependent on the achievement of other learners.

Achievement evaluation in relation to specific criteria rather than other individuals is variously called *objective-, domain-,* or *criterion-referenced* evaluation. Such evaluation is particularly appropriate for instructional programs that allow students to progress at their own rates of learning. Criterion-referenced evaluation usually is concerned with assessment of whether or not a student has achieved enough to satisfy the minimum competency requirements specified in the objective or criterion statement.

There are other differences between norm-referenced and criterion-referenced achievement evaluation, and the issues related to these are discussed more fully in Chapters 2 and 3. Suffice it to say here that most differences are related to uses and interpretation of test data rather than test content, although some technical concerns have developed in regard to item analysis and reliability of tests employed for criterion-referenced evaluation.

Diagnostic function. Tests serving a diagnostic function focus on the *present* and are used to classify students according to their strengths and weaknesses relative to given skills or knowledge. Essentially, diagnostic tests provide an information base on which either to group students for instruction or to individualize instruction for needed remediation or challenges for the learners. Katz (1973) notes that tests used for grouping students usually are *extensive* in nature, whereas tests with a narrower content focus, that is, *intensive* in nature, are more appropriate for assessing an individual's strengths and weaknesses. He maintains that extensive tests, which generally examine strengths and weaknesses over a fairly broad range of subject matter, are usually used for placing students into appropriate instructional groups and basically are used for *inter*-individual comparisons. Intensive tests are designed for *intra*-individual comparisons and usually provide the basis for remedial instruction in the areas of needed skill development. Intensive tests also are considered to be prescriptive aids.

Although Wigdor and Garner (1982) caution that students should be grouped only when there is an instructionally valid reason for it, tests serving the diagnostic function are an important part of most educational programs. Students are grouped according to skills and abilities at virtually all instructional levels. Placement examinations are a standard part of all music programs in higher education. Students often are selected for performance groups and are assigned to parts in bands and orchestras on the basis of auditions. Most undergraduate and graduate programs in the United States use placement examinations in music theory and history. Applied music teachers focus instruction on the basis of their diagnostic evaluations of a performer's strengths and weaknesses. In short, diagnostic evaluation is a critical and everpresent part of any good music program. To the extent that (a) placement examinations are valid, (b) music teachers are accurate in their diagnoses of individuals, and (c) the obtained information is used to select and/or design appropriate instructional sequences for students, the diagnostic function is serving the needs of music teachers.

Aptitude function. The aptitude function involves the use of test and measurement data as a basis for making predictions about students' potential for success in future music learning activities. The aptitude function essentially is a selection function and in many respects serves a placement function. However, a basic difference between an aptitude function and a placement function is that an aptitude function uses *present* performance to predict *future achievement.* A particular value of aptitude assessment is in identifying the talented, in other words, individuals with potential for above-average learning in the skill or academic area under consideration.

To the extent that aptitude tests can predict potential for future learning and identify potential talent, they can be extremely valuable in educational and vocational guidance. However, as Boyle (1982) and Katz (1973) have noted, a primary difficulty in aptitude testing is to select or develop tests of *present* student performance behaviors that actually are valid predictors of potential for learning.

This has been a particular problem with music tests. For example, the literature is rampant with arguments about whether the well-known *Seashore Measures of Musical Talents* are a valid predictor of musical ability. The critics' views, which are summarized by Lehman (1968, pp. 42–45), are that the measures are not valid, whereas Seashore maintained that the measures are valid for what they purport to measure. Further, Seashore did not claim that the measures were predictors of a holistic musical ability; to him, the use of the measures for such a purpose was a *misuse* of the measures. (Misuses of test, measurement, and evaluation data are discussed in Chapter 2.)

A related issue in the prediction of musical behavior is the extent to which nonmusical variables are useful in such predictions. Rainbow's (1965) classic multiple regression study of predictors of musical ability for elementary, junior high school, and senior high school students suggests that, in addition to tonal memory, musical achievement, and interest in music, the variables of academic intelligence, home enrichment, and socioeconomic background are significant predictors of musical ability. Whellams's (1970) discriminant function analysis of below and above average junior musicians at the Royal Marines School of Music corroborates the view that nonmusical variables are useful in identifying talented individuals.

It is common for music conservatories and college and university music schools to use predictive measures in the identification and selection of students with potential for success in musical study, and it appears that most schools use both musical and nonmusical predictors, a practice which appears to strengthen the accuracy of prediction. The judicious use of test, measurement, and evaluation data can be very helpful to both the institutions and the individuals involved, particularly with respect to student selection and vocational guidance in higher education. Careful selection at this level can do much to ensure high level musical standards.

Using aptitude measures to select the musically elite in elementary and secondary schools, however, must be considered in light of a carefully thought out educational philosophy. To deny elementary and secondary students in publicly supported schools an opportunity for music experiences on the basis of a given aptitude measure is a questionable practice.

Attitude function. A fourth broad function of tests for individuals concerns the affective domain. The purpose of evaluating an individual's attitude is to determine what he or she *chooses* to or *wants* to do rather than what he or she is *able* to do.

Attitude is perhaps the most common of a number of terms used to describe the broad spectrum of feeling behaviors that comprise the affective domain. Affective behaviors generally are recognized as including a strong feeling component as well as involving a certain degree of cognition. There is less consensus regarding the importance of cognition in affective behaviors, but it appears that the labels, or psychological constructs, used to infer varying types of affective behaviors necessarily imply different levels of cognition, for example, interest, preference, attitude, value, appreciation, taste, and aesthetic sensitivity. These constructs are examined more fully in Chapter 9, but it is apparent that they reflect, especially in music, either specific educational goals and objectives or at the very least have a direct relationship to learning of musical behaviors that involve more cognitive and psychomotor behaviors.

Taxonomies of educational objectives in the cognitive, affective, and psychomotor domains are useful to educators, but at the same time create more artificiality for educators and psychologists concerned with understanding and development of musical behaviors (Bloom, 1956; Krathwohl, Bloom, & Masia, 1964; Harrow, 1972). Most musical behaviors, and probably most human behaviors for that matter, involve more than a single domain. Learners have feelings of various types and at various levels about the learning activities in which they are engaged, and there is little doubt that feelings, whether they be termed interests, attitudes, values, or some other affective construct, have a strong bearing on the quality and efficiency of learning.

Although educators have recognized the importance of the affective domain for the individual, evaluation efforts apparently have focused more on group assessments and attitudes toward school and particular programs. The authors contend that much greater importance must be placed on assessing individuals' affective behaviors related to music and that affective evaluation should have a greater impact upon both decision making relative to individual learners and to school music programs. Interest inventories, preference surveys, and value scales could provide much data relevant to selection of learning activities or musical repertoire. Further, decisions related to the educational and vocational guidance of students should include affective information as well as cognitive and psychomotor information.

To summarize, the affective function of test, measurement, and evaluation data should be recognized and considered when making decisions regarding instructional strategies and other matters related to the educational guidance of individual music students. Failure to use such information may have a deleterious effect on the quality of the decision, and hence, the quality of future learning experiences for the individual learner.

Functions for Groups and Programs

Whereas individuals usually are evaluated in relation to each other or to instructional objectives, group or program evaluation is usually in relation to educational objectives that are more generic in nature and are broadly concerned with the outcomes of schooling (Payne, 1982, p. 1182). Concern for educational outcomes, usually termed *product* or *summative* evaluation, is an important aspect of program evaluation, but like achievement testing for individuals, appears to focus on the past, often seeking to pinpoint reasons underlying the success or failure of a program as much as to focus on change as a result of the evaluation.

However, Colwell (1982, p. 182), following the position advocated by Cronbach et al. (1980), argues that program evaluation should not only portray the status of the past and present, but should serve to stimulate questions relative to new directions for education programs:

> Good evaluators must take the time to reflect and to consider more than situational success and failures. If public policy for music education is to be questioned, an independent evaluation format is likely to be necessary. . . . (Colwell, 1982, p. 182)

He goes on to suggest that program evaluation data in most educational enterprises should be of general or public concern and should serve as catalysts for action. He maintains that the pressures of school budgets, the search for inefficiency, and the continuing re-establishing of priorities will make evaluative data increasingly important in the next quarter of a century. More will be said of the relationship of evaluative data to public concerns and policy in Chapter 2.

In a sense all program evaluation may serve a planning function, but the present discussion focuses on five particular functions: (a) *accountability,* (b) *instructional effectiveness, (c) teacher effectiveness,* (d) *policy making and management,* and (e) *research and project evaluation.*

Accountability. Accountability has been a buzz word in education since the early 1960s, and although some of the "buzzing" may have been diverted to competency testing (see Chapter 14), virtually everyone agrees that accountability is both necessary and good for the development and maintenance of quality educational programs. The exact nature of what accountability means or implies, however, does not enjoy such consensus. It has been described variously as a state of being, a process, and a product (Gephart, 1975, p. 68). When described in the state-of-being sense, a subjective, qualitative description usually is offered. When viewed as a process, the description focuses on the system, its

that the assessment of teachers' competencies, not only in teaching, per se, but also in terms of musical skills and knowledge, knowledge of psychology, and educational philosophy, methodology, learner characteristics, and teaching techniques, is an important approach to the evaluation of teacher effectiveness.

While it is beyond the scope of the present discussion to examine the various facets of teacher effectiveness, it is apparent that both process and product evaluation data are essential in assessing teacher effectiveness. Perhaps the most difficult task confronting evaluators is to select data relevant to the intended assessment. Prior to that, however, evaluators must identify criteria for effectiveness, often more of a philosophical issue than an evaluation issue.

Policy making and management. Policy and management decisions perhaps have the broadest and most far-reaching effects of any decisions on an educational program. The extent to which evaluative data can and do influence such decisions undoubtedly varies greatly from program to program, but most decision makers want to have an accurate and comprehensive understanding of the variables under consideration. Generally, the more accurate and comprehensive the information available to the decision maker, the more likely he or she is to make the appropriate decision.

Policy and management decisions are of increasing importance to music educators when fiscal constraints are great and when education in general is under close scrutiny from educational critics and the public. Decisions regarding whether to employ music specialists in the elementary schools, when to begin instrumental instruction, or whether to increase or cut back staffing in these and other curricular areas, while necessarily dependent to a degree on financial considerations, may be influenced by information relative to the decision's effects on the students and the total school music program. A music program that has a strong accountability record is in a far better position to get a decision favorable to the program than one that does not have a strong accountability record. Also, if evaluation has been an integral part of the ongoing evaluation program, most necessary data will be readily available.

It is particularly important that evaluative data used for policy and management decisions be broad based and include both formative and summative evaluations. Formative evaluations generally are concerned with program planning and development.

Summative evaluations include not only assessments of performance groups and the achievement of individuals, but may also include attitudinal data from various perspectives: students, teachers, parents, the community, and other members of the profession, both within and outside the school district.

Research and project evaluation. Evaluation is central to any research effort. Without a valid and reliable assessment of the results of research, any conclusions drawn from a study are of dubious value.

Of particular concern for music educators are the evaluations of various types of short-term curriculum projects, often implemented with funding from agencies outside a school district or university. Most funding agencies require that a system of accountability be built into the project, particularly when hundreds of thousands or even millions of dollars are involved.

Isaac and Michael (1981, p. 2), who consider program and project evaluation to be more akin to technology than science, suggest that project evaluation should be concerned with both product delivery (process) and mission accomplishment (product). For them, process evaluation involves *implementation evaluation,* seeking discrepancies between the program objectives and the instructional realities, and *progress evaluation,* the monitoring of progress toward the objectives. The product evaluation examines whether the objectives have been attained. The process evaluation provides information on which project or program managers may base decisions for changes in the instructional curriculum. The product evaluation, often broad based, provides an examination of a program's strengths and weaknesses with respect to the desired outcomes and should be the primary basis for subsequent program modification.

CONCLUDING REMARKS

That evaluation serves many overlapping functions for both individuals and programs is obvious, and too often persons concerned with measurement and evaluation become so involved in the process and techniques of testing and measurement that *evaluation* is overlooked: Evaluation should serve to facilitate and improve the instructional process in the classroom as well as the development and improvement of the overall educational program so as to serve the educational needs and goals of the community.

Colwell (1985) maintains that, to do this, evaluation should be forward rather than backward looking. The bottom line for all educational evaluation should be for instructional and program planning, which should be a continuing, ongoing process. Colwell also argues that product or summative evaluation alone is inadequate and that program evaluation should focus more on *how* and *why* various music courses contribute toward the overall goals of a school music program. The authors concur.

Study Questions

1. List and discuss the overt musical behaviors by which one may reasonably argue that an individual

   (a) is "musically talented,"
   (b) shows "musical aptitude," and
   (c) is a highly accomplished musician.

   Compare and contrast the behaviors.

2. Describe instances in music education in which

   (a) testing may occur without measurement,
   (b) measurement may occur without evaluation, and
   (c) evaluation may occur without either testing or measurement.

3. Describe "real world" instances in which evaluation serves respectively achievement, diagnostic, aptitude, and attitude functions for individuals at the (a) elementary school, (b) secondary school, and (c) collegiate levels.

4. For a school system with which you are familiar, describe the apparent functions that evaluation serves for (a) individuals, (b) the music program, and (c) the school district. Compare these with the functions described in Chapter 1.

REFERENCES

Bloom, B.S. (Ed.). *Taxonomy of educational objectives: Handbook I, cognitive domain.* New York: David McKay, 1956.

Boyle, J.D. Selecting music tests for use in schools. *Update,* 1982, *1* (1), 14–21.

Colwell, R. Evaluation in music education: Perspicacious or peregrine. In. R. Colwell (Ed.), *Symposium in music education.* Urbana-Champaign: University of Illinois, 1982.

Colwell, R. Program evaluation in music teacher education. *Council for Research in Music Education,* 1985, *81,* 18–62.

Cronbach, L. J. *Essentials of psychological testing* (3rd ed.). New York: Harper & Row, 1970.

Cronbach, L. J., et al. *Toward reform of program evaluation.* San Francisco, Calif.: Jossey-Bass, 1980.

Deutsch, D. (Ed.). *The psychology of music.* New York: Academic Press, 1982.

Gephart, W. J. (Ed.). *Accountability: A state, a process, or a product?* Bloomington, Ind.: Phi Delta Kappa, 1975.

Gronlund, N. E. *Measurement and evaluation in teaching* (4th ed.). New York: Macmillan, 1981.

Harrow, A. J. *A taxonomy of the psychomotor domain.* Iowa City: University of Iowa Press, 1972.

Isaac, S., & Michael, W. B. *Handbook in research and evaluation* (2nd ed.). San Diego, Calif.: EdITS, 1981.

Katz, M. *Selecting an achievement test: Principles and procedures.* Princeton: Educational Testing Service, 1973.

Krathwohl, D. R., Bloom, B. S., & Masia, B. B. *Taxonomy of educational objectives: Handbook II, affective domain.* New York: David McKay, 1964.

Labuta, J. A. *Guide to accountability in music education.* West Nyack, N.Y.: Parker, 1974.

Lehman, P. R. *Tests and measurements in music.* Englewood Cliffs, N.J.: Prentice-Hall, 1968.

Leonhard, C. Evaluation in music education. In N. B. Henry (Ed.), *Basic concepts in music education* (The fifty-seventh yearbook of the National Society for the Study of Education). Chicago: University of Chicago Press, 1958.

Mehrens, W. A. Aptitude measurement. In H. E. Mitzel (Ed.), *Encyclopedia of educational research* (5th ed.) (Vol. 1). New York: Free Press, 1982.

Payne, D. A. Measurement in education. In H. E. Mitzel (Ed.), *Encyclopedia of educational research* (5th ed.) (Vol. 3). New York: Free Press, 1982.

Rainbow, E. L. A pilot study to investigate the constructs of musical aptitude. *Journal of Research in Music Education,* 1965, *13,* 3–14.

Tait, M., & Haack, P. *Principles and processes of music education: New perspectives.* New York: Teachers College Press, Columbia University, 1984.

Taylor, R. G. (Ed.). *Documentary report of the Ann Arbor Symposium: Applications of psychology to the teaching and learning of music.* Reston, Va.: Music Educators National Conference, 1981.

Whellams, F. S. The relative efficiency of aural-musical and non-musical tests as predictors of achievement in instrumental music. *Bulletin of the Council for Research in Music Education,* 1970, *21,* 15–21.

Wigdor, A. K., & Garner, W. R. (Eds.). *Ability testing: Uses, consequences, and controversies* (Part I). Washington, D.C.: National Academy Press, 1982.

2

Contemporary Issues in Measurement and Evaluation

Educational measurement and evaluation always have been fraught with criticism and skepticism, if not downright antagonism, and most measurement and evaluation specialists agree that many criticisms are warranted and that there are many problems and issues confronting the field. The nature of testing, measurement, and evaluation is such that many individuals, including students, teachers, parents, curriculum specialists, administrators, and project managers, may feel threatened by the process. Perhaps some fears, negative reactions, and criticisms are a natural outgrowth of the process, but if educators are to use the process effectively for the intended functions, they must be open to evaluation and all that is involved in the process. Without a willingness to make evaluation an integral part of the educational process, it is doubtful that it can be maximally effective.

A major responsibility for changing attitudes toward the evaluation process belongs to the decision makers, that is, the users of test, measurement, and evaluation data. The standards for use of tests prepared by a joint committee of the American Psychological Association, the American Educational Research Association, and the National Council on Measurement in Education (APA, 1974) specify guidelines for the (a) qualifications of users, (b) choice or development of test or evaluation method, (c) test administration and scoring, and (d) interpretation of scores.

Essentially, these standards define the necessary qualifications and responsibilities of persons who use test data, and if the standards were fulfilled by all test users, many of the concerns and issues examined in this chapter would cease to exist. However, as a result of inappropriate uses of measurement and evaluation data, the case of the critics is strengthened, and the purpose of educational measurement and evaluation is weakened, thus undermining the potentially strongest avenue to improving educational programs in schools and universities.

Questions have been raised about test fairness, test bias, limitations of tests, and misuses of measurement and evaluation data. Ebel (1979, p. 5) maintains that most of the criticism comes from three special interest groups: (a) professional educators who are uneasy about the accountability implied by the use of tests and measurements in schools, (b) reformers who regard testing as part of an outmoded instructional process, and (c) free-lance writers whose best-sellers purport to expose scandals in schools and other important social institutions. He questions whether these critics really are concerned with improving tests and making them more useful educational tools and suggests that many critics are more concerned with discrediting tests to minimize their influence or even to eliminate them entirely. Regardless of the critics' motivations, Ebel suggests that the criticisms should be taken seriously.

Contemporary issues and concerns related to measurement and evaluation are broader than just the criticisms, misuses, and limitations of tests. They also include debates over (a) the relative merits and uses of norm-referenced and criterion-referenced measurement, (b) the approach to evaluation in competency-based education and mastery learning, (c) limitations and dangers of testing, (d) variables influencing test scores, and (e) moral, social, political, and legal implications of measurement and evaluation. This chapter examines these general issues as they relate to educational measurement and evaluation in its broader context. Also examined are two other issues of special concern to the measurement and evaluation of musical behavior: (a) the global versus specifics approach to measuring musical behavior, and (b) low versus high inferences from behaviors.

CRITICISMS OF TESTING

Because testing is an integral part of most measurement and evaluation programs, evaluators must examine and respond to criticisms of testing. If the criticisms are justified, measurement and evaluation specialists must take steps to alleviate the criticisms for tests to be viable bases for educational decision making; if the criticisms appear to be unwarranted, measurement and evaluation specialists are obligated to provide data and/or a philosophical basis for refuting them. Although neither data nor philosophical position is likely to alter the views of all critics, re-examining the criticisms ultimately will strengthen testing programs. Colwell (1970, pp. 4–6) argues that many of the criticisms and fears of testing result from misconceptions of evaluation's role. He maintains that teachers need to understand that evaluation is a positive force in education, and once they become accustomed to it and incorporate it into their teaching, many of their fears and criticisms will be alleviated.

Lehman (1968, p. 83) notes that criticisms of tests usually center around two major points: (a) that tests are inadequate and unfair and (b) that test results are misunderstood and misused. Ebel (1979, pp. 5–6) cites criticisms related to (a) test validity, (b) an overdependence on objective tests because they are easily scored, regardless of serious shortcomings of triviality, ambiguity, and guessing, (c) labeling students as a result of test scores and the subsequent distortions of their expectations and efforts, (d) imposing external testing programs that may cause teachers to abandon sound, long-range instruction in order to teach for the test, (e) the harmful stress and unnecessary experiences of failure to which students are exposed, thus destroying self-confidence and undermining the joy of learning, (f) a white, middle-class bias in tests that misrepresents the achievement and potential of cultural minorities, and (g) the need to replace norm-referenced tests with criterion-referenced tests. Gronlund (1981, pp. 419–427) categorizes the critical issues in educational testing in relation to the nature and quality of tests, the possible harmful effects of testing on students, the fairness of tests to minority group members, possible sex bias, and the potential hazards that testing imposes regarding an individual's right to privacy. Following is a discussion of the various criticisms of testing.

Test Quality

Most criticisms about test quality concern matters related to reliability and validity: Does the test measure what it purports to measure and does it measure it consistently and accurately? Few measurement specialists would not agree that tests should be as valid and as reliable as possible, and by and large it appears that makers of standardized tests have gone to great lengths to demonstrate that their tests are valid and reliable.

Gronlund (1981, p. 420) maintains that it is unrealistic to expect tests to be perfect instruments for measuring behavior and that criticisms of tests as being less than perfect instruments are unwarranted. He suggests that a more appropriate comparison than the ideal comparisons of reliability and validity to perfection, that is, reliability and validity coefficients of 1.00, would be to compare them to other measures of achievement and aptitude. He argues that the alternatives to tests are far less reliable and valid than tests and that qualified test users consider possible error in test scores when interpreting test data.

Many criticisms about test validity actually are matters of inappropriate uses of tests, a usage problem rather than a quality problem. There is little question that many tests are used inappropriately, and it is the responsibility of the education profession, particularly measurement and evaluation specialists, to do everything possible to ensure that tests used as bases for educational decision making are appropriate for the decisions. This requires a clear understanding of the nature of the assessment and the functions for which the test is being administered.

Other criticisms related to test quality focus on clarity of directions, format, and ease of administration. While such criticisms may be justified for individual tests, it appears that the makers of most published, standardized tests have gone to great lengths to ensure that directions and format are clear and that the overall "usability quotient" of their tests is high.

The extent to which individual classroom teachers' tests may be criticized obviously varies with the teacher, and undoubtedly many classroom tests warrant criticism regarding their quality. Perhaps the best that can be done to improve the quality of classroom tests is to ensure that teachers develop the necessary understandings and competencies related to test usage and development, with particular focus on development of tests to evaluate achievement in relation to instructional objectives.

Criticisms regarding the overdependence on objective tests certainly would be warranted if such tests were used only because they are easy to score, despite potential triviality, ambiguity, and susceptibility to guessing. However, Ebel (1979, p. 135) notes that multiple-choice test items are the most highly regarded and widely used form of objective test item. He also maintains that they are adaptable for measuring most important educational outcomes, including knowledge, understanding, judgment, problem-solving ability, and making predictions.

Certainly few objective tests are so nearly perfect as to be above reproach from a persistent, perceptive critic, but Ebel dismisses most of the criticisms because they are seldom supported by data and the critics seldom make a good case for a better way of measuring educational achievement.

Criticisms about the triviality or ambiguity of multiple-choice test items may be warranted if the test developer has not followed established principles in test development (e.g. Ebel, 1979, pp. 135–162; Gronlund, 1981, pp. 178–200); however, this again is a matter of usage, and what appears to be the most useful type of item should not be discarded simply because it may be misused by some practitioners. What needs to be done is to make sure that practitioners are knowledgeable of the principles of test construction.

Misuses of Tests

Gardner (1982, p. 323) argues that many criticisms of tests result from misuses of tests and claims that if tests were used only for the functions for which they were designed, many of the criticisms would be alleviated. While all criticisms of tests may not be a direct result of misuse, it is apparent that misuse, or at least naivete in test use and interpretation, gives more credence to criticisms of tests than otherwise might be warranted.

Although the number of criticisms of test use varies from one critic to another, partly depending on the individual critic's perspective and understanding of the functions of educational measurement and evaluation, there are several basic and somewhat generally agreed upon areas of concern: (a) the validity of tests for their designated purposes, (b) meaningful interpretation and reporting of test results, (c) labeling students, (d) tests as external controls on instructional programs, (e) creation of anxiety and destruction of self-confidence, (f) invasion of privacy,

(g) bias against racial, cultural, and socioeconomic minorities, and (h) the effects of coaching on test scores.

Using valid tests.   As apparent in the discussion of the criticisms of test quality, criticisms of inadequate test validity often are usage problems rather than quality problems. Far too frequently tests are used for purposes for which they were not designed, thus rendering the technical data regarding validity totally meaningless. Users must understand clearly the evaluation function that they want a test to serve, and then either select or develop a test that is appropriate for that particular function.

Test users are responsible for selecting appropriate tests and therefore must be cognizant of the theoretical basis, technical characteristics, and purposes for which a test is designed. A common mistake in test selection is to select a test on the basis of its title and whatever the title suggests or implies. Just because a test is labeled as a music achievement test does not mean that it is appropriate for measuring music achievement in every school. Music aptitude tests are even more difficult to select because the test makers' philosophies regarding the constituent behaviors reflecting music aptitude vary considerably from test to test. To use a test because it is well known or is "generally recognized as a good test" without thorough examination of its appropriateness for one's particular purpose constitutes gross professional negligence on the part of the user. Although there are many other considerations in test selection or development, *the primary responsibility of any test user is to ensure that the test is appropriate for obtaining the desired information.*

Interpreting and using test results.   Perhaps the most critical misuses of tests involve interpreting, reporting, and using test data. For some individuals, including teachers, administrators, and critics, there is a certain "concreteness" or permanency about quantitative test scores—something of a "magic in numbers" syndrome. A student achieves a certain score and is immediately categorized as "talented," "intelligent," or "musical," or as a "slow learner" or an "educationally handicapped" student. Publishing schools' mean achievement scores in local newspapers, while intended to provide a certain accountability, actually may lead parents and community leaders to form unwarranted opinions about the quality of schools.

Test scores must be recognized for what they are: samples of behavior under certain conditions at certain points in time. Their primary purpose in schools should be to provide one type of information to use in making decisions to facilitate improved instruction and learning, although it also is understood that they may serve other more specific functions. To the extent that test data are used for purposes beyond the intended, test users will continue to warrant criticism.

It should be noted, however, that some of the most vociferous test critics may misuse test data. Those who would use test data such as the former downward trends in high school students' *Scholastic Aptitude Test (SAT)* scores only to infer that schools are not as effective as they once were need to broaden the data base on which such inferences are made. Many variables may influence the mean *SAT* scores, including the fact that a greater proportion of high school students take the test than was formerly the case.

Controversy about reporting test data has become an increasing concern in recent years, particularly with the increased advocacy of criterion-referenced as opposed to norm-referenced measurement. The basic issue is whether a student's achievement should be evaluated and reported in relation to attainment of a criterion established to provide evidence of instructional achievement or in relation to the achievement of other students, which involves norm-referenced analysis and reporting. The issues involved in the norm- and criterion-referenced evaluation controversy are discussed later in this chapter.

Labeling. Concerns about labeling students as a result of test scores would be particularly warranted if tests were the only bases on which students were labeled. However, it is apparent that teachers, administrators, parents, and virtually everyone continuously make judgments about others, and most of the judgments are made on bases much less valid and reliable than tests. Music teachers in particular are prone to label a student as "talented" or "musical" solely on the basis of subjective evidence that may not be verified by any objective means. Labeling, whether on the basis of tests or other bases, can be a problem if students are unjustifiably treated differently as a result of a label, but to argue that this problem is unique to testing is unwarranted.

The effect of labeling, which essentially creates teacher expectations concerning the achievement of individual students, the subsequent teaching in accordance with those expectations, and, finally, students achieving at their expected level, received much publicity about 15 years ago and became known as the *Pygmalion* effect (Rosenthal & Jacobsen, 1968). Even though the particular study later was discredited thoroughly (Elashoff & Snow, 1971), the view persists that the effect is real. While it may be real in isolated instances, there is no evidence to suggest that it is prevalent in most classrooms or that it is a negative by-product of testing.

External control. The criticism that external testing programs impose external controls on a curriculum and cause teachers to forego instruction leading toward important long-range objectives in order to teach for the test appears to be a problem of test usage that is warranted in many instances. When teachers are expected to teach for a particular achievement test that a school district requires—for example, when all third-, fifth-, or seventh-grade students are given the test and there is the direct or implied indication that the teacher in some way will be accountable for how well the students will score on the test—many teachers feel obliged to spend instructional time coaching students to meet the short-term goals for which the students will be tested rather than perhaps devoting instructional time to other objectives that might, in a teacher's opinion, better meet the needs of the particular students in his or her classroom.

This type of conflict often appears in larger school districts where decisions regarding testing programs are made by administrators or other individuals who are far removed from the classroom, but are required to provide evidence of accountability in a reading, mathematics, science, social studies, or some other general academic program. Another issue besides the testing and accountability program is the amount of autonomy given the individual classroom teacher, and this issue is more a policy matter than an accountability matter. Whether an individual teacher should make all decisions regarding testing or supervisors or administrators should is both a philosophical and a policy matter, and if the decision is made to have external testing programs in order to provide accountability data, specific information should be provided to teachers regarding the extent to which instruction should be focused on teaching for the test. If the test indeed measures achievement relative to the district's instructional objectives, it would appear that teachers should teach for the test; however, if the test assesses behaviors that are not reflected in the district's instructional objectives, serious questions must be raised regarding the validity of the test for the purpose for which it is being used.

The same criticism can also be made in respect to district-wide competency tests in various subject areas when teachers are required to administer the same test to all students at a given grade level, regardless of whether the students in a given class are working at a level that will enable them to have a chance to demonstrate their competencies. Some competencies often are short-term, lower-level cognitive or psychomotor behaviors that require specific knowledge or skills sometimes best developed through rote instructional procedures. A teacher might believe it in the best interest of his or her students to provide broader, richer experiences that may contribute to long-range development beyond the shorter-range behaviors required on a competency test. Again, this is a dilemma in educational philosophy and policy rather than solely a problem of educational evaluation.

Anxiety and self-confidence. Claims that tests create anxiety are no doubt true, but the extent to which this is harmful to students may vary with particular circumstances. Ebel (1979, p. 8) argues that there are no substantial data to support this claim. It is normal and biologically helpful to be somewhat anxious when faced with any test situation, whether in a classroom or any other aspect of life. Children who experience high level anxiety at the prospect of tests in school usually have deeper and broader problems of security, adjustment, and maturity that the tests did not create, and the elimination of tests in school will not resolve these problems. Coping with test anxiety is discussed further in Chapter 11.

Certainly teachers and parents have a responsibility not to put undue pressure on students with respect to performance on tests. Poor test performance usually is a reflection of a broader educational problem for an individual student, and if a student is prepared for a test, his or her anxiety level is unlikely to approach any level that might be construed as harmful. If tests are used for appropriate educational functions and teachers and parents do not place unwarranted pressure on a student to perform on a test, it is doubtful that any harmful stress will result for the student. Harmful stress more likely results from inappropriate usage and unrealistic expectations placed on students by parents or teachers, and again, these are not necessarily problems of tests per se.

Possible damage to students' self-concepts is also more likely to result from a misused test than one appropriately used. Because a student does poorly on a given test does not mean that he or she is any less a person because of it, and teachers should make every effort not to generalize or imply any such thing from a test. Usually this is a problem of labeling and subsequently treating students differentially as a result of the label.

Invasion of privacy. Criticisms of tests as an invasion of privacy usually relate to personality tests and surveys of personal and family relations and attitudes. Whether these types of data are needed for all students is doubtful, and unless there is a particular need for such data for use by qualified counselors and other professionals, using these tests in schools appears unwarranted. Also, all test data and other personal information regarding students should be confidential. They should be shared only with the student, parents, and other qualified professionals in a school district who have a legitimate need for the information. The right to this privacy is protected by federal law.

Bias. Another criticism of tests concerns bias or unfairness to students of racial and cultural minorities and/or of lower socioeconomic status. Criticisms of tests for bias generally have paralleled the public's increased concern for equal rights and opportunities for all U.S. citizens. Gronlund (1981, p. 424) notes that bias may be examined from two perspectives: test content and test usage.

Tests that emphasize white middle-class values, vocabulary, and environment that minority students have not experienced appear to place the minority students at a disadvantage. Tests in one content area that require or imply certain skills or experiences in another area that minority students may be lacking also place the minority students at a disadvantage. The extent to which bias in test content has affected opportunities for minority students is difficult to assess, but the criticisms have prompted test publishers to make special efforts to correct the situation. Most major test publishers now employ staff members of racial and cultural minorities and routinely review tests for content that might be biased against or offensive to cultural and ethnic minorities.

Charges of unfair test usage are most prevalent when tests are used for educational and vocational selection. The controversy focuses on how test fairness is defined. To some, the use of a common cutoff point is fair, but others maintain that fair use of tests for selection involves some adjustment of cutoff scores for minorities. Whether minorities should be ignored or given special consideration in selection decisions is a far broader issue than test usage and requires input from society through the courts for settlement rather than just from educators and psychologists. Perhaps Gronlund (1981, p. 425) summarizes this problem most succinctly: "How can equal educational and occupational opportunities best be provided for members of minority groups without infringing on the rights of other individuals?"

Questions also have been raised about possible sex bias in tests. Critics claim that excessive use of masculine pronouns and the portrayal of women in traditional roles of homemaker, nurse, or secretary is objectionable. Tests of vocational interest have been criticized as unfairly directing females away from certain occupations. Whether females' lower scores on certain occupational tests are a matter of test bias or a result of cultural influences, however, is debatable. Regardless, test publishers, much like textbook publishers, are making efforts to avoid sex role stereotyping.

Coaching. The ready availability of practice manuals for tests used for admissions to college or graduate school—for example, the practice manuals used with such tests as the *Scholastic Aptitude Test* and the *Graduate Record Examination*—suggests that coaching is becoming very important, particularly for those tests used for admission to highly selective programs. This is also apparent in classrooms where teachers are expected to "prepare" students for taking standardized achievement tests through the use of practice tests. While the arguments for using practice tests may be that they exist in order to ensure that students understand the testing procedure, thus maximizing their opportunity to focus on the test content, it appears that, if coaching is effective, it might lead to short-term gains reflected in test scores, thus raising questions about the test's validity for students who have had the benefit of coaching.

Most research on the effects of coaching relates to college admissions tests. Payne's (1982) synthesis of recent research questions whether the amount of coaching necessary to raise scores significantly (a) is worth the time and effort and (b) helps the student perform better in college. Payne argues that time might better have been spent being educated than being coached. He further notes that coaching did not raise scores significantly and thus did not affect the test validity.

The effects of coaching for achievement tests in the elementary and secondary school classroom are unclear; Hopkins and Stanley (1981, p. 144) conclude that unless students are coached on actual test items coaching usually results in small or even negligible gains in test performance over and above the effects of practice in test taking. However, many teachers and supervisors apparently believe that coaching is effective, because it is a prevalent practice. Selective coaching may undermine the purpose of "standardized" testing and offer advantages to students who are the beneficiaries of it. At the very least, it raises questions of ethics and fair play, and professional educators who engage in coaching should reconsider their motives for engaging in the practice.

CRITERION-REFERENCED VERSUS NORM-REFERENCED TESTS

Questions regarding the appropriateness of absolute and relative standards in assessing student achievement have long been an issue in educational testing, but with the formalization of the concept of *criterion-referenced testing* (which is sometimes known as domain- or objectives-referenced testing) and its application to proficiency assessment in the 1960s, there developed a major trend or movement toward use of criterion-referenced tests. With this came intensified debate over the relative merits and functions of criterion-referenced testing and the more traditional norm-referenced testing.

Criterion-referenced testing developed as a part of the accountability movement in the 1960s that emphasized a systems approach to accountability, thus focusing on assessing achievement in relation to specific instructional objectives. Advocates of such accountability systems argued that achievement of individual students must be assessed in relation to pre-specified objectives for a specific instructional domain; the criterion level for achievement must also be established prior to instruction. An individual's achievement is assessed in relation to the criterion levels established for the objectives. In the basic accountability model, a student who is unable to demonstrate achievement or performance at the criterion level is "recycled" to the same or another instructional sequence until he or she achieves the criterion.

It may be argued that criterion-referenced tests are just another way of interpreting test results and that teachers who "grade on the curve," or interpret achievement in a norm-referenced sense by comparing a student's achievement with that of his or her peers, also are concerned with student achievement of instructional objectives. Certainly this is true, and conceivably the same test, assuming that it provides assessment in relation to attainment of prespecified instructional objectives, could be interpreted in either a criterion- or norm-referenced sense, the difference being in the basis on which a student's achievement is interpreted and reported. If it is interpreted only in relation to attainment of the objectives, irrespective of other students, it is criterion-referenced; if it is viewed in relation to other students' achievement, it is norm-referenced. As test makers have refined item development and selection procedures, other differences in test specifications have emerged, but the interpretation of results remains the basic distinction between the two types of tests.

Essentially the decision to use a criterion- or norm-referenced approach for assessing student achievement depends on the particular function that the test is intended to serve. If the concern is to assess the individual student and obtain feedback about his or her achievement of a relatively specific instructional content, the criterion-referenced approach is the more appropriate. If the concern is to assess an individual's general knowledge of a broad content area in relation to some large population, the norm-referenced approach is better because it provides a basis for comparison. Norm-referenced tests also are designed to discriminate among students.

In conclusion, neither criterion-referenced nor norm-referenced tests is superior to the other for all testing purposes; they provide different information, and it is the test user's responsibility to ascertain which type of test is appropriate for obtaining the needed information. If a teacher or school administrator desires to know how students in a particular school or district are achieving relative to students in other schools, a standardized test with appropriate normative data should be used; if the concern is for achievement in relation to specific instructional objectives, a criterion-referenced test should be used.

COMPETENCY TESTING

As might be expected, competency testing has received criticism from many perspectives, and most of the traditional criticisms have also been leveled against competency tests. In addition, critics have argued that education should be concerned with more than just competence. Further, questions have been raised about the appropriateness of particular targeted competencies.

In many respects competency testing is another way of using and conceptualizing criterion-referenced tests, and Berk (1980, p. 5) maintains that competency or mastery tests have become the most frequently used criterion-referenced tests in practice. When criterion-referenced tests are used to determine which students can demonstrate a competency or mastery of a competency, one is engaged in competency testing. What appears to be a primary difference between the traditional conceptualization of criterion-referenced testing and competency testing, however, is the extent to which each stage of instruction must be mastered. In the traditional conceptualization, a student may, for example, achieve criterion for a given instructional domain by meeting a criterion of 80 percent correct responses on a given test, but in competency or mastery testing a student must demonstrate competency of every objective in an instructional sequence before proceeding on to further instruction.* True competency-based educational programs require very careful structuring of content and evaluation of achievement.

Another use of the term competency testing regards admission to or exit from an educational program or a profession on the basis of demonstrated competency. The recently established testing program for certification in music therapy is a reflection of the trend toward the use of competency tests as a basis for admission to a profession (Certification Board for Music Therapists, 1985). A number of states and local school districts have begun to develop competency tests that students must pass before graduation from high school. Colwell (1984) notes that some 30 states require teachers to pass some form of testing prior to certification, and at least one state, Florida, is developing competency tests for use as one standard in identifying teachers, including music teachers, to receive merit pay awards as part of a master teacher program.

Messick (1981) maintains that the controversy and confusion about mastery testing is exacerbated because the terms are used variously as constructs, as standards of performance, and as part of compound constructs such as *minimum competency* or *basic skills mastery*. He notes that even when used as simple or compound constructs the terms have variable meanings, partially depending on the educational or political context in which they are used. He argues that competence is oriented in the present,

---

*Realistically, a "perfect" test score usually is considered impossible for all test takers to achieve (See Chapter 14). Operationalizing "mastery" is a continuing problem.

referring to something one does or can do, as opposed to achievement and aptitude, which have past and future orientations, respectively. Further, he suggests that "competency testing is politically one directional when it should be two directional—pointed not only toward certification for promotion or graduation but also toward diagnosis for remedial action" (p. 16). Messick argues that further complications arise with the use of such terms as minimum competency testing because they compound test interpretation problems by overlaying more than one test interpretation model.

Messick also questions the *meaning* of mastery as used in test score interpretation, asking what it implies above the meaning of the subject matter achievement that is intrinsically compounded with it. Recognizing that mastery is a value-laden term with strong value implications for educational practice, he maintains that test interpreters must delimit the nature of mastery as a construct, which is not always the case in the interpretation of mastery tests. He argues that compound interpretations of mastery tests, as well as competency tests, reflect a kind of nomological looseness that tends not only to undercut meaningful test interpretation, but at the same time to subvert responsible test use.

Regardless of the criticisms of competency tests and the concerns regarding the constructs implied by the terms competency and mastery, it is apparent that competency tests have become an important part of contemporary education. Their role in educational evaluation is controversial, both theoretically and philosophically, and issues related to their use are not likely to be resolved easily or quickly. Educators, state and other agencies that fund educational endeavors, and, to an extent, the general public must recognize the functions of evaluation in education and the role that competency testing fulfills in the overall scheme. Certainly, an overdependence on competency tests for evaluating a school program is questionable.

LIMITATIONS AND DANGERS OF TESTING

As noted in the discussion of test misuses, a test simply provides samples of an individual's behavior under specific conditions at a given point in time, and as such reflects a certain amount of error variance due to the testing instrument and the variable nature of human behavior. (See Chapter 3 for a discussion of error in a test score.) Test users must interpret test scores in light of this, as well as in terms of the function(s) for which a test was designed and validated.

Recognition of test performance as a *sample* of behavior relative to the skill or knowledge under consideration implies further limitations. Unless the test samples a broad range of behaviors and has carefully demonstrated validity for its intended function for the type of student being tested, the types of decisions to be made on the basis of the test also must be limited. The use, therefore, of any single test as the sole criterion for critical decisions relative to any student's educational and/or vocational opportunities must be considered carefully. A single competency test should not be used to determine whether a student should be graduated from high school. *The more critical the educational decision, the greater the potential danger in basing the decision on a single test,* particularly since it appears that cutoff points, or minimum competency standards, are in most cases determined arbitrarily. Glass (1980, pp. 185–193) argues strongly against setting absolute minimum competency standards for high school graduation, and suggests that if a state must use some standard, it should be on a comparative basis, that is, in relation to other students' scores.

A second limitation is that tests assess *behaviors* rather than intelligence, aptitude, competency, ability, or achievement. The latter are psychological constructs *inferred* from test behavior, and the further removed the construct from the test behavior, the greater the inferences must be. As the relationship between the test behavior and the inferred construct becomes less clear, the greater the potential danger the test data may be misused. The well-known debate between Seashore and Mursell about the validity of the *Seashore Measures of Musical Talents,* while aggravated and compounded by misuses of the measures, is an example of this limitation. Mursell and others questioned whether the behaviors required on the Seashore test really could be interpreted as musical "talents." (See Lehman, 1968, pp. 42–45 for a summary of criticisms and responses.)

A third limitation of tests is that they are *tools*—means to an end rather than ends in themselves. Too often classroom efforts focus on preparing for a test, per se, whether an achievement or competency test, a standardized measure of intelligence or musical aptitude, or some type of admissions examination.* There are

---

*Ensemble directors who organize their groups' repertoire around a performance at a contest or rated festival are engaged in preparing for a "test" as an end in itself.

several potential problems inherent in such a misdirected focus. The test score may take on an importance far greater than it deserves, and test anxiety may be increased unnecessarily. Students' and test users' attention may be directed toward the test or test score rather than the instructional content and/or the function the test should be serving in the particular educational context. Some test users may become enamored of the data analysis and give more credence to some norm-referenced analyses than might be warranted. For example, conversion of raw scores to standard scores sometimes appears to "spread" scores on a test, leading a naive test user to assume greater differences among students' test performances than actually exist, particularly when test reliability and measurement error are considered. In short, tests are means, not ends, and to the extent that test users lose this perspective, the danger of misuse increases.

A fourth limitation of tests relates to the claims that testing programs raise and maintain educational standards, a cliché in the literature of most test publishers. Neither a comprehensive testing program nor the extensive use of tests in a given classroom will guarantee an improvement in educational standards. Tests simply provide data, and it is the test user's responsibility to use those data as bases for instructional and/or curricular change. The extent to which educational standards are raised or maintained depends on the quality of the decisions the test user makes relative to instruction and curriculum, as well as on the implementation of the follow-up changes to be made as a result of those decisions. A state-wide competency testing program alone does not raise standards; however, to the extent that the testing program forces educators to make needed changes for improving student competencies, the testing *may* serve to raise and/or maintain standards.

A fifth concern, viewed here as more of a danger than a limitation, is that testing agencies outside of a local school district may have undue influence on the curriculum. Most public schools depend to a high degree on state funding, and states are increasingly concerned about accountability for their educational dollars. Tests are central to most such accountability programs, and the more local school districts are pressured (or at least feel compelled) to teach for these externally imposed tests, the less curricular autonomy they have.

Besides the potential danger from outside funding agencies, there is concern that publishers of instructional materials are increasingly involved in publishing tests (Shulman, 1980). Both are commercial enterprises, and there always is the potential for conflict of interest. Also, some publishers specifically design "standardized" criterion-referenced tests to assess student achievement, often in relation to instructional objectives for their instructional materials. At face value this appears to be a good practice, but the possibility exists for designing tests in such ways that students will appear to achieve at a higher level when using a particular publisher's instructional materials than perhaps when using other instructional materials.

Even with their limitations and potential dangers, tests are an essential part of educational evaluation. Test users and evaluators, however, must recognize test limitations and interpret test data in light of them.

EXTRANEOUS VARIABLES INFLUENCING TEST SCORES

Educators increasingly have recognized that variables other than knowledge, ability, or skill relevant to a testing task may influence students' test scores. Test users must be cognizant of these variables and take steps to minimize their effects if tests are to provide valid samples of behavior relevant to a test's content and function. Hopkins and Stanley (1981, pp. 141–161) provide an excellent review of these variables, and the present discussion is based primarily on their review. Hopkins and Stanley caution that these variables generally affect what Cronbach (1970, p. 35) terms tests of *maximum performance* rather than tests of *typical performance*. Tests of maximum performance include achievement, aptitude, and ability tests, whereas tests of typical performance generally include affective measures and personality inventories.

Perhaps the most influential variable is *test-wiseness*, which reflects a test taker's ability to recognize and use the characteristics and formats of the test and/or test-taking situation to increase his or her score. Test-wiseness reflects the individual's experience in similar testing situations. Test-wise students usually can recognize inadvertent clues in poorly written test items, thus enabling them to answer an item correctly even without knowledge of the item content.

Practice in taking tests can improve test scores, although only to a limited degree. Various studies reviewed by Hopkins and Stanley suggest that practice effects vary for different groups of individuals and that after a certain amount of practice there are no additional practice effects. Practice effects tend to be greatest for people who have had limited experience with tests.

Coaching for tests often is interrelated with practice effects, and Hopkins and Stanley (p. 144) report that gains in test scores over and above practice effects due to coaching usually are slight. Research on coaching effects is much less clear than for test-wiseness and practice effects because the amount or degree of coaching varies greatly from one study to another. As discussed earlier in this chapter, excessive coaching undermines the purpose of "standardized" testing and raises questions of ethics and fair play. Nevertheless, coaching is a prevalent practice and it appears to have some, albeit limited, influence on test scores.

Knowledge of test content or the ability to perform test tasks alone are insufficient bases for a student to give maximum performance on a test; the student must also be *motivated* to succeed. Although it is recognized that the degree of motivation varies widely from individual to individual and among ethnic and social groups, most students appear to be motivated to succeed once they are in a testing situation.* External incentives have little or no effect on normal students who already are motivated to do well on a test (Hopkins & Stanley, p. 145).

Anxiety also may affect test performance, and Hopkins and Stanley report that almost all research on test anxiety reveals a small negative correlation ($-.1$ to $-.3$) between self-report anxiety measures and performance on intelligence and achievement tests. However, one must be careful not to infer *causation* from such correlation studies; they merely indicate that there is some inverse relationship between the two variables. Studies which attempt to induce anxiety experimentally have met with mixed results. Induced anxiety appears to have little or no effect on tests involving only cognitive performance, but when psychomotor performance is required in addition to cognitive performance, one study (Sarason, Mandler, & Craighill, 1952) reported an increase in error rate. Also, Hopkins and Stanley cite several studies that suggest that anxiety influences performance on affective measures more than on cognitive measures. Obviously there is need for much more research in this area, because these assertions regarding the effects of anxiety on psychomotor and affective tests hold implications for the evaluation of musical behaviors.

Response style or *set*, which is defined by Cronbach (1970, p. 148) as "a habit . . . causing the subject to earn a different score from one he would earn if the same items were presented in a different form," also may affect test scores. Several response sets

---

*Some students are more motivated to avoid failure than to attain success (See Chapter 11).

have been identified by Hopkins and Stanley (pp. 146–154): the speed versus accuracy set, the acquiescence set, the positional preference set, the option length set, and the gambling (or guessing) set. While some of these sets affect only certain types of test items, it is clear that they can and do influence test scores. Although a variety of procedures have been devised to correct, or at least control, the effects of guessing, other response sets are more difficult to control, particularly the set to work quickly and with less caution.

Administrative factors also influence test scores. Research on these variables is limited and mixed, but test administrators should be aware of their possible effects. One group of these variables is related to what Lehman (1968, p. 15) calls *"formal validity"* and includes the mode and format of test item presentation, the influences of the test administrator, the setting for the test, the answer sheet format, and scoring procedures. Tests must be presented in modes and formats that are clearly understandable to the test takers and do not distract from the test task. The test setting should be free of disruptive factors and, as nearly as possible, similar to the students' normal classroom setting. Effects of inconsistent oral/verbal directions may be controlled by providing recorded directions. Answer sheet format and scoring also are critical variables. Even with machine-scored answer sheets, substantial scoring errors have been found, usually as a result of problems with marking the answers and with erasures. Studies of hand-scored standardized tests reveal even greater numbers of errors. Chapter 11 examines ways for alleviating some of the problems in test scoring and administration.

Answer changing has been subject to much research, and most of it serves to dispel what Hopkins and Stanley call the "changed-answer myth." Traditional wisdom suggests that test takers tend to obtain higher scores if they follow their first inclination and do not change their answers, but research reviewed by Hopkins and Stanley consistently suggests otherwise. Test takers should not stick with their first response when on second thought they prefer a different one.

A final variable is *cheating*, which Hopkins and Stanley maintain is extremely widespread, virtually at all levels of education from primary through graduate and professional schools. While it may not be possible to prevent all cheating, the test administrator is responsible for making every reasonable effort to reduce it. Conscientious monitoring, structured seating arrangements, and test design are three relatively easy and manageable ways for reducing cheating.

MORAL, SOCIAL, AND POLITICAL IMPLICATIONS

As Resnick (1982, p. 173) has noted, controversy has been a part of educational testing since its inception. Current controversy about testing is focused on social and political implications rather than technical and functional aspects. Gardner (1982, p. 315) reports that a recent Phi Delta Kappa Symposium on "Measurement in Education for the 1980's" stressed the position that problems facing measurement throughout this decade are primarily political rather than technical in nature.

Most criticisms of tests cited earlier in this chapter also relate to misuses rather than technical aspects of tests, and the issues related to uses and misuses that have come to the fore in the past two decades have increasingly reflected concerns about the impact of testing on individuals, social groups, and educational institutions. These issues are complex and intertwined, often reflecting conflicting educational, social, and political concerns. The more that sound professional educational and administrative judgments conflict with prevailing social and/or political concerns, the more complex and difficult the issues become.

With due recognition of the complexities of the issues and the fact that they are not discrete, the present discussion examines them under four broad headings: (a) rights of individuals and minorities, (b) local versus external control, (c) openness in testing, and (d) effects of testing.

Rights of Individuals and Minorities

Hollander (1982, pp. 195–202) notes that through federal legislation of Title VI of the Civil Rights Act of 1964, Section 504 of the Rehabilitation Act of 1973, and the Education for All Handicapped Children Act of 1975 all individuals are provided with the legal right to "fair treatment in assessing educational ability and achievement, and in the subsequent decisions regarding appropriate education" (p. 196). As discussed earlier in this chapter, "fairness" depends on the perspective from which it is viewed. If a common cutoff point is used for competency tests or other tests used for educational and vocational selection, minority groups, who often are educationally disadvantaged, appear to be treated unfairly. On the other hand, is it fair to others to give special considerations to minorities at the expense of individuals who score higher on the tests but are not members of minority groups? Perhaps Wigdor and Garner (1982, p. 18) summarize this issue best: "Translated into political terms, the issue involves balancing the principle of equal opportunity for every individual in society with the reality of unequal background and preparation."

Minimum competency testing programs for high school graduation have especially come under fire, and legal challenges to them are increasing. In a recent case in Florida, *Debra P.* v. *Turlington* (1979), the plaintiff was successful in overthrowing the results of a minimum competency test, partly because it was ruled that the plaintiff had not received equal educational opportunity.

A high school diploma has social and economic implications. Without the diploma, opportunities in the labor force are severely restricted, causing minimum competency tests for high school graduation to have direct economic significance. In addition, higher proportions of black students than white students do not pass these examinations, thus compounding already existing social and economic problems. Competency tests for high school graduation or tests for admission to a profession have significant impact on individuals.

Admissions tests to colleges, universities, and professional schools also are under scrutiny. Are they sufficiently valid bases for making critical decisions affecting individuals' educational and vocational opportunities? Because of the long-term implications for individuals, there is increasing pressure for truth-in-testing legislation that will allow individuals outside of the testing "establishment" to examine such tests closely. (A discussion of openness in testing appears later in this chapter.)

Hollander (1982, p. 202) notes that while in recent years test takers who are members of groups considered vulnerable to discriminatory practices have generally been successful in having their legal rights protected, other test takers have had less success in securing legal rights and remedies. Questions related to test fairness will not be answered quickly or easily. Test users, educational decision makers, and lawmakers must be sensitive to and responsive to the needs of both individuals and society at large. Certainly, fair and accurate educational assessment is a necessary beginning point.

Local versus External Control

Somewhat parallel to questions about the effects of testing on the rights of individuals and social groups is the question of *who* should do the testing and make the related decisions about instruction and curriculum. Traditionally, local school districts have made instructional and curricular decisions within a framework of general state department of education guidelines. Teacher certification is through state departments of education, and most states have mandated high school graduation requirements and general curricular guidelines for elementary and secondary schools and for teacher education programs. Individual school districts have been responsible for determining which students are to graduate. It appears, however, that tradition is changing.

Along with concerns for educational accountability and the back-to-basics movement, there appears to be a rejuvenated "quest for quality" in education among state legislators and departments of education. Many testing programs are outgrowths of these concerns, thus exacerbating many already uneasy relationships between local school districts and state legislatures and/or departments of education. Minimum competency testing programs, which have been adopted by at least 37 states (Hollander, 1982, p. 219), appear to be central to the problem. Should state legislatures and/or departments of education impose a common statewide competency testing program on local school districts, especially when the school districts must serve different and diverse populations? They may have the legal prerogative to do so, even to make some funding contingent upon compliance. What is the impact of this on local school districts? Will it force them to revise curricula to help students develop competencies evaluated by the mandated tests? Specifically, what is the impact on music programs, the content of which is not included on the state minimum competency tests? There is growing fear, and some evidence to support this fear, that emphasis on the basics included in the competency tests will have significant and adverse effects on many music programs.

Openness

The increased social and economic importance of decisions based on tests has led to increased concern about the content, quality, and validity of the tests on which critical educational and vocational decisions are made. Particularly under fire has been the standardized testing industry, most notably the *Educational Testing Service* (ETS). A 564-page document, entitled *The Reign of ETS* (Nairn & Associates, 1980) and better known as the Ralph Nader Report on the Educational Testing Service, served as a catalyst for much of the truth-in-testing legislation that has been enacted in recent years.

Dwyer (1982, p. 17) notes that, while the movement for test disclosure has focused on post-secondary school admissions tests, the issues also are germane to standardized achievement tests. Test makers have argued against test disclosure both for financial and technical reasons, but Dwyer reports that, as of 1981, most test developers had complied with legislated test disclosure requirements.

Truth-in-testing legislation and other "sunshine laws" that affect the standardized testing industry, while perhaps reflecting radical departure from past policies and practices, are intended to protect individuals from alleged misuses of tests in deciding the future educational opportunities young people will have. Whether this proves to be the case, only study of changing practices over a period of time will tell.

Effects of Testing

Tests have become an increasingly important part of education over the past quarter century, and it appears that they will continue to be an integral aspect of educational evaluation in the decades ahead. Obviously, the effects of testing are neither all positive nor all negative, but as Gardner (1982, p. 331) notes, "they [tests] are the most publicly acceptable, politically viable, and probably most technically appropriate instruments we have."

Claims regarding the effects of testing within schools and particularly beyond school settings are difficult to document, although most would agree that testing does have specific influences on individuals, groups of individuals, school programs, and even beyond school settings. Kellaghan, Madaus, and Airasian (1982, p. 261) conclude from their own research, as well as from their review of other research on the effects of tests, that information from standardized testing tends to be assimilated into a broader knowledge that a teacher develops about his or her students through a variety of evaluative procedures, both formal and informal, and because of this, standardized testing has little day-to-day impact on students in schools. Perhaps the more critical effects of tests tend to be in terms of their potential limiting effect for educational and vocational opportunity, many of which are beyond the elementary and secondary school levels.

The negative effects of testing claimed by critics rarely are the result of the quality of the testing instruments per se, but most often stem from a combination of two basic problems: (a) misuses of tests in educational decision making and (b) inadequate policies for making decisions when test data suggest *educational* decisions that are in conflict with *social* and/or *political* policies that have impact both within and beyond educational institutions.

Resolutions to these problems are not simple. The problem of misuses is largely a matter of educating the professionals responsible for administering, interpreting, and making decisions based on tests. Resolving conflicts of educational and social or political concerns is far more complex. However, recognition of the conflicts is a first step, and responsible professionals, both in education and in the broader arena concerned with the social and political welfare of individuals and social groups, must recognize the nature of the conflicting issues and take action to deal with the conflicts.

SPECIAL ISSUES IN MUSIC TESTING

Previous sections of this chapter have examined issues related to educational measurement and evaluation in a broad context, but two issues should be examined as they relate to music testing: (a) global versus specific evaluation and (b) interpretation of test results as behavior or cognition.

Depending on an individual's philosophical and psychological persuasions, the measurement and evaluation of musical behaviors may involve assessment of complex holistic behaviors, such as musical performance, analytical skills, composition, or some other complex musical behavior that requires integration of many skills. Advocates of such a position usually are concerned with evaluation through auditions or critiques of performances or compositions, reflecting a *global* approach to the assessment of musical behavior. Mursell (1937) referred to this approach as the *"omnibus"* approach.

Others, of whom Carl Seashore was a primary proponent, are concerned more with measuring isolated behaviors in the belief that this is the more scientific approach to the measurement of musical behavior. This approach, labeled the *specifics* approach, focuses on testing isolated discrimination skills such as recognition of differences between two pitches, two loudness levels, or two timbres.

The question of which approach to use has centered around

test validity, the claims made regarding what a test is measuring. Mursell questioned whether Seashore's measures of isolated pitches or other tonal attributes were measuring *musical* behaviors and argued that more global measures of musical behavior should be used. The authors' position is that the approach should depend on the purpose of the assessment and the use to be made of the data. It is not an "either–or" situation; rather, more of an "it depends" situation. There are times when one needs to assess basic aural discrimination skills, and it may be more appropriate to do this with isolated tonal stimuli. At other times one is clearly concerned with assessing responses to musical stimuli, and in these situations more global behaviors should be assessed in a musical context.

The particular function for which a test is being used would be an important determining factor in selecting global or specific testing tasks. Many diagnostic functions require specific isolated assessments. Measurement of aptitude also might require assessments of specific aural acuities, although some evaluators might argue that it is necessary to obtain some broader, more global measures of musical experience as part of aptitude assessment. Achievement behaviors tend to require more musical behaviors than isolated behaviors. However, as noted above, the extent to which teachers and professional test makers emphasize global or isolated musical behaviors often is a function of philosophical and psychological persuasion, even when the assessments are to serve a given function.

A second issue in the assessment of musical behaviors is in the degree of inference to be made from the behavioral assessment. Clearly, tests assess *behaviors,* but the extent to which test makers and test users infer that the behaviors reflect covert cognitive or affective constructs varies greatly. As noted in the discussion of musical behavior in Chapter 1, many of the constructs traditionally assessed by music tests, for example, talent, aptitude, and musical ability, are highly inferential and lack consensus regarding definition. Covert responses to music, or constructs used to describe responses to music, are inferred from overt test behavior.

The behavior versus cognition or affect inference issue is somewhat related to the global versus specifics issue. Users of music tests must understand and define clearly what they are attempting to assess and select or develop tests or other evaluative procedures appropriate to obtaining the desired information. Problems arise when naive test users select a test based only on its title or someone's recommendation that it is a "good" test and do not ascertain that the test's theoretical basis and required test behaviors are indeed appropriate for inferring the cognitive or affective construct(s) the test purportedly measures. Test makers and users vary greatly in how much they are willing to infer beyond the testing task itself. Responsible test use demands a strong theoretical basis for inferring covert cognitive or affective constructs; otherwise, a test user should be extremely cautious in making such inferences.

SUMMARY

This chapter examined criticisms of tests and selected issues related to educational measurement and evaluation. Most criticisms of tests focus on uses of tests rather than their technical aspects. Misuses include (a) selection of inappropriate tests, (b) erroneous and naive interpretations of test results, (c) labeling students on the basis of tests, (d) allowing external tests to control a curriculum, (e) creation of undue anxiety among students, (f) invasion of privacy, (g) bias against minorities and the educationally disadvantaged, and (h) excessive coaching for tests.

Other general issues include (a) use of norm- and criterion-referenced tests, (b) minimum competency testing, (c) limitations and dangers of testing, (d) extraneous variables influencing test scores, and (e) moral, social, and political implications of testing.

Two issues of particular relevance to music testing are (a) the global versus specific approaches to music testing and (b) the matter of inferring covert cognitive and affective constructs from overt test behavior.

Study Questions

1. Discuss the potential effects of misuses of tests on children's

    (a) musical achievement,
    (b) opportunities for participation in "special" performance ensembles and programs for the "musically talented," and
    (c) self-concepts and confidence with respect to their musical ability.

2. Discuss the issues and problems inherent in the development of a music competency test for graduation from high school.

3. Suggest ways for alleviating the limitations and dangers inherent in testing.

4. Identify extraneous variables that may influence test scores and discuss the relative degree of influence of each. What are some ways for minimizing the effects of extraneous variables on test scores?

5. Consider the moral, social, and political implications of testing, especially with regard to the rights of individuals and minorities, and suggest strategies for resolving some of the issues at the local, state, and national levels.

REFERENCES

American Psychological Association, American Educational Research Association, & National Council on Measurement in Education *Standards for educational and psychological tests* (Rev. ed.). Washington, D.C.: APA, 1974.

Berk, R.A. (Ed.). *Criterion-referenced measurement: The state of the art.* Baltimore, Md.: Johns Hopkins, 1980.

Certification Board for Music Therapists. *Program for certification in music therapy: Candidate handbook.* Philadelphia: Certification Board for Music Therapists, Inc, 1985.

Colwell, R. *The evaluation of music teaching and learning.* Englewood Cliffs, N.J.: Prentice-Hall, 1970.

Colwell, R. *Music teacher education: Program evaluation.* Paper presented at the meeting of the Music Educators National Conference, Chicago, March 1984.

Cronbach, L.J. *Essentials of psychological testing* (3rd ed.). New York: Harper & Row, 1970.

Debra P. v. *Turlington,* Case No. 78-892-Civ-T-C. Miami, Dade County, Fla., 1979.

Dwyer, C.A. Achievement testing. In H.E. Mitzel (Ed.), *Encyclopedia of educational research* (5th ed.) (Vol. 1, pp. 12–22). New York: Free Press, 1982.

Ebel, R.L. *Essentials of educational measurement* (3rd ed.). Englewood Cliffs, N.J.: Prentice-Hall, 1979.

Elashoff, J.D., & Snow, R.E. (Eds.). *Pygmalion reconsidered.* Worthington, Ohio: Charles A. Jones, 1971.

Gardner, E. Some aspects of the use and misuse of standardized aptitude and achievement tests. In A.K. Wigdor & W.R. Garner (Eds.), *Ability testing: Uses, consequences, and controversies* (Part II). Washington, D.C.: National Academy Press, 1982.

Glass, G.V. When educators set standards. In E.L. Baker & E.S. Quellmalz (Eds.), *Educational testing and evaluation: Design, analysis, and policy.* Beverly Hills, Calif.: Sage, 1980.

Gronlund, N.E. *Measurement and evaluation in teaching* (4th ed.). New York: Macmillan, 1981.

Hollander, P. Legal context of educational testing. In A.K. Wigdor & W.R. Garner (Eds.), *Ability testing: Uses, consequences, and controversies* (Part II). Washington, D.C.: National Academy Press, 1982.

Hopkins, K.D., & Stanley, J.C. *Educational and psychological measurement* (6th ed.). Englewood Cliffs, N.J.: Prentice-Hall, 1981.

Kellaghan, T., Madaus, G.F., & Airasian, P.W. *The effects of standardized testing.* Boston: Kluwer-Nijhoff, 1982.

Lehman, P.R. *Tests and measurements in music.* Englewood Cliffs, N.J.: Prentice-Hall, 1968.

Messick, S. Evidence and ethics in the evaluation of tests. *Educational Researcher,* 1981, *10* (9), 9–20.

Mursell, J.L. *The psychology of music.* New York: W. W. Norton, 1937.

Nairn, A., & Associates. *The reign of ETS* (The Ralph Nader report on the Educational Testing Service). Washington, D.C.: Ralph Nader, 1980.

Payne, D.A. Measurement in education. In H.E. Mitzel (Ed.), *Encyclopedia of educational research* (5th ed.) (Vol. 3). New York: Free Press, 1982.

Resnick, D. History of educational testing. In A.K. Wigdor & W.R. Garner (Eds.), *Ability testing: Uses, consequences, and controversies* (Part II). Washington, D.C.: National Academy Press, 1982.

Rosenthal, R., & Jacobsen, L. *Pygmalion in the classroom.* New York: Holt, Rinehart & Winston, 1968.

Sarason, S.S., Mandler, G., & Craighill, P.G. The effect of differential instructions on anxiety and learning. *Journal of Abnormal and Social Psychology,* 1952, *47,* 561–565.

Shulman, L.S. Test design: A view from practice. In E.L. Baker & E.S. Quellmalz (Eds.), *Educational testing: Design, analysis, and policy.* Beverly Hills, Calif.: Sage, 1980.

Wigdor, A.K., & Garner, W.R. (Eds.). *Ability testing: Uses, consequences, and controversies* (2 vols.). Washington, D.C.: National Academy Press, 1982.

3

Psychometric Foundations

Psychometrics is a discipline that concerns itself with the construction, evaluation, and theoretical bases of psychological measures. By extension, many of its theories and principles apply to the measurement and evaluation of musical behavior. Knowledge of certain psychometric phenomena is essential to a musician seeking to construct or interpret tests, evaluation programs, and audition procedures. This chapter presents practical information for describing a distribution of scores, assessing the adequacy of a measure for a particular purpose, interpreting scores, and distinguishing among measures on the basis of the intended use of the data. Since most of the information is widely known to students of testing and measurement, little specific documentation is necessary. Students who are familiar with elementary statistics may wish to omit the opening sections. Others are invited to enter a world of numbers.

DISTRIBUTIONS

Values obtained from a measurement process, whether they be test scores, judges' ratings, or the measures of some physical attribute, may be arranged into a *distribution* of those values. For example, if one were to administer a test of 20 items that required naming staff lines and spaces to five graduate students in musicology, one probably would obtain a distribution of

20, 20, 20, 20, 20.

A test requiring five third graders to label 20 bassoon tones as typical of the American, French, or German tonal concept could yield a distribution of

0, 0, 0, 0, 0,

although some students might guess the correct tonal concept for a few items.

More realistically, five freshmen music majors asked to classify 20 musical excerpts as typical of the baroque, classical, romantic, or twentieth-century eras might yield the distribution

12, 14, 9, 17, 8.

LEVELS OF MEASUREMENT

Distributions of numeric values may be at one of four commonly recognized levels of measurement. The permissible mathematical operations and the permissible logical statements vary with the level.

Nominal measurement merely employs numbers as names or labels. Nothing can be said about differences in amount of some property represented by the numbers: The measurement serves a categorizing or sorting function. Team player numbers are a classic example; on a football team, number 89 is not necessarily a better or worse player than number 7, although, in the numbering scheme common in American football, number 89 probably plays an end position and number 7 probably is a quarterback. Coding male music students as 1 and female students as 2 (or vice versa) says nothing about the musical abilities or experience of those students.

Ordinal measurement yields rank orders. Nothing is known about the *amount* of difference between any two ranks, but there are clear differences in the property in question. Traditional chair orders within a band or orchestra section exemplify ordinal measurement: The 15 members of a band's clarinet section may be seated in accordance with the results of an audition. The first chair player may be clearly superior to the second chair player, who in turn is only slightly better than the third chair player. Ranks do not represent any constant distance between the ranked persons or objects.

Most educational and psychological applications assume *interval* measurement. A constant unit interval means that there is an equal difference between test scores of 46 and 41 and scores of 36 and 31. Scores may be added and subtracted, and all of the test statistics discussed below may be applied. One can *not* assert that a score of 80 is "twice as good" as a score of 40, however, because interval scales have an arbitrary zero point. A test score of zero rarely if ever represents complete lack of knowledge; had different procedures been employed (possibly much simpler questions), the person scoring zero may have earned a few points. Zero amounts of intelligence or other psychological constructs are difficult to conceive. The Fahrenheit and Celsius temperature scales are excellent physical examples of arbitrary zero points; temperatures colder than Dr. Fahrenheit could obtain in his laboratory or the freezing point of water are possible. One can not say that 90°F is "twice as hot" as 45°F. Similarly, one can not say that a person with a score of 100 on a musical aptitude test has "twice as much aptitude" as a person with a score of 50.

One *can* make "twice as much" and "half as much" statements with *ratio* measures, where there is an absolute zero point that represents a genuine absence of the property in question. The Kelvin temperature scale includes an absolute zero, a point at which molecular motion theoretically ceases, resulting in an absence of heat. A sensation scale, such as the sone scale of loudness, could have a total absence of sensation.

In practice, the most commonly used measurement levels in musical applications are ordinal and interval. For example, adjudicators' ratings generally are treated as ordinal data and scores on tests of musical achievement, as well as most other written tests, are treated as interval data.

CENTRAL TENDENCY

Any set of scores or other distribution of numerical values may be examined for a point around which the numbers tend to cluster or center. Three common indexes of central tendency in a distribution of measured values are the mean, median, and mode.

Mean

The term *mean* almost always refers to the arithmetic average of a set of values. Such a mean technically is an *arithmetic* mean; it is found by summing all the values and dividing that sum by the number of values. In symbolic terms,[*]

$$\overline{X} = \frac{\Sigma X}{N}$$

where

$\overline{X}$ is the arithmetic mean,

X is any particular value in the distribution,

Σ is the *summation operator,* the symbol which instructs one to add the designated values,

and

N is the number of values.

The respective means for the three distributions described above are 20, 0, and 12.

The mean is the most commonly employed measure of central tendency for research and evaluation purposes. It is sensitive to each value in the distribution; if, in the distribution of stylistic classification scores noted above, the 8 were replaced by a 7, the mean would become 11.8. Means provide an easy way to compare the "average" performance of different groups, although average can be misleading.

If a constant is added to or subtracted from each term in a distribution, as might be done to make a group of numbers have no negative values or be in a more convenient range, the mean will change by an identical amount. If 7 were subtracted from each term in the freshman music major distribution above, the "new" mean would be 5.

Means other than the arithmetic mean include the harmonic, whole, and geometric means; the geometric mean will receive some attention in Chapter 8's discussion of *magnitude estimation.*

---

[*]These symbols are in common use, but there is no standardization of statistical symbols. They differ among textbooks; some make symbolic differences between population and sample statistics.

Median

The *median* is a distribution's midpoint. It is the middle value in a distribution containing an odd number of values; for the three five-value distributions noted above, the respective medians are 20, 0, and 12. In a distribution containing an even number of values, the median is the mean of the two middle values.* For example, if the 17 were deleted from the above stylistic classification distribution, the median of the remaining four values would be $(12+9) \div 2 = 10.5$.

The median does not change with each change in a distribution's values. Changing the 8 to a 7 in the stylistic classification distribution lowers the mean, but it does not change the median. The lack of sensitivity to each value makes the median useful for expressing the central tendency of a distribution where atypical values might "pull" the mean to one misleading extreme or the other. For example, if the five cellists in a small high school orchestra own cellos assessed at $500, $300, $700, $600, and $7,900, the mean value of $2,000 gives a distorted view of the cellos' "average" assessed value. The median of $600 is more typical of the cello section.

One must be careful to ascertain that the median is in fact reported rather than the mean (or vice versa) in a particular situation. As indicated above, the mean is more common.

A comparison of a distribution's mean and median provides some evidence of the distribution's symmetry. On a typical classroom achievement test, the mean is below the median: A few low scores, possibly from students who did not study, "pull down" the mean. The resulting distribution has a *negative skew*. A *positive skew* results when the mean is higher than the median; this could happen on a classroom test if the teacher had been effective for only a few superior students, whose relatively high scores "pull up" the mean.

The distribution's degree of skewness, that is, its amount of departure from symmetry, may be quantified when the deviation of each individual score from the mean and the distribution's variability (see the section that follows) are known. Also, a distribution's tendency to be "squeezed toward the middle" or "stretched at its ends" (*kurtosis*) may be quantified (Ghiselli, Campbell, & Zedeck, 1981, pp. 47–49). However, for most classroom testing applications, awareness of the skew is sufficient.

---

*When one is dealing with data grouped into class intervals, interpolation procedures that take into account class boundaries are used. Since the authors believe that modern computation aids make data grouping procedures unnecessary, those procedures are not discussed here. Interested readers may consult a statistical text such as Minium (1978).

Mode

The *mode* is the most commonly occurring value in a distribution. Many distributions have no mode. Some have several values sharing most common occurrence; the term then loses any practical significance. For a large distribution, knowledge of the existence and value of a mode may be of some worth, but the mode is of little interest in most measures of musical behavior.

VARIABILITY

Countless phenomena vary. If musical behaviors did not vary, there would be no need for measurement. Just how much a distribution's values vary from one another is important; distributions with common central tendencies may be very different in terms of variability.

Consider the following three distributions of scores earned by three groups of five students each who took a 10-item test of music recognition:

5, 5, 5, 5, 5

6, 5, 5, 5, 4

10, 6, 5, 3, 1

A quick inspection of the scores shows that one group has zero variability, another has a relatively small amount, and the other has a relatively large amount. Computation of the mean yields $\overline{X} = 5$ for each distribution, but the intra-distribution difference between the highest and lowest score ranges from 0 to 9.

Variance

Variance refers to the "spread" of a distribution. The distribution *characteristic* which is called variance is a measure of *how* spread or scattered the values are. It is defined as the mean of the squared deviations from the distribution mean.

Deviation is the difference between a particular value and the distribution's mean. In the music recognition test distribution 6, 5, 5, 5, 4, the mean is 5 and the respective deviations are 1, 0, 0, 0, and −1; the mean of those squared deviations is 0.4. In terms of a definitional formula,

$$s^2 = \frac{\Sigma(X - \overline{X})^2}{N},$$

where $(X - \overline{X})$ refers to a deviation between a score and the mean, s^2 is the variance, and the other symbols are as above.

Variances usually are computed directly from the individual distribution values. A common computational formula[*] is

$$s^2 = \frac{\Sigma X^2}{N} - \frac{(\Sigma X)^2}{N^2},$$

where the symbols have the same meaning as above. If one computes the variance for the 6, 5, 5, 5, 4 distribution, it is found to be 0.4.

Variances probably are more meaningful when several are compared. In addition to their utility for comparing distributions, variances are the bases for various statistical comparisons. For example, one can assess the effects of an experiment by determining how much of the observed variability in subjects' scores is due to experimental treatments and how much is due to other factors; this is known as analysis of variance.

Standard Deviation

A distribution's variability often is expressed by a yardstick of variability called the *standard deviation*. The standard deviation (s) is found by extracting the square root of the variance (s^2). For the 6, 5, 5, 5, 4 music recognition test distribution, $s = \sqrt{.4}$ or .632.

Adding or subtracting a constant to each term in a distribution will not change the variance or standard deviation. Multiplication or division of each term by a constant will cause the variance to be multiplied or divided by the *square* of the constant. The standard deviation will be multiplied or divided by the constant. In the above example, if all terms were divided by 2, making the distribution 3, 2.5, 2.5, 2.5, 2, the "new" variance would be $.4 \div 2^2 = .1$. The "new" standard deviation would be $.632 \div 2 = .316$.

According to Popham and Sirotnik (1973, p. 20), the standard

---

[*]This is a computational formula for a population variance, not a sample variance. The distribution of interest is considered a population to be described, not a sample for use as a basis of inference about some larger population. This generally is the case with a set of test scores.

deviation is a linear measure of variability; it is in terms of the distribution's original units of measurement. The variance, in terms of squared measurement units, is analogous to a surface area, thereby accounting for "spread" in more than one direction. The standard deviation is more likely to be used as a measure of variability in a distribution of test scores; the variance is more likely to be used in research settings where one wishes to determine sources of variability.

Standard Error of Measurement

The *standard error of measurement* is an estimate of the variability in an expected distribution of a given individual's score if that individual's particular knowledge, skill, or attitude were to be measured repeatedly many times. Theoretically, errors of measurement would cause an observed score to fluctuate around some "true" score (which never is known for certain), even if the individual's knowledge, skill, or attitude did not change. The standard error of measurement, which is the standard deviation of the distribution of sample test scores that would result from repeated testing of the individual, is given by

$$s_m = 2 \sqrt{1-r},$$

where

s_m = standard error of measurement,
s = the test's standard deviation, and
r = the test's reliability. (True score and reliability are discussed in the following section.)

As an example, consider again the above 6, 5, 5, 5, 4 music recognition test distribution. The standard deviation is .632. Short tests given to a small group with little variability usually have a low reliability; by the split-halves method (see discussion, under "split-halves reliability," which follows) it might be .40. Substituting in the formula yields a standard error of measurement of .490.

As a more realistic example, consider a 100-item multiple-choice music history final examination with a standard deviation of 6.25 and a reliability of .90. Substituting in the formula yields 1.98. The standard error of measurement, an index of *intra*individual variability, always will be smaller than or equal to the standard deviation, an index of *inter*individual variability, some of which presumably is due to differences in true scores as well as measurement error.

The standard error of measurement often is estimated from the test group's standard deviation and the test reliability. This may be questionable in situations where the test group is rather heterogeneous, as in a case where a freshman music appreciation test is developed for a compulsory university-wide course. Individual standard errors of measurement may be determined (Mehrens & Lehmann, 1973, p. 106).

The more reliable the test, the lower the standard error of measurement; the smaller the region of possible variations around the true score. If one assumes a normal distribution, one can say that a true score lies within +1 or −1 standard errors of measurement of the observed score with "68 percent certainty." With 95 percent certainty, the true score lies within +2 or −2 standard errors of the observed score. Regardless of quantitative specificity, the existence of a standard error of measurement well suggests the imprecision and lack of finality of *any* particular score.

Range

The difference between the highest and lowest value in a distribution, the *range,* may be reported as a crude measure of variability, especially for gross comparisons of large distributions.

The range can be misleading. Consider two distributions resulting from two groups of five freshman theory students who took a 20-item test of aural recognition skills: 15, 14, 14, 12, 3, and 15, 12, 11, 8, 3. In each case, the range is 12. The respective standard deviations are 4.41 and 4.07; the first group is somewhat more "spread out." As a more extreme example, consider the distributions 17, 15, 12, 11, 9 and 17, 9, 9, 9, 9: The range is 8 in each case, but the first distribution obviously has a greater variety of values.

Quartile Deviation

When the median is the measure of central tendency, the *quartile deviation,* also known as the *semi-interquartile range,* is an appropriate measure of variability. Just as the median is the distribution's midpoint, the first quartile (Q_1) is the point below which 25 percent of the values lie, and the third quartile (Q_3) is the point below which 75 percent of the values lie. The quartile deviation then is

$$Q = \frac{Q_3 - Q_1}{2}.$$

In an asymmetrical distribution, the distance from the median to Q_1 may be different than the distance from the median to Q_3. Then, the median plus or minus the computed Q will not be a strictly accurate description of the distribution.

RELIABILITY

Definition

Reliability is defined as the *consistency* with which a measuring instrument measures. If such an instrument consistently yields the same result when it is used to measure the same thing, the instrument is reliable. A good thermometer will give a consistent reading for a given air condition, a good tape measure will give a consistent reading for a given table length, and a good musical aptitude measure will give a consistent reading for a given level of musical aptitude. Of course, if what is being measured changes, as often is the case in educational and psychological measurement, "inconsistent" measures are not necessarily due to unreliable measurement.

A more technical definition of reliability refers to the proportion of variance in a set of values that is due to genuine variability in what is being measured (Stanley, 1971). In symbolic terms,

$$r_m = \frac{\sigma_T^2}{\sigma_X^2},$$

where

r_m = reliability of the measure,
σ_T^2 = variability due to genuine differences in the measured values,
σ_X^2 = observed variability in the measured values.

One never knows for certain the variability due to genuine differences (the *true* variance) although, as illustrated below, there are ways to estimate it. The *observed* variability is simply the variance provided by the formula for s^2 earlier.

Suppose a test requiring classification of musical excerpts as stylistically representative of the baroque, classical, romantic, or twentieth century periods is administered to a freshman music appreciation class. The scores vary; most of the variability should be due to differences in the students' abilities to classify the excerpts. The remaining variability may occur due to momentary inattention, differences in willingness to guess, ambiguities and distractions in the testing environment, unclear excerpts, and reasons that no one would be likely to identify. Such remaining variability is called *error* variance. So, the music appreciation scores vary due to true variance (σ_T^2) in stylistic classification ability and to error variance (σ_E^2). In symbolic terms, $\sigma_X^2 = \sigma_T^2 + \sigma_E^2$. The greater the proportion of observed variability due to true variance, the more reliable is the test.

Just as the overall variance theoretically may be allocated to true and error components, an individual test score may be considered to have a true component, representing what the individual truly "knows," and an error component, representing influences serving to enhance or depress the true score due to measurement inconsistencies.

Reliability Estimation

A perfectly reliable test, which is impossible, has a reliability of 1.00. In such a test all the observed variability is due to true variability in what is being measured. A perfectly unreliable test, one with a reliability of .00, yields scores which vary entirely because of error variance. The band in which a reliability estimate theoretically may fall then is between .00 and 1.00.* The closer to 1.00 the estimate, the more reliable is the test.

Techniques for reliability estimation examine consistency between test versions, between administration times, and within the test. A discussion of the common techniques, usually applied to paper-and-pencil measures, follows. Reliability based on consistency among judges (so-called *interscorer* reliability) is discussed in Chapter 11.

---

*It is possible to obtain a negative reliability estimate, particularly with a short test administered to a very small (N<10) group. Such statistical artifacts are rare and, for practical purposes, may be interpreted as indicative of very questionable reliability.

Parallel Forms Reliability. Theoretically, there are many ways to measure a given property. A person could measure the width of a residential sidewalk with different yardsticks, meter sticks, or tape measures. Each measuring device is a parallel form of the other measuring devices. Similarly, a person could identify 200 musical excerpts for freshman music appreciation students to classify by style period. One hundred excerpts could be assigned randomly to Form A and 100 to Form B. The two test forms, if equivalent, should yield similar results when administered to the same group of students if the test is reliable. The relationship between the two sets of scores is an estimate of the test's reliability.

The *correlation coefficient* (r) expresses parallel forms reliability, as well as test–retest reliability and, as will be seen, an "uncorrected" split-halves reliability. Since the correlation coefficient between the two supposedly parallel measures' scores *is* the reliability, this is an appropriate time to discuss correlation, but correlation is not limited to parallel forms reliability: It is a key concept of descriptive statistics. Readers who are familiar with correlation may skip ahead.

A correlation coefficient is a number that indicates the size and direction of relationship between two sets of scores. The number may range from -1.00, a perfectly negative relationship, to 1.00, a perfectly positive relationship.* A perfectly negative relationship $(r = -1.00)$ is illustrated by the following situation:

Student	Score on X	Score on Y
Albert	8	3
Flora	7	4
Maude	6	5
Paul	5	6
Zelda	4	7

Albert, who is highest on the measure of X is lowest on Y. Zelda, lowest on X, is highest on Y. The higher the rank on X for anyone, the lower the corresponding rank on Y. A perfectly positive relationship $(r = 1.00)$ is illustrated by:

Student	Score on X	Score on Y
Clark	9	10
Donald	7	8
Mary	6	7
Phyllis	5	6
Sandor	4	5

---

*Both "perfect" relationships are equally strong. The closer to positive *or* negative 1.00 the correlation coefficient is, the stronger the relationship.

Here, the higher the X score, the higher the Y score will be, and the difference between the corresponding scores is consistent. Clark is highest in both distributions; Sandor is lowest.

A more realistic example might be provided by correlating scores on Forms A and B of the music appreciation test mentioned earlier. To keep the numbers small, we shall assume a small class in which no one scores well on either form:

Student	Score on Form A	Score on Form B
Barbara	10	9
Frank	7	7
Jennifer	6	7
Quinn	6	5
Walter	4	3

There are minor inconsistencies between the forms in all but one student's scores. A somewhat different rank ordering exists between the forms. The correlation coefficient is the reliability estimate.

A common computational formula for the correlation coefficient usually used with such data (the Pearson product–moment correlation coefficient) is

$$r = \frac{N\Sigma XY - (\Sigma X)(\Sigma Y)}{\sqrt{[N\Sigma X^2 - (\Sigma X)^2][N\Sigma Y^2 - (\Sigma Y)^2]}}$$

where

r = the correlation,
N = the number of *paired* scores,
ΣXY = the sum of the products of corresponding X and Y scores,
ΣX = the sum of the X scores,
ΣY = the sum of the Y scores,
ΣX^2 = the sum of the squared X scores,
ΣY^2 = the sum of the squared Y scores,
$(\Sigma X)^2$ = the squared sum of the X scores,

and

$(\Sigma Y)^2$ = the squared sum of the Y scores.

The appropriate values for the above data, with Form A designated as the X scores and Form B designated as the Y scores, are:

$$N = 5,$$
$$\Sigma XY = 223,$$
$$\Sigma X = 33,$$
$$\Sigma Y = 31,$$
$$\Sigma X^2 = 237,$$
$$\Sigma Y^2 = 213,$$
$$(\Sigma X)^2 = 1089,$$

and

$$(\Sigma Y)^2 = 961.$$

Substituting the values into the formula and solving for r yields a correlation coefficient between the two test forms of .92; this is the estimate of parallel forms reliability. There is no universally recognized minimum acceptable reliability, but .92 is quite reliable.*

Test-Retest Reliability. Another means of estimating reliability is correlating the scores from a first administration with the scores from a second administration. If the test is measuring consistently, there should be a strong positive relationship, as indicated by the correlation coefficient, between the Time 1 and Time 2 scores, *provided* that what is being measured has not changed. In some educational measurement situations, test–retest reliability may be inappropriate because of the opportunity for students to learn (or forget) between the two administering times.

Split-halves Reliability. This technique often is used to estimate the reliability of a one-time teacher-made test. The test is divided arbitrarily into two sections, usually the odd numbered and even numbered items, and the resulting two sets of scores are correlated. Then the correlation is "boosted" to provide the reliability estimate via the twofold increase case of the Spearman–Brown prophecy formula,

$$r_{TT} = \frac{2r_{HT}}{1 + r_{HT}}$$

where

$$r_{TT} = \text{reliability of the total test,}$$

---

*The scores and group sizes in this example are small for illustrative purposes. The principles remain the same regardless of score values and group sizes.

and

r_{HT} = reliability of "half" of the test, i.e., the correlation coefficient resulting from correlating the two halves.

The rationale for the "boost" is that the test was shortened artificially by the odd–even split, and the formula projects the reliability back to the full-length value.

A split-halves reliability estimate is easy to compute, but it can give spurious results when many test takers omit numerous items—there is considerable "consistency" in omitted items, distributed evenly among the two test halves. Furthermore, the odd–even split is arbitrary—there are other ways of halving the test, all of which may yield different results. Because of such factors, split-halves reliability probably should be considered a relatively liberal estimation—the "true" reliability usually will not be higher.

A further word regarding the Spearman–Brown prophecy formula is in order. The formula above is a special case for predicting the reliability of a test lengthened by a factor of two. In general terms, the formula is

$$r_{TT} = \frac{nr_i}{1 + (n-1)r_i}$$

where

r_{TT} = the projected reliability,
n = the multiple by which the test is lengthened,

and

r_i = the reliability of the unlengthened test.

Note that (a) the formula can be used to predict what will happen to the reliability if the test is lengthened by *any* multiple and that (b) the original reliability estimate may be obtained by *any* means. The reader must not think that Spearman–Brown and split-halves are synonymous.

Internal Consistency Methods.   Reliability may be conceived as a matter of the relationship between individual items or interitem consistency. The average interitem correlation may be estimated by *coefficient alpha.* In symbolic terms,

$$r_{TT} = \frac{I}{I-1}\left(1 - \frac{\Sigma\sigma_i^2}{\sigma_X^2}\right),$$

where

r_{TT} = reliability of the test,
I = the number of test items,
$\Sigma\sigma_i^2$ = the sum of the item variances,

and

σ_X^2 = the variance of the overall scores.

The variance of any test item is found in the same manner that an overall score variance is found; the individual terms are the individual scores for that item and are plugged into the variance formula. Calculations necessary for coefficient alpha can become rather laborious if no calculator or computer is available, but the technique is one of the few that can be used with tests containing variable point items, such as found in many attitudinal measures, which have no "right" answers.

When a test consists of dichotomous items (each has a "right" answer and anything else is "wrong"), the internal consistency may be estimated by the Kuder–Richardson formula 20

$$r_{TT} = \frac{I}{I-1}\left(1 - \frac{\Sigma p_i q_i}{\sigma_X^2}\right),$$

where

p_i = the proportion of examinees answering item i correctly,
q_i = the proportion of examinees answering item i incorrectly,

and the remaining symbols mean what they do in the coefficient alpha formula. Note that one multiplies p_i and q_i for each item and sums the individual products. That sum is divided by the overall variance as part of the computational process.

According to Nunnally (1970), the internal consistency method is in reality estimating the correlation of a test form with a hypothetical alternate form. The technique should not be used when test items are rather heterogeneous in nature.

A less well-known method for estimating test reliability is Hoyt's (1941); it yields results identical to those of the above internal consistency methods. Hoyt's procedure uses an analysis of variance approach, in which total score variability is partitioned among variability attributable to test takers, to items, and to measurement error—the less the error, the higher the portion of variability attributable to deliberate manipulation and to the test takers, hence the higher the test reliability.

Factors Influencing Reliability

As indicated above, reliability is conceived as the proportion of score variance attributable to genuine differences in what is being measured. To what extent do score differences reflect "genuine" differences? To what extent do they reflect differences in other characteristics? To what extent do they reflect idiosyncrasies of the measurement situation? These questions never can be answered with absolute accuracy, but consideration of variability and its sources can improve reliability.

In general, the more varied the score distribution, the more reliable the test. A restricted range of scores will lower the reliability. Hence, a test comprised of items that are appropriate regarding content and comprehensibility will be more reliable than a test of needlessly difficult or easy items.

Individuals may vary in the extent to which they comprehend directions and can read and interpret the items. Directions, including whether one should guess, peculiarities of machine-scorable answer sheets, whether or not every choice in a matching item should be used, and specifications of what an essay item seeks, should be as clear and distinct as possible. (With some groups, especially younger pupils, it may be wise to talk through the test as the pupils work.) Ideally, items should be written so that a person who "knows" the material will see quickly just what is expected. Needless verbiage should be avoided.

Guessing may be a problem in tests where the examinee selects rather than constructs an answer. In the "real world," one occasionally must operate with educated guesses, so a teacher may choose to ignore the variance introduced by differences in tendencies toward and success in guessing. So-called guessing formulas presume an equal likelihood to select each choice; this usually is an unrealistic presumption, particularly for students who have partially mastered the material. One should avoid two-choice items because of the fifty–fifty possibility of a correct guess for those who do guess at random; a "?" or "Don't know" option may alleviate some guessing. People who are cautious test takers may be discouraged from guessing by applying a scoring formula in which the number of wrong answers is subtracted from the number of right answers so that a wrong answer hurts more than an omitted answer. An illuminating discussion of scoring formulas, philosophical arguments, and instructions to examinees appears in Thorndike's (1971, pp. 59–61) lengthy footnote addressing the problem of guessing.

Individuals vary in what sometimes is called "test-wiseness," which is the ability to detect certain cues which suggest a correct answer, especially on a paper-and-pencil test. Music history test items occasionally may be answered by matching composers and titles on the basis of nationality or language. A multiple-choice item stem ending with "an" may point to the one choice which begins with a vowel. Answers to a later item may appear inadvertently in an earlier item. A true–false item or a multiple-choice option that appears unusually long or full of qualifications may attract undue attention to form rather than content. Items should be written in such a way as to avoid enabling the test taker to discern the correct answer by analyzing the item's structure.

Although evidence regarding effects of distraction is mixed and people vary in their ability to stay on task, the test administrator should strive for a comfortable environment, taking into consideration temperature, light, and quiet. Musical examples should be free from distortion and played at a comfortable loudness level. Aside from legal and moral implications, test security and prevention of cheating may help prevent reliability loss—and why tempt people?

Other factors being equal, a longer test will be more reliable. There is a practical limit, of course; a test that hardly anyone can finish may look spuriously reliable, especially by the split-halves method. It may be wise with multiple-choice tests to consider writing three-choice rather than four- or five-choice items; more material can be covered in the same testing time with no loss of reliability (Asmus, 1978).

To promote test reliability, then, one should strive for simple and clear directions, potential for a wide range of scores, a comfortable environment, test items with no "giveaways," and as long a test as practical.

Reliability is a complex and somewhat controversial topic among psychometricians; readers interested in the rationale behind the

particular estimation techniques and the reliability recommendations should consult Stanley's (1971) classic chapter.

VALIDITY

Definition

Validity refers to how well a measure measures what it is
supposed to measure. A validity estimate is, in a sense, an estimate
of "truth in measurement." A measure that is invalid for the alleged
purpose will yield false and even bizarre results.

Validity is a particular problem in the measurement of musical
behavior. An aptitude or "talent" test may be a valid measure of a
particular skill, such as pitch discrimination or tonal memory, and
yet be invalid as a measure of likely success in formal music
instruction because the test is not sufficiently comprehensive and
does not consider important but nonmusical aspects of formal
instruction. Many college and high school students' complaints
about "unfair" tests can be viewed as validity problems—the tests
did not measure what the students were led to believe would be
measured.

Reliability is a necessary but not sufficient prerequisite for
validity. A highly reliable test of achievement in undergraduate
music theory is not valid as a measure of skill in playing the oboe.
The time-honored rated music festival, probably valid as a measure
of planned well-rehearsed performance of a few selections, is quite
invalid as a measure of the performers' general musical knowledge.

Validity Estimation

Unlike reliability estimates, validity estimates usually are qualitative rather than quantitative. Terminology used to refer to different
types of validity varies; the authors have elected to discuss *content,
predictive*, and *construct* validity. A few other related terms are
used as merited.

Content Validity. How well does a test sample the domain of
logically related observables? Do test items provide adequate
coverage of the supposedly tested material? These are the sorts of
questions answered positively by a test that has content validity.

For example, a valid test of this chapter would include items related to central tendency, variability, reliability, validity, norms, and the test classifications discussed near the end of the chapter. Within each major section, attention would be given to the stressed subsections, such as types of central tendency, reliability estimates, and norms.

It is important to provide a balanced representation of material among the items in a test purported to have content validity. A recommended procedure, especially useful with multiple-choice tests, is to determine the test length appropriate to the purpose and the relative proportions of instructional material, as represented by the amount of textbook pages, lecture time, and/or assignments, which are devoted to particular topics. If roughly one-fourth of the instructional material in a music history unit is devoted to Beethoven symphonies, then roughly 20 items of an 80-item unit test should be devoted to Beethoven symphonies. Prior to actual item writing, the test writer can construct a matrix with item numbers running along one dimension and aspects covered in instruction along the other dimension. Such a matrix will help with balancing the test content.

Content validity should not be confused with *face* validity, which is simply a judgment that a measure "looks" like a measure of whatever it is supposed to measure. A balanced representative sampling of what *could* be measured is the criterion for content validity.

Content validity is the most logical means of justifying the validity of an achievement measure. Written achievement tests should contain a representative sampling of the instructional content; performance achievement tests should require performance of what the performer has been expected to study and practice.

Predictive Validity. To the extent that a measure is accurately able to predict the outcome of another measure, it has predictive validity. One might wish to predict success in formal music instruction, college, or an occupation. The correlation between scores on the predictive measure and on the criterion measure provides a quantitative indication of validity. Predictive validity is an important consideration in using a measure as a basis for selecting students for future instruction.

Consider a measure of skills such as pitch discrimination, loudness discrimination, tonal memory, and rhythm pattern discrimination. How could its validity as a predictor of success in learning to play an instrument be established? One way is to administer the measure to a large group of people representative of those for whom the measure is intended. In many school settings, instrumental music lessons begin in fourth or fifth grade, so the test could be administered to many fourth and fifth graders prior to the onset of instruction in instrumental music. The students' performing abilities could be assessed after one or two years of study, and the performance scores could be correlated with the test scores. A strong positive relationship might indicate good predictive validity. It also might indicate that some other factor or factors is or are jointly responsible for high test scores *and* the ability and stamina necessary to succeed with an instrument. Nevertheless, although strong correlation does not indicate a cause and effect relationship, a strong correlation between predictor and criterion is a good sign that the predictor will indicate more about future criterion behavior than will random guessing.

Criterion-related and *empirical* validity are other terms used for predictive validity. When the criterion is not in the future, the term *concurrent* validity may be used; a new test may be validated by correlating the new test's scores with scores on an older recognized measure of the behavior in question. One always may wonder about the validity of the criterion, especially when the criterion is another test.

Construct Validity. A *construct* is a somewhat abstract concept or organizational perception of a psychological trait. One can con*struct* for himself or herself a *con*struct of musical ability, intelligence, rhythmic perception, or some other trait. Constructs may be linked together in a theory. To the extent that a measure yields results as predicted or presupposed by a theory, that measure has construct validity.

For example, consider a theory that says that ability to recall and recognize tonal sequences is an important component of musical ability, one which is related directly to success as a performing musician. The better performers then should score well on an appropriate test of tonal memory; weaker performers should score poorly. If that is the case, the tonal memory test *may* have construct validity as a performance measure. If the relationship is not as it should be, the test may be invalid, or the theory may be invalid.

Establishing construct validity is a lengthy and difficult process, involving careful construction of a requisite theoretical framework. At present, construct validity is less important than content or predictive validity in the measurement of musical behavior, but as researchers attempt to build theories enabling prediction and explanation rather than just description of human musical activity, construct validity may become increasingly important. (One possible important use is discussed later under "Criterion-referenced Tests.")

NORMS

In many instances of educational and psychologial measurement, the information provided by the raw score (usually the number of items answered correctly) is insufficient. If Jimmy recognizes 15 of 20 excerpts on a "drop the needle" test, that may be "good," but is it? What if Jimmy is one of 50 students, and the other 49 earned scores of at least 18? What if Jimmy is the class "star," and no other student recognized more than 10 excerpts? How does Jimmy's relative performance on this test compare with his performance relative to students in other classes?

Comparisons among individuals are facilitated by *norms*, which should be interpreted as representative scores. Norms are established by administering a test to a large sample of representative people and equating the raw scores with one or more forms of equivalent scores. Commonly used equivalents include standard scores, age scores, and percentile ranks. There are other types of norms; a standard reference such as Mehrens and Lehmann (1973) may be consulted.

Norms are obtained from a designated population sample. Information regarding the size and constitution of the norm group is necessary for a test user to interpret fully the meaning of his or her scores in relation to the reference group. Groups are not representative merely by being large or available; Angoff (1971, pp. 550–557) discusses various procedures for selecting norm groups in order to enhance their ability to represent accurately the population under consideration. Even with meticulous sampling procedures, norm groups' scores become obsolete due to demographic and philosophical changes in education.

Standard Score

A standard score is based on the number of standard deviations by which a particular score deviates from the mean of a given distribution. In the "basic" form, known as the z-score, the formula is

$$z = \frac{X_i - \overline{X}}{s},$$

where

X_i = the score in question,
$\overline{X}$ = the mean of the distribution,

and

s = the standard deviation.

For example, if the mean of Eddie's test is 12 and the standard deviation is 3, Eddie's z-score corresponding to his raw score of 15 is 1.00. Relative to his class, Eddie has done rather well; he is one standard deviation above the mean. Comparisons may be made on a standard deviation scale with Eddie's other test scores and scores of his classmates.

In the case of a large representative group, the z-score corresponding to a particular raw score becomes a norm. Then, in the future, for as long as the representative group may be considered a valid representation of the population in question, one who earns the particular raw score can be compared in terms of standard deviation to the representative group. Those who approach mean or "average" performance of the group will have z-scores near 0.00. Those who are truly exceptional will have z-scores approaching 2 or more standard deviations (+2.00 or −2.00). Z-scores may be interpreted in accordance with a normal curve (see Chapter 8).

Other forms of standard scores are derived from z-scores. The T-score* is derived by multiplying the z-score by 10 and adding 50. This may make the standard score "look" better; negative T-scores are rare, and the decimal places usually are fewer. The T-scores that correspond to the z-scores of −1.50, −0.83, 0.00, 1.00, 1.88 are, respectively, 35, 41.7, 50, 60, and 68.8. One may multiply the z-score, which is in relation to an arbitrary mean of zero in a distribution with an arbitrary standard deviation of 1, by any number, which will represent the new standard deviation, and add any number, which will represent the new mean. Standard scores in the *Music Achievement Tests* (Colwell, 1969), for example, have a mean of 500 and a standard deviation of 100.

---

*The T-score should not be confused with the inferential statistical technique called the *t*-test.

Age Score

In a test appropriate to differing chronological ages, one can determine the age equivalents that are most common for particular raw scores. If the mean age that earns a score is 12 years and 4 months, the norm for that score is 12.3 (*not* 12.4!). One also could express the raw score or derived score that is typical of a given age. Age scores can be very deceptive because considerable variability may exist in the ages of representative people who earn a given raw score. With the tremendous divergences found in child development and social environment, it may be wise to avoid norms in the form of age scores.

Of course, one can determine norms for a *particular* age group, just as one can determine norms for any population or subset of that population from an adequate sample. With norms for a particular age group the question is "How does Arthur compare with other students of his age?" regarding percentile rank or standard score rather than "What age does Arthur's score represent?" or "What is the age equivalent of Arthur's score?"

Percentile Rank

There is a certain clarity and concreteness in saying that a person earned a score that equals or exceeds a certain percentage of the test scores or the scores within a reference group. The *percentile rank* enables this; it is the sum of the percentage of scores below the particular score plus one-half of the percentage the particular score comprises. The formula is

$$P_X = 100 \left[\frac{N_{<X}}{N} + .5 \left(\frac{1}{N} \right) \right],$$

where

P_X = the percentile rank for score X,
$N_{<X}$ = the number of scores lower than score X,

and

N = the number of scores.

Suppose 10 people take a test. Jimmy and Jane each earn a score that exceeds five others (the actual score value is not necessary for determining percentile rank). Their percentile rank is

$$100 \left[\frac{5}{10} + .5 \left(\frac{1}{10} \right) \right],$$

or 55. If Marla earns the highest score, her score exceeds nine others; her percentile rank is 95.

The size of the reference group will alter the possibilities of percentile ranks; a larger group has more possibilities. A person (i.e., his or her *score*) who exceeds 996 of 1000 scores will have a percentile rank of 99.65.

Percentile ranks may function as norms when a given raw score is equated with the percentile rank in a reference group. Sometimes plain "percentile" is used; properly speaking, percentile refers to the actual score that has a certain percentile rank: In the example above, if Jimmy and Jane's raw score is 53, the score of 53 is the fifty-fifth percentile.

THREE TYPES OF TESTS

Norm-referenced Tests

If a test's primary purpose is to discriminate among individuals, the test is norm-referenced. The discriminating power of individual items (see Chapter 5) becomes very important, and interpretation of scores on a relative basis is critical.

In the norm-referenced situation, *how* good is "good" depends upon the performances of the test taker's peers. In the event that Herman answers 60 of 100 items correctly, Herman is a "star" if no one else in a class of 50 earned a score higher than 45. Herman is spectacularly unsuccessful if everyone else earned at least an 80. Regardless of how much a person "knows" about the material in question or how skillfully he or she can perform in a designated situation, the judgment of that person's endeavor depends upon where he or she stands within the group of interest.

Norm-referenced tests are useful, if unpopular, for comparisons among schools. Even though a school's pupils may be reading "below national norms," that school may be the best in an impoverished urban system—when all the other schools in the city are further below the norms. The rated music festival, while presumably judged on the basis of rigidly designated standards, in reality operates on a partially norm-referenced basis. Ratings assigned to performers appearing later in the festival almost always are influenced by ratings assigned to earlier performers. In short, when one wishes to make relative comparisons among individuals, groups, or institutions, a norm-referenced approach is appropriate.

Criterion-referenced Tests

Criterion-referenced testing appeared in the psychometric literature in the 1960s and was of considerable interest in the early 1970s. In the authors' opinion, no really adequate definition has been offered; Glaser's (1963) distinction of a criterion-referenced test as one that makes comparisons with an absolute standard while a norm-referenced test makes comparisons with a relative standard probably is useful. The distinction in practice must be in terms of the *use* made of the test data.

The standard, or criterion, to which a criterion-referenced test "refers" must be fixed in relation to some arbitrary standard. If an instructor develops a series of tests for a music literature class, and sets grading criteria as

93% of all items answered correctly for an A,

84% of all items answered correctly for a B,

72% of all items answered correctly for a C,

and

63% of all items answered correctly for a D,

the testing may be said to be criterion-referenced: Scores are interpreted in relation to the instructor's arbitrary criteria. Individual grades will not be influenced by any sort of interindividual comparisons; grade assignment is strictly a matter of where each student stands in relation to the criteria.

Criterion-referenced testing may be especially appropriate in "pass-fail" or "can do–can not do" situations, particularly those requiring demonstration of a clear-cut skill. Either the French horn player can or can not string a valve. The clarinetist either can or can not demonstrate chromatic fingerings. A marching band member either can demonstrate the dance routine in correct sequence or can not. In all cases, the individual meets or does not meet an arbitrary criterion, regardless of how many other people do or do not.

Certain psychometric issues remain unresolved for criterion-referenced tests. One issue is reliability. Classical reliability techniques, well-established in the literature and discussed earlier, depend to some extent on variability. Another is item discrimination. An item may be extremely difficult or easy and hence not discriminate among the test takers, and thus be a poor norm-referenced item, but that item may be related very closely to criterion attainment.

Various solutions for the reliability problem exist. No one solution has earned widespread acceptance, partly because of conceptual differences and mathematical intricacies. Hambleton et al. (1978) identified three conceptual approaches to criterion-referenced test reliability. One considers the consistency with which the test classifies its test-takers as "masters" or "nonmasters" in accordance with an arbitrary cutoff score. Another considers the reliability of the test scores themselves; the scores' deviations from the criterion or cutoff score are important. The third approach considers the consistency of scores across two forms without regard for a particular cutoff score.

Subkoviak (1980) examines in detail four methods for estimating the consistency of mastery–nonmastery classifications. If a test consistently classified examinees in accordance with a specified minimal criterion for mastery, alternate forms of that test theoretically would lead to identical classifications. The proportion of examinees consistently classified by two forms of a criterion-referenced test, $\hat{p}_0$ in Subkoviak's notation, is

$$\hat{p}_0 = \sum_{k=1}^{m} p_{kk},$$

where

$m =$ the number of classification categories

and

$p_{kk} =$ the proportion of individuals consistently classified in category k on both test forms.

For example, suppose that 20 students take two parallel ten-item tests that have arbitrary minimal criterion scores ("mastery" scores) of 8. There are two classification categories, mastery and nonmastery. If 6 students earn scores of 8 or better on both tests, 2 students earn scores of 8 or better on just one test, and the remaining 12 students earn scores below 8 on both tests, the two forms have classified 18 students consistently. The two consistent classification proportions are 6/20 and 12/20 or .30 and .60, so $\hat{p}_0 = .90$.

In addition to the classification consistency statistic, coefficient kappa ($\hat{\kappa}$), which modifies the observed consistency by deleting the consistent decisions expected by chance alone, is of interest. First, the expectancy for classification by chance alone, $\hat{p}_c$ in Subkoviak's notation, is computed by multiplying (a) the proportion of mastery classifications on form one by the proportion of mastery classifications on form two and (b) the proportion of nonmastery classifications on form one by the proportion of nonmastery classifications on form two, and then adding the products. For example, suppose that the 2 students in the above example who were classified inconsistently earned scores of 8 or better on form one but not on form two. Then form one classified 8 students as masters and 12 students as nonmasters; form two classified 6 as masters and 14 as nonmasters. The corresponding mastery proportions for the two forms are 8/20 or .40 and 6/20 or .30, the corresponding nonmastery proportions are 12/20 or .60 and 14/20 or .70. $(.40 \times .30) + (.60 \times .70) = .12 + .42 = .54$, the value of $\hat{p}_c$. The formula for coefficient kappa is

$$\hat{\kappa} = \frac{\hat{p}_0 - \hat{p}_c}{1 - \hat{p}_c}$$

In this case, substituting .90 for $\hat{p}_0$ and .54 for $\hat{p}_c$ yields a coefficient kappa value of .78. Coefficient kappa presumably measures test consistency solely on the basis of the test itself; the particular mastery–nonmastery composition of the tested group is negated. Whether one should use $\hat{p}_0$ or $\hat{\kappa}$ is determined by a judgment of whether overall classification consistency for whatever reason or classification consistency of the test itself is of primary importance.

One of the four methods Subkoviak discusses is the Swaminathan, Hambleton, and Algina (1974) method, which requires computational steps identical to those above that exemplify computing $\hat{p}_0$ and $\hat{\kappa}$. It requires two parallel test forms; to the present authors' knowledge, it is undetermined whether one can divide a single form in half to obtain two forms. The other methods, which require just one test form, include the Huynh (1976), Subkoviak (1976), and Marshall–Haertel (cited by Subkoviak from an unpublished 1976 manuscript) methods; these are computationally tedious, and, to the probability theory tyro, mathematically foreboding. In a lengthy study comparing the four methods, Subkoviak (1980, pp. 147–150) found that the Swaminathan et al. method gave relatively large standard errors of estimate* but gave unbiased estimates of $\hat{p}_0$. The other methods had smaller standard errors of estimate but tended to give biased estimates of $\hat{p}_0$. Subkoviak recommends the Huynh procedure because its estimates are conservative, it requires only one test administration, and it is mathematically elegant. Interested readers may consult the Subkoviak and Huynh references.

Brennan (1980) presents two procedures for estimating criterion-referenced (in his view, "domain-referenced") test reliability (in Brennan's view, "dependability") on the basis of just how deviant the test scores are from an arbitrary criterion. One "dependability index" yields values that vary with the particular criterion score; it supposedly indicates the dependability of decisions based on the testing procedure. The other index estimates the particular test's contribution to the dependability of decisions. Brennan's indexes are based on conceptualizing universes of items and persons, person–item interactions, and associated variance components. The mathematical exposition is lengthy and, in Brennan's notation, requires an intricate array of Greek letters, apostrophes, and wiggly lines.

An approach similar to Brennan's first index is that of Livingston (1972), who makes the assumption that a norm-referenced test is a special case of a criterion-referenced test in which the *mean* is the criterion. His formula is

$$r_L = \frac{r_{TT}\, \sigma_X^2 + (\overline{X} - C_X)^2}{\sigma_X^2 + (\overline{X} - C_X)^2},$$

where

r_L = Livingston reliability,
r_{TT} = reliability of the test as estimated by one of the "standard" methods,
σ_X^2 = test variance,
$\overline{X}$ = test mean,

and

C_X = the arbitrary criterion.

---

*The standard error of estimate may be considered as the standard deviation of a distribution of predicted values centered on a true value. In Subkoviak's study, $\hat{p}_0$ values for a large (N = 1586) population were known and were estimated via the four methods using 50 samples each of sizes 30 and 300.

The results obtained with Livingston's formula will vary with where the criterion is in relation to the mean. If criterion and mean coincide, the r_L will of course be equivalent to the "standard" reliability estimate. If the criterion and mean deviate slightly, the "standard" reliability will be reduced drastically; as the deviation increases, the r_L will pass the "standard" reliability estimate and can go well beyond it. For example, suppose that on a certain test the mean is 65, the variance is 12, and the reliability estimate by the split-halves technique is .80. If the criterion were set at 66, the r_L would be .15. With criteria of 68, 70, 72, 75, and 90, the respective r_Ls would be .47, .70, .82, .90, and .98. The Livingston technique is controversial, partly because test reliability seems to hinge on how badly a tested group performs in relation to the criterion.

In situations where a test is used in a pre–post instruction situation, the Cox–Vargas (1966) index may be useful as an indication of "good" items, where "good" items are those which virtually all uninstructed test takers miss and virtually all instructed test takers answer correctly. It is simply a matter of subtracting pretest item difficulty from posttest item difficulty. (See Chapter 5 for details of item difficulty indexes.)

Although the validity of a criterion-referenced test may be in terms of its content or its ability to predict attainment of some "real-world" criterion, Haertel (1985) argues for a type of *construct validity* in which one may generalize beyond the domain of possible test items to an interpretation of what testable achievement means regarding real world achievement beyond what is or can be tested. This requires the creation of "achievement constructs," that is, intended consequences of planned instructional experiences. A large number of empirical studies from several perspectives, then, are necessary to validate how well the constructs were predicted and supported by test scores.

Objectives-referenced Tests

Akin to the criterion-referenced test is the test that is based on a specific set of objectives peculiar to a given instructional or research setting. All tests are based on objectives that are at least implied, but in *objectives-referenced* testing the specific items largely are in one-to-one correspondence with objectives. A particular use of objectives-referenced tests is in evaluating an instructional program. Results often are reported in terms of how many people could answer a particular question or perform a particular task. Scores generally are not compiled by adding item scores together; individual test takers' scores may or may not be important. Examples of objectives-referenced testing in music, although the terms may not have been used by the practitioners, include the tests keyed to the Kansas music curriculum guide, the Seminar on the Evaluation of Comprehensive Musicianship (Boyle & Radocy, 1973), and the National Assessment of Educational Progress.

SUMMARY

The major points of Chapter 3 include the following:

1. A set of measurements may be arranged into a *distribution* of values.

2. Distributions may be based on values obtained from *nominal, ordinal, interval,* and *ratio* measures; most educational applications employ interval measures.

3. A distribution's *central tendency* is usually expressed by its *mean* or arithmetic average; other measures of central tendency include the *median* or midpoint and the *mode* or most common value.

4. A distribution's *variability* may be expressed via the *variance, standard deviation, range,* and *quartile deviation;* the variance and standard deviation are more useful.

5. A measure's *reliability* is the consistency with which it measures, or the proportion of observed variance that is due to genuine differences in what is measured.

6. In addition to test score variation due to genuine differences or "true" scores, there will be variation due to measurement *error.*

7. The variability of an individual's possible test scores around his or her "true" score may be estimated via the *standard error of measurement.*

8. One never knows test reliability, but it can be estimated by the *parallel forms, test–retest, split-halves,* and/or *internal consistency* methods.

9. *Correlation,* on which reliability estimation methods rely, is a technique for showing the size and direction of a relationship between two sets of values.

10. *Reliability* may be strengthened by adequate length, proper

testing conditions, clear instructions, and avoiding cues to the test-wise.

11. *Validity* is the extent to which a measure measures what it is supposed to measure; reliability is a necessary but not sufficient prerequisite.

12. Validity of a measure in terms of how well the relevant material is sampled and presented is *content* validity.

13. Validity of a measure in terms of how well the measure predicts some criterion is *predictive* validity; there are alternate names.

14. Validity in terms of how well a test supports theoretical predictions is *construct* validity.

15. Scores earned by large representative groups that then provide a basis for comparison are *norms;* common norms include *standard scores, age scores,* and *percentile ranks.*

16. In a *norm-referenced* test, a relative standard is employed and people are compared with each other.

17. In a *criterion-referenced* test, people are compared with an absolute standard.

18. Criterion-referenced reliability estimation techniques still are under development; the Swaminathan et al. and Livingston techniques are relatively easy to use but require possibly controversial assumptions.

19. In an *objectives-referenced* test, percentages of people able to attain designated objectives are reported.

Study Questions

1. In your own words, what does each of the following statements mean?
    A. The mean on the test was 52, but the median was 56.
    B. Sam's score has a percentile rank of 72.
    C. The standard deviation on the first midterm was 3.85, but it was 7.26 on the second midterm.
    D. If he really grades on the curve, some people have to fail, but some will get As.
    E. She's throwing out the test because of low reliability.
    F. A music history test says nothing about how much people enjoy music from any particular historical period.

2. What type of test is most appropriate for each of the following situations? Why?

    A. Determining what proportions of the eighth graders in a school system meet each objective in the music curriculum guide
    B. Selecting a proportion of sophomore music majors for participation in an advanced theory seminar
    C. Deciding whether applicants for a music teaching position have enough general musical knowledge to qualify for further consideration
    D. Discovering whether freshman music majors are ready to begin music theory classes or require remediation
    E. Ranking a group of sixth graders regarding their knowledge of music notation

3. The following data are for a 36-item junior high general music test:

Student	Score on Odd Items	Score on Even Items	Total Score
Andrea	17	16	33
Clyde	15	16	31
Donald	7	10	17
Esther	11	11	22
Herman	15	17	32
Ida	14	15	29
Martin	16	18	34
Mary	13	14	27
Phyllis	8	8	16
Waldo	5	4	9

    A. What is the mean?
    B. What is the median?
    C. What is the mode?
    D. What is the range?
    E. What is the variance?
    F. What is the standard deviation?
    G. What is the reliability?
    H. What is the standard error of measurement?
    I. Does the test have a positive, negative, or no skew? Why?
    J. If the instructor set an arbitrary criterion of 32, what is the Livingston reliability?

REFERENCES

Angoff, W.H. Scales, norms, and equivalent scores. In R.L. Thorndike (Ed.), *Educational measurement* (2nd ed.). Washington, D.C.: American Council on Education, 1971.

Asmus, E.P., Jr. *The effect of altering the number of distractors on test statistics: Is 3 better than 5?* Paper presented at the meeting of the Music Educators National Conference, Chicago, April, 1978.

Boyle, J.D., & Radocy, R.E. Evaluation of instructional objectives in comprehensive musicianship. *Council for Research in Music Education,* 1973, *32,* 2–21.

Brennan, R.L. Applications of generalizability theory. In R.A. Berk (Ed.), *Criterion-referenced measurement: The state of the art.* Baltimore, Md.: Johns Hopkins, 1980.

Colwell, R.J. *Music achievement tests.* Chicago: Follett, 1969.

Cox, R.C., & Vargas, J.S. *A comparison of item selection techniques for norm-referenced and criterion-referenced tests.* Paper presented at the meeting of the National Council on Measurement in Education, Chicago, February, 1966.

Ghiselli, E.E., Campbell, J.P., & Zedeck, S. *Measurement theory for the behavioral sciences.* San Francisco: W.H. Freeman, 1981.

Glaser, R. Instructional technology and the measurement of learning outcomes: Some questions. *American Psychologist,* 1963, *18,* 519–521.

Haertel, E. Construct validity and criterion-referenced testing. *Review of Educational Research,* 1985, *55,* 23–46.

Hambleton, R.K., Swaminathan, H., Algina, J., & Coulson, D.B. Criterion-referenced testing and measurement: A review of technical issues and developments. *Review of Educational Research,* 1978, *48* (1), 1–47.

Hoyt, C. Test reliability obtained by analysis of variance. *Psychometrika,* 1941, *6,* 153–160.

Huynh, H. On the reliability of decisions in domain-referenced testing. *Journal of Educational Measurement,* 1976, *13,* 253–264.

Livingston, S.A. Criterion-referenced applications of classical test theory. *Journal of Educational Measurement,* 1972, *9,* 13–26.

Marshall, J.L., & Haertel, E.H. *The mean split-half coefficient of agreement: A single administration index of reliability for mastery tests.* Unpublished manuscript, University of Wisconsin, 1976.

Mehrens, W.A., & Lehmann, I.J. *Measurement and evaluation in education and psychology.* New York: Holt, Rinehart, and Winston, 1973.

Minium, E.W. *Statistical reasoning in psychology and education* (2nd ed.). New York: Wiley, 1978.

Nunnally, J.C., Jr. *Introduction to psychological measurement.* New York: McGraw-Hill, 1970.

Popham, W.J., & Sirotnik, K.A. *Educational statistics: Use and interpretation* (2nd ed.). New York: Harper & Row, 1973.

Stanley, J.C. Reliability. In R.L. Thorndike (Ed.), *Educational measurement* (2nd ed.). Washington, D.C.: American Council on Education, 1971.

Subkoviak, M.J. Estimating reliability from a single administration of a mastery test. *Journal of Educational Measurement,* 1976, *13,* 265–276.

Subkoviak, M.J. Decision-consistency approaches. In R.A. Berk (Ed.), *Criterion-referenced measurement: The state of the art.* Baltimore, Md.: Johns Hopkins, 1980.

Swaminathan, H., Hambleton, R.K., & Algina, J. Reliability of criterion-referenced tests: A decision-theoretic formulation. *Journal of Educational Measurement,* 1974, *11,* 263–267.

Thorndike, R.L. (Ed.) *Educational measurement* (2nd ed.). Washington, D.C.: American Council on Education, 1971.

4

Types of Music
Test Behaviors

A variety of schemes may be employed for classifying music tests. Previous books concerned with music tests generally have classified them according to what the tests purported to measure—usually aptitude, achievement, performance, and various types of affective behavior (Lehman, 1968; Colwell, 1970; Whybrew, 1971; George, 1980). Although performance generally is recognized as achievement, it is treated separately from other types of musical achievement, perhaps because most books were concerned with classification of existing tests, which were usually labeled as one or another of these types.

Writers of books concerned primarily with constructing general educational tests, however, classify tests differently. Ebel (1979, p. 56), for example, recognizes three major types: objective tests, mathematical problems, and oral examinations. Gronlund (1981, p. 135) recognizes two general types of items: objective and essay. Cronbach (1970, p. 35), perhaps thinking less in terms of item type than Ebel and Gronlund, classifies tests under two broad categories. Tests of *maximum* performance include tests of aptitude, ability, achievement, and any other measure that assesses the test taker's best possible performance. Tests of *typical* performance are concerned with what the test taker will do of his or her own volition when there is no pressure, internal or external, to "do well" on the test. Tests of this nature generally include such affective measures as attitude, interest, value, or preference, as well as measures of various other traits such as personality or habits.

Still other schemes appear to be appropriate for classifying tests. An argument could be made for classifying tests according to the methods by which the test data are analyzed: norm-referenced or criterion-referenced. Music tests also could be classified as musical or nonmusical, that is, whether they involve an audible musical stimulus or response versus no audible musical stimulus or response. Whatever classification scheme is used, it must be recognized as a framework or convenience for discussion rather than a reflection of any particular theory (Cronbach, 1970, p. 35).

Music tests also may be classified according to the nature of the behavior required. One approach might be to classify them by the three broad behavioral domains of the taxonomy of educational objectives: cognitive, affective, and psychomotor. However, as noted in Chapter 1, the range of behaviors that may be called musical is great, both in type and complexity, and often involves highly complex integration of various levels of cognitive, affective, and psychomotor behaviors. Consequently, classifying musical behaviors and music test behaviors according to the three taxonomic domains is both difficult and inadequate.

Musical behaviors might better be classified under four broad headings reflecting those which music teachers are most concerned their students develop: (a) performance behaviors (instrumental or vocal), (b) reading and writing behaviors, (c) listening behaviors, and (d) other cognitive behaviors relative to music, musicians, and musical phenomena. These categories certainly are not discrete, because the overt behaviors have underlying, albeit generally subconscious, perceptual, cognitive, and affective bases. Also, as shown in Figure 4.1 (Boyle, 1974, p. 81), there is much obvious overlapping and combining of behaviors under the four broad categories.

With respect to the assessment of musical behaviors, there is some question whether to attempt to isolate and assess specific musical behaviors or to examine more global musical behaviors, but as noted in Chapter 2, it need not be an either–or situation; a test maker should use or lean toward one or the other approach depending on the nature of the musical behavior to be assessed and/or the test's intended function. (The global versus specifics approach to assessment of musical behaviors offers still another possible classification scheme.)

With due consideration of potential test categorization schemes,

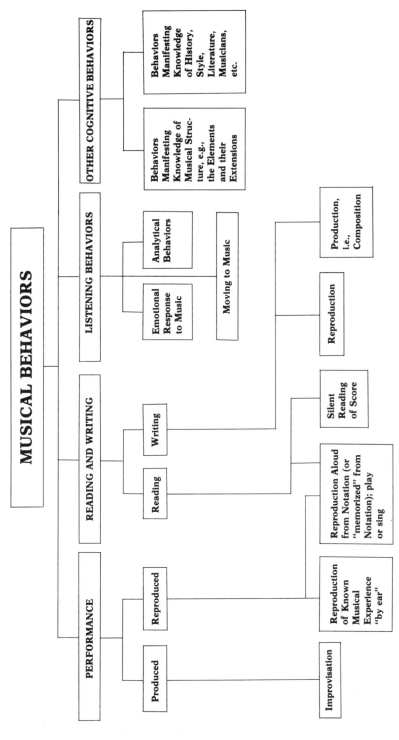

Figure 4.1: Taxonomy of Musical Behaviors

87

and of Cronbach's somewhat pragmatic view that some categorization system is a necessity, the present discussion examines music test behaviors as they relate to two underlying dimensions of the behavioral task: (a) the response behavior and (b) the response methodology. These dimensions are similar to those used by Johnson and Hess (1970, pp. 12–33) in their response taxonomy for tests in the arts. Essentially, the response behavior, which Johnson and Hess labeled "response construct," reflects *what* the test actually measures, and the response methodology reflects the *method* used to assess the response behavior. Much of the following discussion is based on Johnson and Hess's taxonomy for classification of music tests (pp. 24–26). The value of the scheme is not in the scheme itself. The scheme provides a framework for analyzing the appropriateness of existing and potential music test tasks for assessing designated musical behaviors.

RESPONSE BEHAVIORS

Johnson and Hess (1970, p. 25) identify and define nine response behaviors that had been used in at least one of the 30 music tests they reviewed:*

1. Aural Discrimination: The ability to note differences between two or more pitches, rhythms, harmonic phrases, melodies, etc.

2. Aural Identification with Note Reading: The ability to read and identify sounded pitches, rhythms, melodies, etc.

3. Aural Recognition and Identification: The ability to recognize and identify specifically aural (musical) stimuli.

4. Background Knowledge: Manifest knowledge of music history, terminology, composers, compositions, etc.

5. Compositional: The subject is required to compose a piece of music.

---

*Johnson and Hess listed 73 music tests but indicated that they had examined only 30 of them; it was not clear which 30 tests had been examined, but one must assume that some of the tests were not published, standardized tests. Many of the 73 tests listed were tests used in research, achievement tests from local school districts, and even some "promotional" tests available from musical instrument manufacturers. Nevertheless, their sample appeared to be sufficient for deducing the music test response behaviors and methodologies described here.

6.   Emotive: Manifest expressions of "feelings" about aspects of music.

7.   Note Reading: The ability to read notes.

8.   Playing Proficiency: The ability to play a musical instrument successfully.

9.   Preference: To choose or esteem certain musical works above others.

When the music test response behaviors are juxtaposed to the musical behavior classification scheme shown in Figure 4.1, it is apparent that, except for improvisation, performance "by ear," and moving to music, at least some effort has been made to devise music tests or subtests to assess the general types of musical behaviors that music teachers consider important for their students to develop. The most commonly used music test response behaviors were, in order of frequency, tasks involving background knowledge, aural discrimination, aural recognition and identification, and note reading.

RESPONSE METHODOLOGIES

Johnson and Hess's review of music tests also revealed nine basic response methodologies that have been used in assessing musical behaviors. The methodologies and their definitions are:

1.   Pair Comparisons: Stimulus items are presented in pairs to the subject to evaluate along some polarized dimension, e.g. same–different.

2.   Successive Categories: Judging each of several musical stimuli as belonging to one of a limited number of categories.

3.   Standard Objective: Questions requiring [paper-and-pencil] answers of the true–false, multiple-choice, matching, or fill-in-blanks nature.

4.   Reproduction: Subject is required to reproduce a given musical stimulus.

5.   Production (written): Subject is required to demonstrate a particular ability by correct placing of notes, time signatures, etc.

6. Melody Composing: Subject is required to compose a melody.

7. Verbalization: Subject gives a verbal response to questions or stimulus items presented to him.

8. Singing: Subject is required to respond by singing.

9. Instrument Playing: The subject is required to play a particular musical instrument. (Johnson & Hess, pp. 25–26)

The most commonly used response methodologies were, in order of frequency, pair comparison, standard objective, and successive categories.

TAXONOMY OF MUSIC TEST RESPONSES

Johnson and Hess developed a taxonomy of music test responses based on their analyses of the response behaviors and methodologies in the tests they examined. (See Figure 4.2 and 4.3.) Essentially, Figure 4.2 shows the response methodologies that had been used for each of the response behaviors, and the matrix in Figure 4.3 shows the frequency with which the respective response methodologies were used in conjunction with each of the nine response behaviors. For example, the pair comparison methodology was most frequently used for assessing aural discrimination behaviors, standard objective items such as true–false, multiple choice, matching, or fill-in-the-blank were most used to assess background knowledge, and the successive-categories method was most frequently used to assess aural recognition and identification behaviors. As apparent from examination of Figure 4.3, most of the music tests examined by Johnson and Hess used only a few of the response behaviors and methodologies.

A cursory examination of the content analysis of 12 published, standardized music tests reviewed by Boyle (1982) suggests that it is possible to classify most music test behaviors into the Johnson and Hess taxonomy. Except for one rhythm subtest, which asks respondents to count silently at an established tempo until instructed to stop and then to indicate the number to which they had counted, all test and subtest tasks of the 12 tests were conveniently classified into the various taxonomic categories, although some subtests required more than one type of response. The most frequently used response behaviors were aural dis-

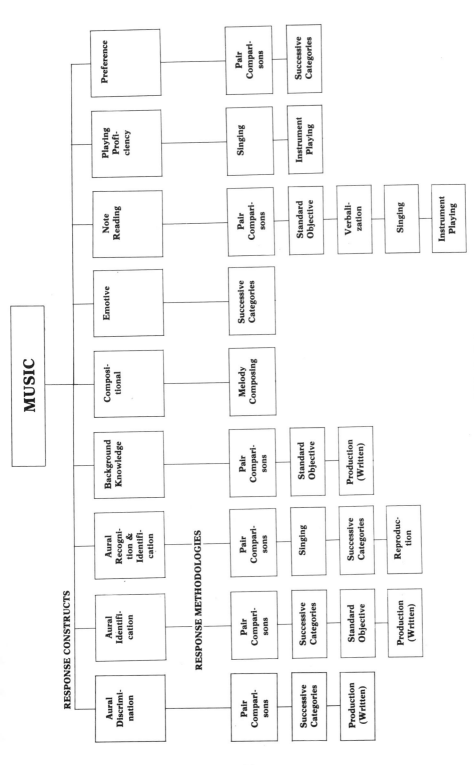

Figure 4.2: **Taxonomy of Music Test Response Behaviors and Methodologies**

91

Response Behavior	Response Methodology								
	PC	SC	SO	RE	PR	MC	VE	SI	IP
Aural Discrimination	17	2			1				
Aural Identification with Note Reading	2	1	1		1				
Aural Recognition & Identification	3	10		3				1	
Background Knowledge	1		15		5				
Compositional						1			
Emotive		1							
Note Reading	1		5				1		
Playing Proficiency								1	4
Preference	3	3							

Figure 4.3: **Music Test Response Matrix**

crimination, aural recognition and identification, and aural identification with note reading. The most frequently used methodologies were pair comparisons and successive categories.

Whether "what is" (regarding the frequency of use of the response behaviors and methodologies) is what "should be" is questionable. Other response behaviors and methodologies certainly are available to music test makers;* also, persons concerned with the evaluation of musical behavior and music programs often may desire to assess behaviors that do not require response to or knowledge about musical stimuli and therefore will require other response behaviors and methodologies. Undoubtedly the response behaviors and methodologies selected for use in music tests will vary with the test's functions, the nature of what a test maker is seeking to assess, and many other variables, including the philosophical and psychological persuasions of the test maker and user.

---

*Chapters 8 and 9 examine some specific techniques for assessing musical performance and attitudes that do not fit conveniently into Johnson and Hess's taxonomy.

DECIDING WHICH MUSIC TEST BEHAVIORS TO ASSESS

Whether concerned with developing tests for evaluating instruction or with assessing some other psychological construct such as aptitude, ability, or attitude, the prospective test maker must determine which specific behaviors to include on a test. At first such decisions might appear obvious and simple, but the prudent test maker will consider many variables during the process of test development.

Many specific suggestions are provided throughout this book for developing tests for particular functions, but the purpose of the present discussion is to offer some general principles for music test construction. In addition to the general principles for music test design and construction, this section examines several particular variables that must be considered when making decisions regarding the particular behaviors to be assessed by a music test.

Principles Underlying Music Test Design

Virtually this entire book is devoted to examining issues, guidelines, and procedures relevant to test selection, design, and usage, and to attempt to reduce guidelines for test design to a few basic principles is both presumptuous and hazardous. Nevertheless, several underlying principles should be apparent, and it might be helpful to list them here.

1. *Music test content and design must reflect the particular function a test is intended to serve.* The first step in designing any test is to define clearly the test's function. Without a clear understanding of the test's purpose and the intended uses of the test data, a test maker has little basis for making necessary subsequent decisions about test content, scope, item format, or response methodology. It is particularly important that the test be designed to elicit information that is relevant to the types of educational decisions to be based on the test.

2. *The scope and specificity of a music test's content must be appropriate and relevant to the test's function.* Achievement tests generally are designed to assess achievement in relation to specific instructional objectives, although the data analysis

sometimes may be norm-referenced rather than criterion-referenced. Achievement tests for specific instructional units usually are rather narrow and specific in content, whereas general standardized achievement tests tend to include a much broader range of content. Aptitude tests usually have a particular theoretical basis that serves to define and delimit the nature of the test content. Performance tests may assess specific performance behaviors such as sight-reading skill, or they may take the form of general auditions, where each test taker is allowed to select his or her own pieces for performance. Attitude tests usually are designed to assess attitudes toward some specific musical composition, style, or phenomenon. Whatever the test's function, the test content should be specifically relevant to that function, and content designed to elicit extraneous information should be avoided.

3. *Music test content and design must reflect consideration for the general developmental level, academic level, and test taking experience of the test takers.* The primary implication of this principle is that the test results should reflect the test takers' knowledge, skills, or attitudes relevant to the required test behaviors rather than other variables such as ability to follow or read test directions.

4. *The level of cognitive, affective, or psychomotor behaviors required in the test tasks should be appropriate to the test's function and the test takers' general level of experience with the musical behaviors under consideration.* This is a particular concern for tests designed to evaluate instruction. (See Chapter 5.) Tests serving other functions also should reflect appropriate levels of questioning. Tests used to screen students for admission to graduate school or to place them in music history classes should require more than low level knowledge of names and dates. Music discrimination tasks on music aptitude tests should be particularly relevant to the theoretical constructs of the test. When auditioning students for a special choral group, the evaluative criteria should reflect the conductor's specific bases for selection, whether they be sight-reading skill, voice quality, or even dancing skills.

5. *A music test must be designed to provide a balanced sample of behavior relevant to the test's function.* If a test is serving to diagnose music theory skills, the test maker must assess the test takers' skills that relate specifically to the skills needed

for success in music theory; a dictation test alone does not provide an adequate sample of behaviors relevant to success in music theory classes. In achievement testing it is particularly important that the test reflect a balanced sample of the instructional objectives and content; only to the extent that it reflects a representative sampling of the instruction may it be said to have content validity.

6. *A music test must be efficient.* With due respect to the function a test is serving and the decisions to be based on the test, test makers also must give consideration to providing the maximum amount of information in the most economical way. A four-hour individually administered test might provide highly reliable and valid information relevant to a given function, but given present-day administrative costs, it might also prove to be impractical. Test makers must weigh the merits of increased depth and scope of information to be gained from such a test against a number of administrative considerations, such as test taker's time, administrator's time, test cost, and data analysis expenses. Overly expensive and inefficient tests, while perhaps technically flawless, are rarely used. On the other hand, tests that fail to provide adequate samples of behavior relevant to a test's function, hence failing to provide adequate information for making an educational decision, are also inefficient.

7. *A music test must be technically adequate.* Besides having evidence of reliability and validity, music test directions, item format, and, where appropriate, recording quality must be such that they do not interfere with the test takers' responses to the test content.

Principles for Determining Music Test Behaviors

Even with adherence to the general principles discussed above, a test maker still is faced with determining the test's specific response behaviors and methodologies. The principles for making these decisions are rather straightforward, but variables that intertwine with them tend to complicate the decision-making process.

1. *The response behavior(s) required in a testing task should reflect as directly as possible the knowledge, skill, or value*

being assessed. In other words, the response behaviors should not require high inference interpretations by the test user. For example, if one is interested in diagnosing an individual's music theory skills, a first step is to ascertain the specific skills that one can accept as evidence of music theory skills. Rather than seeking to determine whether the individual has a "good understanding of harmony" and a "good ear," the test maker should define clearly the types of behavior he or she accepts as *evidence* of such. If the test is for college admission or placement in music theory, the test should have an appropriate range of tasks that will allow for clear-cut decisions regarding admission or placement. Does having a good ear imply the ability to recognize aurally presented intervals that are the same (even though on different pitch levels), to name aurally presented intervals, or to notate aurally presented intervals, having been given the name of the lower pitch? Also, should the assessment be in terms of successive or simultaneous intervals?

While many would say that any of the above responses to intervals reflect an individual's "interval perception" ability, the three tasks in fact reflect three quite different cognitions and require three different response behaviors. To recognize that two intervals presented on different pitches are the "same" or "different" is essentially an aural discrimination task. It can be accomplished by individuals with no knowledge of interval names or of musical notation. However, to name aurally presented intervals is an aural recognition and identification behavior and would be impossible for an individual without prior learning regarding interval names. The third task, notating an aurally presented interval when given the lower of the two pitches, reflects still another type of response behavior, aural identification with note reading. Without belaboring the point, it should be apparent that a test maker undertaking to develop a diagnostic test for music theory must clearly define what he or she wishes to assess and then select the appropriate response behavior.

The interval discrimination/recognition tasks are but three potential behaviors for assessing a "good ear," so the developer of a diagnostic test for music theory must consider just as carefully the other behaviors that will provide "evidence of a good ear." Similarly, "a good understanding of harmony" may require more than one response behavior, possibly involving note reading, compositional, and/or background knowledge behaviors, depending on what the test maker is willing to accept as evidence of "understanding harmony."

If a test maker plans in terms of the type of response behaviors desired on a test, he or she is less likely to use vague, ill-defined constructs requiring high inference interpretation. A cursory examination of tests used in research over the past two decades reveals an overdependence on such terminology, possibly reflecting the trend toward cognitive psychology and away from behaviorism. The authors appreciate and are sympathetic with the concern for understanding cognitive processing of musical stimuli; further, they recognize that many carefully designed and controlled testing procedures allow inferences to be made concerning perceptual and cognitive processing strategies. However, they are concerned with the loose application of the term *perception* to many tests that clearly require performance tasks as a response behavior. While a performance task *may* reflect perception, failure to perform does not necessarily indicate failure to perceive; it may be that the respondent lacks the necessary performance skills. To belabor the interval example further, just because an individual can not sing a tritone does not mean that he or she can not discriminate between a tritone and a perfect fifth or recognize and name a tritone when he or she hears one.

2. *Whenever possible, evaluation of musical behaviors should involve response to (or production of) aural musical stimuli.* Perhaps this is obvious, but too often music teachers rely on paper-and-pencil tests of knowledge about music as a measure of musical achievement rather than on response to music. Whether this is a matter of objective selection or response behavior selection is uncertain, although it is conjectured that it is probably a little of both. Objective selection is a matter of philosophy and will not be considered here. Response behavior selection, however, is a testing problem, and all too often even teachers who spend most of the instructional time involved in music making resort to paper-and-pencil tests, usually of background knowledge or notation, musicians, composers, or musical styles. Such knowledge is important, but if the test does not adequately sample the instructional activities, a general principle of test design is being violated.

Also, for most school testing situations it is more appropriate to assess musical behaviors in a *musical* context rather than in response to isolated tonal stimuli. Many test makers continue to follow the practice of Carl Seashore and other early leaders in the field of music psychology and measure responses to isolated tonal stimuli. While this is appropriate in some instances, it also creates questions of test validity if one wants to generalize to more global musical behaviors. For the most part music teachers are concerned with response to music, and therefore whenever possible the testing and evaluation of musical achievement, aptitude, or attitude should be in relation to musical stimuli.

3. *The response methodology required on a test should minimize the effects of irrelevant skills and knowledge.* The most obvious concern is to design response formats that do not offer advantages to the test-wise student. Poorly written objective items are particularly susceptible in this respect, and Chapter 5 offers guidelines for avoiding such problems. Also, if the intent of a test is to assess a given response behavior, the response methodology should not require other response behaviors that some students may be able to demonstrate while others can not.

APPLICATION OF PRINCIPLES TO TEST DESIGN

Although subsequent chapters examine test item development and other assessment techniques for specific evaluation functions, the principles just outlined appear to be basic to test design for most specific evaluation functions. Once a test maker perceives a need to obtain data relative to a given function, he or she must (a) consider to whom the test is to be administered, (b) determine the nature, scope, and general level of the behavioral domains the test is to sample, and (c) develop test items that will yield adequate, representative, and efficient samples of relevant test-taker behaviors. The response behaviors and methodologies for the test items and/or other evaluation procedures also must be appropriate for the information sought.

Undoubtedly there are a number of approaches to ensuring that a test meet the criteria implied by the principles. Also, technical requirements will vary for tests serving different functions as well as for tests used in different testing situations. Whatever approach a test maker uses, there should be some systematic way for ensuring that the principles of test design are given due consideration, whether one is developing a college admissions test, a classroom achievement test, an audition or performance achievement procedure, or perhaps a new standardized music aptitude or achievement test. For illustrative purposes, approaches to the development of an achievement test and an aptitude test will be considered.

Basic to the development of either test is the need for a systematic approach, and the following illustrates one sequence that might be followed in designing a test. The sequence assumes (a) that the need for information relative to educational decisions for students and/or programs already has been established, (b) that existing data are inadequate, and (c) that tests and/or other procedures for obtaining valid data are not available. The sequence of steps in designing a music test might include the following:

1. The test maker must define clearly the test's intended function. Without a clear understanding of the function a test is to serve, there is little point in proceeding further. Such decisions are not always as clear-cut as they might seem. For example, many aptitude tests clearly assess behaviors that reflect learning, which may or may not include formal learning or achievement. To the extent that a test maker believes that previous achievement is an indicator of potential for further learning, he or she will include test items reflecting achievement on an aptitude test. To distinguish clearly between a diagnostic and achievement function is even more difficult. Therefore, determining the primary test function must be the overriding concern for a test maker. Further, a test maker should avoid attempts to develop tests to serve multiple functions. It must be clearly ascertained whether a test's primary function is to assess (a) specific or general past learning (achievement), (b) present ability to demonstrate specific behaviors (diagnostic), (c) potential for further learning (aptitude), or (d) attitudes, interests, or values relative to some aspect of music.

2. Once a test's function is clearly ascertained, the test maker's next task is to define the population for whom the test is intended: general students or selected music students; preschool, primary, intermediate, junior high, senior high, or college level students. Many standardized music aptitude tests developed in the past have sought to be useful with anyone

from about age eight through adult, but some of these tests were inappropriate for certain segments of the population with which they were used. Often the tasks were too difficult to yield any meaningful results for younger test takers. Makers of music tests might well consider the practice of makers of standardized general intelligence, aptitude, and achievement tests where it is common to develop different forms of the tests for use with different age or grade levels.

Certainly some music test response behaviors and methodologies are appropriate for use with test takers of widely varying intellectual and musical skills, but current understanding of child development suggests that some tasks appropriate for teenagers and adults are inappropriate for preschool and elementary children. Music test makers therefore must be cognizant of the populations for whom a test is intended and allow for this in the subsequent stages of test development.

3. Once a test's function is clearly defined and the potential testing population is ascertained, the test maker should establish parameters for test construction and administration or, if these matters are not all under his or her control, determine general parameters. The parameters for construction of a unit test to assess achievement for third-grade students in a given teacher's classroom are much different than for a district-wide music competency test to be administered to all sixth-grade students in a large school district. The time and other resources available to the individual classroom teacher are necessarily limited; also the primary requirements of a unit test are that it have content validity for classroom instruction and that it adequately sample students' achievement in relation to the instructional objectives. The district-wide test may also require the establishment of competency standards and perhaps norms and behavior profiles. Certainly it will require more than one person's subjective view of test validity; further, the time and expense required to develop a district-wide test are no small matter.

    Test administration parameters must also be considered. How much student and teacher time can be devoted to test administration? Are there minimum and maximum time requirements for obtaining the needed information? How do these time requirements fit into a school day? Must the test be a group test? Will there be sufficient numbers of students and items to warrant making it machine scored? Are adaptions for special populations necessary?

Without some perspective on the parameters for test construction and administration, a test maker may be engaged in an exercise in futility. Also, an understanding of these parameters may force early decisions in the development process regarding the test's limitations. The extent to which real world restraints of test development and administration should limit the scope of a test is debatable, but they are nevertheless real.

4. The next step, perhaps the most critical step in test development, is determining the domain of behaviors relevant to the test's function. For achievement tests to assess student learning of a relatively limited instructional unit, this is no major problem. One must examine the instructional objectives for the unit, and, assuming that they were well defined, select a balanced and representative sample of the items to be evaluated. An often used procedure for this is to develop a matrix listing the objectives and the types of behaviors one desires to assess relative to each objective.

For tests serving other purposes the problems are considerably more complex. The types of behaviors included on an aptitude test, for example, often are a matter of theoretical perspective. The test maker must establish a rationale for types of behaviors to include, especially since aptitude is one of those convenient yet difficult-to-assess theoretical constructs used to classify individuals. A test maker totally committed to the position that previous achievement is the best predictor of future achievement might actually construct a test reflecting musical achievement to serve as an aptitude measure. Those following in Seashore's tradition will assess basic aural acuities such as pitch discrimination, loudness discrimination, and rhythm discrimination in contexts isolated from musical structure. Others might be concerned that the test assess response to musical structure.

Regardless of the test's intended function, a test maker still must decide which response behaviors and methodologies to include. As noted above, the three guiding principles for determining which response behaviors and methodologies to include are that (a) the behaviors should reflect as directly as possible the knowledge, skills, or values being assessed, (b) whenever possible, the behaviors should involve response to (or production of) aural musical stimuli, and (c) the response methodology should minimize the effects of skills and knowledge irrelevant to the given response behavior.

A recommended approach for selecting response behaviors and methodologies is to create a matrix listing the behaviors on one axis, the response methodologies on another, and then to select the response behaviors one wishes to assess. Either concurrently or after decisions have been made regarding the behaviors, one can indicate the response methodologies to be used for each of the selected behaviors. The response methodologies identified by Johnson and Hess (1970) might serve as a starting point for the development of such a matrix, but an individual test maker may wish to supplement those categories; also, a test maker might list specific item types or variations under the respective categories, especially for the standard objective category.

A next step might be to determine the tentative test proportion to be allocated to the respective categories of response behaviors and methodologies. Some tests will require only a single type of response, especially if the test is to assess a particular skill. Others may include a variety of response behaviors and methodologies—although one should avoid using a variety of methodologies just for the sake of using them.

Great care must be taken in the design of the response structure. Sometimes slight variations in the structure of a given response methodology can effect significant changes in the apparent test results. For example, Sergeant and Boyle (1980) examined the effects of task structure, those used in five published, standardized tests, on pitch discrimination for a common set of frequency stimuli using a counterbalanced design with a group of sixth-grade students as subjects. There were statistically significant differences among the group's means for the five task structures, suggesting that the differences were due to the contextual configuration of the response methodologies.

5. Before constructing and administering a test, a test maker should decide what type of data analysis is appropriate, particularly for an achievement test. A criterion-referenced test will involve different criteria and procedures for item selection than a norm-referenced test. Further, will there be sufficient bases for analyzing subsection scores? Are subsection

scores necessary and/or desirable? If so, will the data analysis yield both a profile and a total score? Whichever, a rationale for the decision needs to be established a priori rather than a posteriori.

6. Before finalizing a test for use, some judgment must be made regarding test validity for the function it is intended to serve. If the test is a teacher-made test for use in assessing student achievement with respect to instruction in the teacher's own classroom, the necessary type of validity is content validity, which he or she can establish through a careful analysis of the test items vis-à-vis the instructional objectives and/or activities. Should the test be serving some broader purpose or as a dependent variable in a research study, it is imperative that steps be taken to establish item discrimination and difficulty indices and test (also subtest where appropriate) reliability and empirical validity. (Test reliability and validity are examined in Chapter 3; item analysis is examined in Chapter 5.) Figure 4.4 summarizes the above steps.

SUMMARY

Music tests may be classified in a variety of ways, including item type, typical versus maximum performance, norm- versus criterion-referenced, the nature of the behavior required in the testing tasks, taxonomic domains of educational objectives, and specific versus global behaviors.

Music tests are classifiable in terms of Johnson and Hess's (1970) taxonomy of response behavior and response methodology. Response behaviors in the taxonomy include aural discrimination, aural identification with note reading, aural recognition and identification, background knowledge, compositional, emotive, note reading, playing proficiency, and preference. Response methodologies include pair comparisons, successive categories, standard objective, reproduction, production (written), melody composing, verbalization, singing, and instrument playing.

Seven principles underlying music test design are:

1. Music test content and design must reflect the test's intended function.
2. The scope and specificity of a music test's content must be appropriate for and relevant to the test's function.

STEP:

1. **Specific Test Function:** _____

_____

2. **Potential Testtakers:** _____

_____

3. **Parameters:**
   Test Design: _____

   _____

   Test Administration: _____

   _____

4. **Possible Response Behaviors and Methodologies:**

| | *Response Methodology* | | | | | | | | | |
Response Behavior	**PC**	**SC**	**SO**	**RE**	**PR**	**MC**	**VE**	**SI**	**IP**	**Other**
Aural Discrimination										
Aural Identification with Note Reading										
Aural Recognition & Identification										
Background Knowledge										
Compositional										
Emotive										
Note Reading										
Playing Proficiency										
Preference										

5. **Data Analysis:** _____

6. **Validation Procedures:** _____

Figure 4.4: **Checklist for Music Test Design**

3. Music test content and design must reflect consideration for the general developmental level, academic level, and test-taking experience of the test takers.

4. The level of cognitive, affective, and psychomotor behaviors required in the test tasks should be appropriate to the test's

function and the test takers' general level of experience with the musical behaviors under consideration.

5. A music test must be designed to provide a balanced sample of behavior relevant to the test's function.

6. A music test must be efficient.

7. A music test must be technically adequate.

Three general principles to guide the selection of response behaviors and methodologies are:

1. The response behavior(s) required in a testing task should reflect as directly as possible the knowledge, skill, or value being assessed.

2. Whenever possible, evaluation of musical behaviors should involve response to (or production of) aural musical stimuli.

3. The response methodology required on a test should minimize the effects of skills and knowledge irrelevant to the given response behavior.

Study Questions

1. Make a list of ten widely varying musical behaviors, classify them according to the four broad categories of musical behavior, ask several colleagues or classmates to categorize them according to the four categories, and compare the ways in which you and they classified them.

2. Classify each of the following according to response behavior:

   (a) a "drop the needle" listening identification test,

   (b) a test asking respondents to discriminate between two pitches,

   (c) a test asking respondents to indicate which of two renditions of a composition they like better,

   (d) a sight-reading test,

   (e) a part-writing examination in music theory,

   (f) an "error detection" test comparing a taped performance with a musical score, and

   (g) a "typical" music history test.

3. Classify the test behaviors listed in question two according to response methodology.

REFERENCES

Boyle, J.D. (Comp.). *Instructional objectives in music.* Vienna, Va.: Music Educators National Conference, 1974.

Boyle, J.D. Selecting music tests for use in schools. *Update,* 1982 *1* (1), 14–21.

Colwell, R. *The evaluation of music teaching and learning.* Englewood Cliffs, N.J.: Prentice-Hall, 1970.

Cronbach, L.J. *Essentials of psychological testing* (3rd ed.). New York: Harper & Row, 1970.

Ebel, R.L. *Essentials of educational measurement* (3rd ed.). Englewood Cliffs, N.J.: Prentice-Hall, 1979.

George, W.E. Measurement and evaluation of musical behaviors. In D.A. Hodges (Ed.), *Handbook of music psychology.* Lawrence, Kans.: National Association for Music Therapy, Inc, 1980.

Gronlund, N.E. *Measurement and evaluation in teaching* (4th ed.). New York: Macmillan, 1981.

Johnson, T.J., & Hess, R.J. *Tests in the arts.* St. Ann, Mo.: Central Midwestern Regional Educational Laboratory, 1970.

Lehman, P.R. *Tests and measurements in music.* Englewood Cliffs, N.J.: Prentice-Hall, 1968.

Sergeant, D., & Boyle, J.D. Contextual influences on pitch judgement. *Psychology of Music,* 1980, *8* (2), 3–15.

Whybrew, W.E. *Measurement and evaluation in music* (2nd ed.). Dubuque, Iowa: Wm. C. Brown, 1971.

5

Developing Tests for Evaluating Instruction

Constructing a test may seem burdensome. The prospective test maker certainly should consider many things, and preparation of a good test of any instructional aspect of music is not simply a matter of writing a few questions. Testing in some form nevertheless is essential for evaluating the results of musical instruction. This chapter discusses determining objectives and what to test, aspects of item writing and analysis, and certain considerations involving musical examples. It is oriented toward paper-and-pencil rather than performance measures, which are covered elsewhere.

OBJECTIVES

Definitions

An *objective* is a relatively specific target toward which an organization or an individual works. One may have a biological objective, such as obtaining a drink of water, a learning objective, such as becoming able to make an oboe reed, or an affective objective, such as choosing to hear a favorite piece of music. In all cases, there is a specific want or need toward which purposeful behavior is directed. A *goal* is a more long-range target, one that requires attainment of numerous objectives to reach. One may have a goal of living a long and healthy life, becoming an oboe

107

virtuoso, or obtaining daily pleasure. Little, if anything, is gained by arguing whether a particular desired behavior or set of behaviors is an objective or a goal; it is a matter of relative specificity of the target and the observer's perspective.

Behavioral Objectives

A useful outgrowth of expanding educational technology and curriculum revisions in the 1960s is the *behavioral* objective. Mager's (1962) landmark publication was followed by numerous other works; Boyle (1974) prepared a summary compilation regarding behavioral objectives applied to music education. Behavioral objectives certainly were no educational panacea, but neither did they dehumanize education. They *are* valuable for the test maker because they suggest ways of demonstrating particular knowledge or attitudes that lend themselves to test items.

The key to a behavioral objective is the verb. Objectives calling for students to "recognize," "appreciate," "know," or "understand" are nonbehavioral because they do not indicate how an observer will "know" that the students recognize, appreciate, know, or understand. Objectives calling for students to "write," "list," "sing," or "clap" are behavioral because an observer can observe the specified action. Behavioral objectives may be more useful if they include criterion statements, as in

> The student will clap correctly at sight at least 90 percent of the rhythm patterns, on a list compiled by the instructor at a tempo of ♩ = 72.

> Given a random list of Italian terms denoting tempo, the student will rewrite them in order from the slowest to the fastest in no more than one minute, with no more than two errors.

The "clapping" and "rewriting" are the observable behaviors, of course, and the objectives specify criteria for the behaviors and conditions under which they are to occur.

Behavioral objectives are not limited to relatively straightforward cognitive and performance behaviors. Elusive affective and aesthetic objectives can be stated in behavioral terms; the objective writer must decide what he or she will accept as evidence that the desired affect or aesthetic experience occurs. For example, what might a 13-year-old boy *do* if he "appreciated" a variety of musical styles? He might spend a portion of his allowance on recordings, few of which are alike. He might attend concerts of varied performances, even when he is not excused from school to go. He might frequently retune his radio as he seeks changes in background music. In conversation, he might name composers and/or performers in each of several styles. All such activity can be observed. If particular examples of observable behaviors are not valid indicators of appreciation, the objective writer can select others—if "something happens" when appreciation occurs, that "something" can be manifested in some observable way. If no valid behavioral indicators of some desired condition exist, either the condition does not exist or it is useless as an instructional objective or goal.

SAMPLING BEHAVIORS AND OBJECTIVES

In any instructional situation beyond the most trivial, many events, relevant and irrelevant, occur. Many instructional outcomes are planned; some are spontaneous. It rarely (if ever) is possible to test everything, so what material should be tested? Of all the conceivable relevant behaviors, which ones should a measurement procedure sample? Instruction and evaluation thereof should be guided by comprehensive objectives, but decisions regarding the relative importance of objectives and potential test items inevitably are subjective judgments.

Deciding What's Important

What are the "really important" things to test? Of all the material pertinent to an instructional unit on, say, Beethoven, what did the instructor teach? In his or her best professional judgment, what does the instructor–testmaker believe the particular students should "know" about Beethoven and/or his music? Are biographical data, such as Beethoven's lifespan and approximate age at the onset of deafness important? Should students be prepared to recite a catalog of Beethoven's works by categories? Should they recognize excerpts from Beethoven's works, and, if so, how specifically should they identify the excerpts' sources (i.e., titles, movements, theme numbers)? All such decisions ultimately fall to the person responsible for instruction: He or she is obligated to prepare a test in such a way that it reflects the content as it was presented. Content validity is essential for tests that purport to evaluate instruction; the student who studies Beethoven in accordance with the instructor's requirements should recognize the Beethoven of the test as the Beethoven of the classroom. Biographical and publication data and thematic recognition should be important during testing to the extent to which they were important during teaching.

Although this chapter is oriented primarily toward testing achievement that results from specific instruction, the question of what is important applies to aptitude, affective, and performance measures as well as classroom achievement measures. On the basis of knowledge, experience, and a sampling of available research, the would-be test maker must answer questions such as: What must a person do to be a musical success? How essential are nonmusical indicators of potential musical success? What are the indicators of a positive attitude toward a school music program? In what musical styles should a comprehensive musician be able to perform? These and similar rhetorical questions have no simple or general answer—the test maker must decide subjectively what to measure in the particular situation.

Note that from the standpoint of test construction "what is important" refers not to whether something should be *taught* or *characteristic of people,* but rather to what should be *tested, given* that something *has* been taught or *may* be characteristic of people.

Comprehensive Treatment of Important Aspects

Once he or she has decided what is important, the test maker is obligated to represent that importance in a comprehensive manner. All the objectives related to a particular corpus of material require some representation on a test of that material. A list of objectives, chapters in a text, or segments of a study guide must be represented in a balanced manner that fits constraints of time and the sophistication of the learners.

Constructing a detailed test plan can enable the test maker to cover the material sufficiently. Such a plan requires representing the corpus of the material to be tested, perhaps in the form of a list of objectives, numbers of pertinent pages in books, or a set of study questions. It also requires allocating the objectives, pages, or questions among particular test items or sections.

For example, suppose that an examination is supposed to cover three chapters of a music appreciation text. The chapters are respectively 30, 27, and 18 pages long. If the test maker determines that the test should contain 36 multiple-choice items balanced among the chapters, a preliminary plan might reason that the total number of pages is 75, so the chapters should occupy respective proportions of .40, .36, and .24. Therefore, 40 percent of the test (14 items) should relate to the first chapter. Similarly, 36 percent (13 items) should relate to the second chapter, and 24 percent (9 items) should relate to the third. Within each chapter, one can construct a list of key points to determine the content of specific items. Adjustments in chapter proportions may be made if the test maker decides that there are more important points in a shorter than in a longer chapter.

As another example, consider a unit on basic properties of sound waves. Objectives may pertain to the students knowing (a) a definition of a wave, (b) factors influencing the frequency, speed, and direction of a wave, (c) components of a wave, and (d) conditions distinguishing a wave resulting from a musical tone from other waves. A test maker could itemize each major point and write corresponding objective test items. Possibly one comprehensive essay item requiring description of a wave's origin, its travel, and events that may occur as it travels would suffice. If multiple test items are necessary, proportional representation of perceived relative importance should determine how many items to write regarding each point. Naturally, there should not be slavish adherence to number—if the test maker believes one objective, such as indicating that a sound wave is the travel of disturbances rather than particles, is especially important, that objective may merit more test items than some other objectives.

This section's important point is that the test maker should *lay out the priorities*. The test must reflect what has been taught and how it was taught.

Taxonomies

A *taxonomy* is an ordered classified grouping within a subject field. In education there is the well-known Bloom (1956) taxonomy of cognitive objectives and the Krathwohl, Bloom, and Masia (1964) taxonomy of affective objectives. Psychomotor taxonomies are less well known; Colwell (1970) presented a largely perceptually based psychomotor taxonomy developed by Elizabeth Simpson at Illinois. Harrow (1972) developed a largely movement-based psychomotor taxonomy. All such taxonomies represent attempts to order possible educational objectives along a continuum ranging from simple tasks requiring very little skill to complex tasks requiring extensive experience and use of intellectual, affective, or physical resources.

The Bloom taxonomy identifies six major categories of objectives: knowledge, comprehension, application, analysis, synthesis, and evaluation. There are subcategories within all but the application category, and even sub-subcategories within the knowledge subcategories. The simplest type of objective relates to knowledge of specific facts, such as knowing that an oboe is a double reed instrument. The most complex objective requires judgment in terms of external criteria, as in evaluating a set of published school orchestra programs to judge the balance of literature to which the students are exposed.

The Krathwohl et al. affective taxonomy runs from receiving through responding, valuing, and organization to characterization by a value or value complex, with subcategories in all categories except the last. Passive willingness to listen to "classical" music exemplifies the simplest level. Electing to listen to music when several other options are available indicates more than passive interest. A person who virtually organizes his or her life around opportunities to perform or listen to violin music would exemplify characterization by a value or value complex.

Simpson's psychomotor taxonomy begins with perception and is followed respectively by set (mental, physical, or emotional), guided response, mechanism, complex overt response, adaptation, and origination. The category boundaries are somewhat blurred; perceptual tasks can be rather sophisticated. Furthermore, as the term "psychomotor" implies, the cognitive aspect of a motor behavior may be extremely difficult to analyze.

Harrow (1972) developed a six-level taxonomic model based on a continuum of movements, discriminations, and manipulations. She defines psychomotor behaviors as "observable voluntary actions or action patterns performed by the learner and designated by the educator as being an essential portion of the educational goal of his [sic] particular curriculum" (p. 32). The first level, called Reflex Movements, contains respective levels of Segmental, Intersegmental, and Suprasegmental Reflexes. Harrow's second level, Basic-Fundamental Movements, includes Locomotor, Non-Locomotor, and Manipulative Movements. In order, Kinesthetic, Visual, Auditory, and Tactile Discrimination plus Coordinated Abilities comprise Perceptual Abilities, the third level. Physical Abilities—Endurance, Strength, Flexibility, Agility—constitute the fourth level; the fifth level, Skilled Movements, includes Simple, Compound, and Complex Adaptive Skills. Harrow's sixth and highest taxonomic level includes Expressive and Interpretive Movement together as Non-Discursive Communication. There are subdivisions within most divisions at all levels, and even sub-subdivisions within a few subdivisions. As with all taxonomies, there are inevitable overlaps. Cognitive and affective aspects will relate to many voluntary movement-based behaviors.

One can waste considerable time in attempting to classify particular objectives or test behaviors exclusively and/or exhaustively into taxonomic categories; most musical behaviors involve complex combinations of domains and categories. Nevertheless, taxonomic structures are valuable for the test maker because they indicate various levels of knowledge, ability, and/or interest, all of which may suggest particular item types. Testing recall of many musical facts may indicate the degree of knowledge about those facts, but it may say little about how the test taker can *use* those facts. Testing interest in attending a particular concert for which the test taker may be excused from school will say little about a long-standing attitude toward music. Behaviors that fall relatively low in the taxonomic structure may be tested objectively and precisely; multiple-choice, completion, or observation items can easily be constructed to assess knowledge of musical facts or receptivity to a stimulus. Examining a student's evaluation of a musical composition or commitment to a value requires that the examiner make a more subjective judgment. As one considers various item types, one should be aware that the types of items and scopes of particular items may be suggested by a taxonomic structure.

ITEM WRITING

The advantages and disadvantages of various item types are discussed below, and the authors offer some general suggestions based on their experiences. The item writer must consider carefully the background and sophistication of the intended test takers as well as the test's purpose in relation to instruction. The needs for reliability, validity, and adequate coverage of objectives exist regardless of item type.

Wesman's (1971) chapter on item writing is a detailed discussion of short-answer, alternate-choice (true–false), correction, multiple-choice (in several versions), and matching items. The present authors' approach is focused toward assessment of musical behaviors, but it acknowledges the comprehensive treatment by Wesman, as well as Gronlund's (1981) principles for item construction.

Multiple Choice

The multiple-choice item is ubiquitous in educational and psychological measurement. It is highly useful for testing specific knowledge and application thereof. Although the emphasis here is on cognitive items, multiple-choice items may assess attitude or affect when a series of answers ordered on a continuum can be constructed. Multiple-choice items are easily scorable by machine; hand scoring is not especially formidable with group sizes less than 50, although obtaining desired test statistics may be.

Multiple-choice items consist of an opening question or stem followed by a set of alternate answers. Although items may be written to have more than one correct answer, if the examinee is told that he or she is to indicate all "correct" answers, it is customary to have one correct or "best" answer.

There is little or no agreement regarding the optimal number of choices. In theory a greater number of choices should reduce the likelihood of guessing the correct answer and increase the reliability. There are practical limitations regarding test and item length; extra choices (often called "distracters" or "foils" as well as "wrong answers") require extra reading time, and writing additional plausible choices can become difficult. Wesman (1971, p. 101) indicates that four- or five-choice items are the rule, except for younger (approximately six- or seven-year old) children. Ebel (1969) demonstrated that the greatest increase in reliability comes from an increase from two to three choices and that the longer the test, the less the effect of increasing item choices. Asmus (1978) demonstrated that reducing the number of answer choices would not necessarily reduce reliability because more items could be written. The present authors believe that the fewer-choices, more-items option is desirable. Three choices generally are quite sufficient for most multiple-choice tests.

Given the appropriate content area, one must consider certain caveats in writing multiple-choice items. Consider the following item:

The nineteenth century saw the development of an extensive instrumental form known as the symphonic poem; one of that form's leading composers was

A. Richard Strauss.
B. Johannes Brahms.
C. Felix Mendelssohn.

The brief music history lesson is unnecessary. It adds reading time, and in the event that any choice was not active in the nineteenth century it might provide clues to test-wise students. If the test writer wants the examinee to select Strauss from among a group of nineteenth century composers on the basis of the symphonic poem, all he or she should write as a stem is "A leading composer of the symphonic poem was". If the test writer also wants to assess knowledge that the symphonic poem arose in the nineteenth century or that it is an instrumental form, those concerns may be addressed in separate items.

Extraneous words within item choices lengthen test forms and are inefficient. Consider:

> The two main factors determining the reverberation time of a room are
>
> A. the absorption in the room and the shape of the room.
> B. the absorption in the room and the volume of the room.
> C. the shape of the room and the volume of the room.

It is much more efficient to say:

> The two main factors determining a room's reverberation time are the room's
>
> A. absorption and shape.
> B. absorption and volume.
> C. shape and volume.

The principle is to avoid excessive articles and prepositional phrases and state any information that applies to all answers in the item stem.

Grammatical and linguistic cues may lead a test-wise respondent to the correct answer. Incorrect use of an article can hasten elimination of an otherwise carefully planned foil, as in

> Japanese music often is associated with playing a
>
> A. oboe.
> B. aulos.
> C. koto.

Answers A and B are grammatically incorrect; the simplest solutions are to substitute *the* for *a* or incorporate the correct article in each answer. A bit more subtle might be the item

The composer of *Rigoletto* is

A. Georges Bizet.
B. Richard Wagner.
C. Giuseppe Verdi.

A student sensitive to the appearance of Italian names might make the educated guess that the only Italian composer available is the correct answer. Providing Italian foils, such as Rossini and Puccini, would solve the problem and might require more musical discrimination.

It generally is stock wisdom, although not clearly authenticated through research, that the following points should be observed in constructing multiple-choice items:

1. Individual answer choices that appear substantially longer or shorter than the others should be avoided.
2. A predictable answer pattern (e.g., ABC, ABC, ABC) should be avoided.
3. All available letters should be used more or less equally; for example, one should not write a test of 40 ABC items in which C is used only 5 times.
4. Answers such as "all of the above," "none of the above," and "some of the above" should be avoided unless there is a specific reason for encompassing or eliminating the designated answers; they should not be used to avoid writing additional substantive foils.
5. Obviously absurd choices, in relation to the test takers' knowledge and sophistication, should be avoided because they effectively narrow the number of choices.*

The authors strongly recommend instructing the examinee to select the "best" rather than the "correct" answer, especially on tests where there is legitimate debate about the ultimate truth of an answer. Furthermore, this allows for asking learners to recognize synonyms or alternate ways of stating particular facts.

A related argument-avoiding recommendation is to introduce an item with "According to . . ." when one specific but not universally accepted theory or viewpoint is the subject of the item. To ask

The number of choices in a multiple-choice item should be
A. 3.
B. 4.
C. 5.

---

*If providing a touch of humor overrides total concern for psychometric excellence, a test writer may include a few comical answers in a test intended for his or her own students.

is unfair because all three choices are defensible (see earlier discussion). If a particular authority took a position, it would be acceptable to ask "According to . . . , the number of choices . . . ." "According to" items are particularly useful in reference to a designated text, to what a particular music critic has said, or to what any particular authority (including the test writer) believes.

A well-constructed multiple-choice test can require substantial knowledge of specific information and the ability to use it. While one's communication skills may not be enhanced by selecting rather than constructing a response, the skillful limitation of selections to plausible but not quite "right" answers in addition to "right" answers is a time-honored way of assessing acquisition of information. In introductory music appreciation classes, in general music situations, in music theory, indeed in any situation where relatively specific recognition and use of musical terminology is necessary, the multiple-choice item is valuable. One sacrifices creativity, expression, and synthesis for precision and relative objectivity.

Matching

Relating one subcategory to another within one general category is the basis for matching items. Particular examples of matching items on music tests might include matching composers with compositions, measurement units (e.g., Hertz, decibels, cents) with tonal properties, performers with performance media, and compositions with styles. Here is an example of a matching item deliberately constructed to exemplify the genre positively:

> Match each musician in the left-hand column with the musical medium or style for which the musician is best known, according to our class discussion and listening assignments, from the right-hand column. Only one letter should be placed in a blank; it is possible that the same letter would fit more than one blank correctly.

_____ 1.	Johann Strauss	A. opera
_____ 2.	Merle Haggard	B. symphony
_____ 3.	Johannes Brahms	C. jazz
_____ 4.	Richard Rodgers	D. musical comedy
_____ 5.	John Philip Sousa	E. country-western
_____ 6.	David Brubeck	F. rock
_____ 7.	Robert Schumann	G. cantata
_____ 8.	Giuseppe Verdi	H. musique concrete
_____ 9.	Michael Jackson	I. marches
_____ 10.	J.S. Bach	J. waltzes

In the above item it is clear that only one letter is to be placed in a blank. While it is possible to require more than one answer (if Mozart were listed, it would be difficult to justify forcing a choice between A and B), the examinee should know if that is a possibility in the particular matching item. Although the number of blanks and choices is equivalent (it need not be), there is no way that one answer may be right automatically by elimination (B should be used twice; H fits none of the listed musicians). The examinee is aware that simple elimination will not work because he or she is told that a letter could be used more than once. The length is manageable (one should avoid having a matching item requiring more than one page), and the distance from each blank to the correct choice varies. The item is relatively homogeneous in the context of a comprehensive survey of musical styles and musicians, including composers and performers from different eras.

Linguistic cues can be a problem in a matching item, as in matching an author and a music history source or a composer and a composition on the basis of foreign language similarities.

Matching items are a useful way to investigate whether learners can make a correct series of relationships or associations within some logical category. They are as objective as multiple-choice items and can easily be scored by hand, although some respondents' printed or cursive letters may be ambiguous. Machine scoring may be difficult without adaptation of score sheets.

True–False

True–false items may be deceptively simple to write. Lehman (1968, p. 31) discusses the difficulties of constructing nonambiguous true–false items and the relative ease with which a person might guess the correct answer. Wesman (1971, p. 92) also discusses the ambiguity problem and recommends (p. 94) "unless there are truly compelling reasons to do otherwise, the test constructor would do well to favor other forms of items." Despite authoritative warnings the true–false item remains popular in some teacher-made tests, so it is discussed here.

A good true–false item must be defensibly true *or* false in the context in which it is used. The truth or falsehood of "Sibelius was a great musician" could be assessed in the context of his *not* being a carpenter, playwright, or general—then it is obviously true. However, one could focus on "great"—"great" in whose opinion? Sibelius is revered in Finland and certainly is well known to some orchestra enthusiasts, but was he "great"? His "greatness" was and is too ambiguous to judge on a yes–no basis. "The clarinet is a band instrument" is, of course, true in the sense that concert bands usually contain clarinets, but the clarinet also is an orchestral, a chamber music, and a solo instrument. "The saxophone is an orchestral instrument" is false, unless one's orchestral experience includes works such as Ravel's orchestration of Mussorgsky's *Pictures at an Exhibition,* Ravel's *Bolero,* Milhaud's *La Creation du Monde,* or Prokofiev's *Lieutenant Kijé Suite.* Qualifying words can decrease ambiguity, as in

> Sibelius's career was that of a musician.
> Some conductors, performers, record producers, and other musical authorities believe that Sibelius was a great musician.
> Concert bands are very likely to contain [or not contain] clarinets.
> The saxophone usually is not [or is] part of a symphony orchestra.

Care should be taken that qualifying words do not make true items long in relation to false ones.

That which is not completely true is false. That point must be made to examinees, especially younger ones.

In the interest of reliability it may be worthwhile to print T–F in front of each item for examinees to circle. Then there is no question of whether a person has written or printed a T or an F. Some test makers may prefer that examinees write "true" or "false," but that procedure is slightly more time consuming. With machine scoring of answer sheets, true–false items may be treated as two-choice multiple-choice items.

Guessing *may* be discouraged by using a guessing formula that penalizes a wrong answer more than an omitted answer; a ? option may be provided for the unsure student. (However, see Chapter 3.)

True–false items may be combined with other item types. An essay item could be built around an explanation of why a particular statement, even an ambiguous one, is likely to be true or false. Examinees may be asked to rewrite false statements, thereby combining true–false with short answer items and requiring response construction as well as classification. One point may be awarded for each correct decision, and, for each false item, one point may be awarded for a correct rewrite. When this option is elected it is wise to underscore or italicize particular words for which change is allowed (in true as well as false items!) in order to avoid a situation such as

> "Allegro ma non troppo" means "fast but gradually slow down"

being rewritten to become true as

> "Allegro ma non troppo" does not mean "fast but gradually slow down."

Yet another option is to turn a true–false item into a type of multiple-choice item by requiring true–false decisions about several segments, as in

> The solo concerto for a wind or string instrument was a
> <u>   </u>
>   A
> common form in the eighteenth century; one of the principal
> <u>   </u> <u>   </u>
>
> composers of solo concerti was Franz Schubert, and another
> <u>   </u> <u>   </u>
>   B   C
> was Wolfgang Mozart.
> <u>   </u>
>
> A. T   F
> B. T   F
> C. T   F

In general, the authors believe that the difficulties of true–false items outweigh their usefulness. In a conventional multiple-choice item, the examinee really is evaluating the truth or falsehood of each particular choice, yet the "best answer" criterion allows selection of the "most truthful" (or most defensible) answer. While acquisition of musical factual information can be assessed via true-false items, confusion of facts with likely misunderstandings is better assessed through multiple-choice items. Construction of a response is better assessed through the item types we now discuss.

Completion

In a *completion* item, the test taker supplies a word or words to fill a blank or blanks in a sentence. Obviously, the given statement must contain enough words so that a knowledgeable person would be able to see what is required. All blanks should be of equivalent length, and there should be no grammatical cues.

> Consider the following completion items:
> 1. _____ composed *The Rite of Spring*.
> 2. The four major woodwind instruments in standard symphony orchestra instrumentation (i.e., "woodwinds in pairs") are the _____, _____, _____, and _____.

3. A solo concerto is most likely played by a solo instrument and an _____.

4. _____ was (is) a composer of atonal music.

All of these items "look" all right; the blanks are of equal length, and particular words would complete the sentences. Closer examination indicates that the first two items only could be answered correctly in the expected way, but what does one do with partial answers or misspellings? Is "Igor" alone sufficient for the first answer? The third item clearly contains a grammatical cue that "band," "quartet," "chorus," or "piano" is not the answer. Does one accept "ensemble" or "accompaniment"? The fourth item's use of "was (is)" forces the examinee to consider living as well as dead composers, but there clearly is more than one correct answer that the test scorer must be prepared to accept. What happens if the examinee is familiar with an obscure composer of atonal music who is unknown to the scorer?

Clearly, completion items can tap knowledge that is organized logically in a sentence format. While obviously ambiguous and overly leading [to the correct answer] items can be avoided, the test maker must be prepared for unexpected but correct answers and must have a consistent procedure for handling alternative spellings. The need to interpret answers makes using different readers to score identical tests less reliable. Machine scoring is impossible, unless the test is administered via computer-controlled word processing and text editing.

Completion items may be especially valuable in the context of formative evaluation. Completed answer blanks may be compared for alternative correct answers. If knowledge of exact spelling and ability to write terms are considered important, completion items are viable. However, they generally are impractical for testing large groups, and their use in summative evaluation where a grade or a curricular decision is at stake should be approached with considerable caution.

Short Answer

What the authors call a *short-answer* item is a request for a relatively small amount of specific information in an unstructured format. There are varying degrees of specificity, and the amount of information can vary. When a short-answer item requests a narrative description of specific facts, as in requesting a citation of five twentieth century composers of art music with a brief indication of why each is important, the item may in fact be a short essay item. As with completion items, ambiguity must be avoided and the reader must be prepared to evaluate unexpected but veridical answers. Here are a few examples:

1. Name four composers active during the baroque era.
2. List in score order the four voice ranges commonly found in an adult mixed chorus.
3. List six songs that we sang in class this semester.

The second and third items have definite answers. The first also does, but an examinee may name an obscure (to the scorer) but nevertheless "active" baroque composer.

It is possible to have multisectional short answer items. An item could request four composers and three compositions by each. A student could list instruments or voices and notate a playing or singing range. (In a way, the time-honored exercises of melodic and harmonic dictation are short-answer items; if some notation is provided they may be completion items.)

A type of relatively structured short-answer item provides the information in a scrambled order. If one wants a student to "know" tempo markings, he or she could request a list of the terms (in which case it is only fair to specify how many terms) and definitions, test definitions for each term (or terms for each definition) through multiple choice or completion, request matching of terms with definitions, or provide the terms and request an ordering, as in

Arrange the following terms in order from the slowest to the fastest:
   Andante
   Allegretto
   Largo
   Moderato
   Presto
   Allegro

Short-answer items can assess how well the examinee can produce something rather than only recognize it. They may be useful where the test takers should "know it cold." They are relatively quick to write, but they are time consuming to score. (Machine scoring is not possible except with sophisticated equipment.) The number of possible points may vary among short-answer items; the scorer must determine how many points are possible and on what basis each point will be awarded. When time permits and construction of a detailed list or set of exemplars is deemed important, short-answer items are potentially useful.

Essay

There are reasons to avoid essay examinations as a means of evaluating instruction. Different readers may assign widely varying ratings to an identical essay. A fluent writer may write an elaborately impressive but shallow answer. A person who has learned a considerable amount may not be able to show it because he or she can not write well or the corpus tapped by the item does not require much of what was learned. An essay may be read with a positive or negative bias because of what the reader knows about the writer; this is the "halo effect." The essay item nevertheless is a traditional examination mode, especially in higher education, and a well-constructed essay can be a valuable learning experience. There are particular steps in constructing essay items that can enhance the quality of an essay examination.

The "halo effect" may be avoided by having essay writers identify themselves only by a code to which the reader will not refer until the essays are read and evaluated. Test takers could use student or social security numbers. They might designate a particular combination of letters, numerals, and symbols to which the reader will not refer until the essays are scored. An assistant instructor or paraprofessional might remove names and assign each paper a code number that is not revealed to the evaluator until the scoring is complete. Having all students write on identical paper with same-color ink may prevent some identity clues. In small classes, handwriting recognition may be an insurmountable problem unless typing is feasible.

It is important that the essay writer have a fair chance to know what is expected and to organize the essay into an acceptable form. This requires a certain amount of structure in the "question." Consider the following examples:

1. Discuss how a person hears and organizes music.
2. Indicate how to tune an instrument.

While a student might know more from the context of the examination and previous instruction than is evident here, these are both "wide open" items that could elicit divergent answers. Is the "discussion" of a physiological or perceptual nature? Is one to "discuss" the basic hearing process? Is one to consider different sources of music? Does organization mean conceptually or in some physiological way? Does organization mean conception of musical structures, such as melody, classification of styles, recognition of form, or something else? *What* instrument is to be tuned, or does it matter? Is "have someone tune it for you" an acceptable answer? Are tuning mechanics all that is required or is one supposed to evaluate different types or frequencies of tuning standards? The items are far more clear regarding what is expected when written in this way:

1. (Part A) Describe the basic hearing process involved in listening to music. Account for reception and transmission of the sound wave through the ear, perception of tonal properties, and relaying a sensory message to the brain.
   (Part B) Describe several principles by which a listener organizes auditory input to the brain as music. Consider melody, harmony, form, and rhythm.
2. Describe the procedures by which you would tune a brass instrument. Account for a tuning standard, mechanical adjustments to the instrument, and adjustments made by the player while playing.

While room for diversity remains, what is expected is far more clear as a result of the item writer's guidelines.

A model answer constructed by the test writer may guide the reading of the essays as well as reveal unexpected sources of difficulty or a need to provide further guidance. Model answers also can provide useful feedback to the students.

Essay examinations should be read while the reader is reasonably alert and free from distractions, which requires allowing adequate time. One should read question by question rather than examination by examination and avoid assigning final grades until all responses to a particular essay item are read. Evaluative criteria should be based on accuracy, organization, and completeness of the requested information, not on length or neatness. If time permits, a rereading of the essays and/or reading by more than one knowledgeable person to arrive at a consensus may enhance reliability.

When a group of readers are to score an essay independently, guidelines may be useful. Sample "good," "bad," and "indifferent" answers may be provided; a list of events or phenomena that the writer should discuss may focus the readers' attention. In general, all responses to a particular essay item should be read by all readers to avoid introducing further extraneous variance or bias, as would be the case if only the "hard" graders read one item while a mixture of "hard" and "easy" graders read another. If there are too many papers for any one person to read all responses to a given essay item, some other testing procedure should be employed.

Unless the essay must contain an exact amount of specific facts, scoring an essay item is a matter of judgment and/or categorization. Scoring usually is based on matching an overall impression of the essay with a score or grade rather than on counting right answers. An ABCDF or ESU (excellent–satisfactory–unsatisfactory) classification could be employed. An essay could be allocated a maximum number of possible points, with that number being an upper limit, as in scoring a gymnastics event or round of a prize fight. Generally grades or points should not be assigned until all the essays are read unless criteria are detailed and rigid. Much of the material in Chapter 8 is relevant to making a "judgment call" on an essay.

Verbal skills, written as well as spoken, are crucial in higher education and many careers. There comes a time in the study of music theory, history, acoustics, psychology, sociology, and pedagogy when it is important for the student to synthesize, evaluate, and prioritize in a way that cannot be done "objectively." The essay examination thus is essential, despite its difficulties. Coffman (1971, p. 300), in his treatise on essay examinations and their inherent problems, concludes:

> There is little doubt that for many purposes, particularly when large numbers of candidates are to be examined and when the measurement involves subject-matter knowledge, objective testing is more efficient than essay testing. On the other hand, when questions are carefully constructed and focussed on performances involving the communication of complex relationships among ideas and when carefully planned scoring procedures designed to minimize systematic and variable scoring error are applied, essay examinations can provide reliable and valid evidence of achievement.

WHAT ITEM TYPES SHOULD BE USED?

The types of items that a test writer employs are a function of the subject matter, the learners' experience, developmental stage, and sophistication, and the test writer's objectives and beliefs. Multiple-choice items are especially useful in many situations and may be the best overall item type for assessing factual information and specific relations among facts. General musical knowledge, fundamentals of notation, facts of music history and theory, pedagogical questions, and anything where logical accurate and inaccurate responses to stimuli can be categorized are appropriate areas for multiple-choice items. Where construction of a response is desirable, as it may be when accurate use of musical vocabulary and musicians' names is of concern, completion and short-answer items are appropriate. If synthesis and application of information from diverse sources is important, there is no substitute for an essay examination. It is possible to mix item types within one examination; a music history final examination might include multiple-choice items assessing relations of factual information, matching items regarding composers and compositions, and an essay item regarding stylistic contrasts and similarities among three compositions. In any case, the test writer is responsible for professional judgments regarding item selection and construction, and he or she must be prepared to defend those judgments, with consideration of the learners and the subject matter.

ITEM ANALYSIS

Item analysis refers to evaluating individual objective test items for their difficulty and their ability to discriminate among the examinees. Such statistics help the test writer retain, reject, revise, and/or defend particular items. With modern computational aids, both statistics are easy to obtain, and they may be very informative. Teachers can build an extensive item file and gradually improve the quality of their tests through item analysis.

Item Difficulty

An item's difficulty customarily is expressed as the proportion of respondents who answer the item correctly. The possible range thus is from 0.00, for an item that no one answers correctly, to 1.00, for an item that everyone answers correctly. (The *larger* the number, the *easier* the item.)

While computing item difficulty is simple, interpretation may be more intricate. A "hard" item may indicate failure to study, poor teaching, or ambiguous item writing. An "easy" item may indicate successful study or teaching or trivial measurement. Items with difficulty indexes of 0.00 or 1.00 are nondiscriminating; this is bad from a norm-referenced standpoint, because individuals are not separated by the item, but good from a criterion-referenced standpoint, because it is clear that pertinent criteria are or are not met. A few easy items at the beginning of a test may give examinees confidence. In any case, there is no universal rule regarding optimal item difficulty or the optimal mix of difficulties within a test. The test writer must consider the particular advantages of hard or difficult items in the context of the test's purpose(s).

Item Discrimination

To *discriminate* means to separate according to some criterion, so *discriminating* items separate test takers, presumably according to differences in their performance. One may adopt the conceptual position that overall group tendencies in relation to some absolute standard are more important than separating individuals (the criterion-referenced approach), but item discrimination indexes still can provide useful information regarding what items seem to be the most related to overall test performance. When a test is to be norm-referenced, item discrimination data perhaps are the most significant for selecting and refining items.

The authors recommend item-total correlation as an index of item discrimination because the correlation coefficient reveals the strength and direction of the relationship between success on the particular item and success on the total test. The stronger the correlation (in either direction), the more the item relates to the total test scores' ability to classify individual test takers. When items are scored on a right–wrong basis, the point-biserial correlation,

$$r_{PB} = \frac{\overline{X}_1 - \overline{X}_o}{S_x} \left(\sqrt{\frac{N_1 N_o}{N(N-1)}} \right),$$

where

$\overline{X}_1$ = mean total test score of persons answering the item correctly,

$\overline{X}_o$ = mean total test score of persons answering the item incorrectly,

S_x = standard deviation of the distribution of total test scores,

N_1 = number of persons answering the item correctly,

N_o = number of persons answering the item incorrectly,

and

$$N = \text{total number of respondents}$$

is recommended. When items are scored on a multipoint basis, as in 1–5 Likert scale items, the product–moment correlation, discussed earlier regarding reliability, is recommended. The theoretical range of item discriminations parallels the correlation coefficient range; perfect discrimination, positive or negative, is virtually impossible.

To illustrate the technique and show some relationships to item difficulty the following examples are provided. Consider a 10-item test given to 10 individuals that yields the following "response strings," in which a 1 represents a correct answer and a 0 represents an incorrect answer:

Examinee (Item)	1	2	3	4	5	6	7	8	9	10	Total Score
E1	1	1	0	1	1	1	0	1	0	0	6
E2	1	1	1	1	1	1	1	1	0	1	9
E3	1	0	0	0	1	1	1	0	0	0	4
E4	1	1	1	1	1	1	1	0	0	1	8
E5	1	0	1	0	1	1	1	0	0	0	5
E6	1	1	1	1	1	1	0	1	0	1	8
E7	1	0	1	1	1	1	1	0	0	1	7
E8	1	1	0	0	1	1	1	0	0	0	5
E9	1	0	0	0	1	1	1	0	0	0	4
E10	1	0	0	0	0	1	1	0	0	0	3

Item difficulty:

1.00 .50 .50 .50 .90 1.00 .80 .30 .00 .40

Items 1 and 6 were answered correctly by everyone. Regardless of the values of $\overline{X}_1$, S_X, and N in the above formula, the facts that N_o is 0 (no one missed either item) and $\overline{X}_o$ is nonexistent means that the discrimination index is .00. Similarly, item 9, where no one answered it correctly, N_1 is 0, and $\overline{X}_1$ is nonexistent, will have no discriminating power. Logically, if *everyone* is labeled as successful *or* as unsuccessful, there is no discrimination.

Now consider item 10, where E2, E4, E6, and E7, the four individuals who answered the item correctly, earned the four highest total test scores. The item discrimination index (point-biserial correlation) is .94. In item 5, where only E10 missed the item, the index is .43; E10 earned the lowest total test score. Items 2, 3, and 4 all have *difficulty* indexes of .50, but their respective *discrimination* indexes are .71, .82, and .93. Although the proportion of examinees answering correctly or incorrectly remains the same, the particular individuals in each proportion vary. The greater the tendency of the successful (on the item) proportion to include the higher overall test scores, the greater the discrimination index.

Item 7 exemplifies an undesirable situation. The discrimination index is −.23; E1 and E6, with respective total scores of 6 and 8, are the two examinees who answered incorrectly. Their mean item score is 7.00, which is above the overall test mean of 5.90 and the mean of the eight people who answered the item correctly of 5.63. When the "better" students, who presumably are more knowledgeable in general, miss an item, it may indicate that something about the item is misleading the students. Perhaps a foil intended to be clearly wrong has a degree of rightness apparent to the more perceptive students. Perhaps, too, there were some mechanical errors in scoring or marking an answer sheet, or E1 and E6 just did not know the particular information, but, in any case, a negatively discriminating item indicates at least a need for the test maker to reconsider the item.

Item discrimination is not limited to right–wrong items. Attitudinal items that have no right answer but solicit degrees of agreement with some position can be related to an overall score distribution by means of product–moment correlation.

Difficulty and Discrimination in Multipoint Items

The concept of item "difficulty" becomes ambiguous when there is no "right" answer, as in attitudinal items. The proportion of examinees selecting any particular choice still can be a descriptive statistic, of course.

In a short answer or completion item where two or more specific correct answers are sought, one must determine whether the entire item or the individual answer is the unit of analysis. For example, one could ask for a listing of the instrumentation of a standard woodwind quintet. The totally correct answer, worth "5 points" in many scoring schemes, is flute, oboe, clarinet, bassoon, horn. Perhaps students remember certain instruments more easily than others; the respective "difficulty indexes" for each instrument may show that. In the event that the entire item is considered totally right if all five instruments are listed and totally wrong if any one is missing, the item becomes a dichotomy and the index applies in the usual manner.

Discrimination indexes can be computed for any part of a multipoint item. For example, when there are choices A, B, and C, a point-biserial correlation between total score and selection–nonselection of the answer will show the relationship between overall test scores and selecting the particular answer. When there are attitudinal items, such as extent of agreement items on a 1–5 scale, the item scores may be correlated with total scores via product–moment correlation. In any case, item discrimination measures the contribution of an item toward determining the total score.

USE OF RECORDED MUSICAL EXAMPLES

Recorded musical examples obviously are essential for many forms of musical measurement. The test maker needs to consider the appropriate use of musical examples, taping mechanics, the sound environment, and copyright.

Appropriate Use

In the interest of testing efficiency, a musical example should exemplify what it is supposed to exemplify, be of sufficient but not excessive length, and be as "musical" as possible. The examples must be subservient to the purposes of the test.

If a student is to recognize a particular musical work, the chosen excerpt must reflect the test constructor's desired recognition ability level. Is there a particular "great moment of music" or well-known theme, such as the second theme from the first movement of Schubert's "Unfinished"? Do the recognition requirements extend to different portions of a lengthy work? Is the excerpt in the instrumentation in which the music customarily is performed? In the interest of "musicality," the excerpt should start and stop at a musically logical place; a gradual fade in and/or fade out is desirable to avoid an abrupt beginning and/or end when there are no appropriate silent spaces in the music.

When the particular piece is irrelevant but the test taker must recognize a particular style, section, or compositional device, care obviously must be taken that the excerpts clearly exemplify the style. If one is testing meter recognition, for example, polymetric excerpts and excerpts with peculiar syncopation patterns may be needlessly difficult. Musical examples that are atypical of a style or period should be avoided in items testing style or period classification. Yet, in the interest of musicianship and generalization, musical dimensions that are irrelevant to the test task should vary, especially as students acquire increasing musical sophistication. A test of classification according to different periods of music history should use instrumental and choral music. A test of instrument identification should include the target instruments in varied solo and exposed ensemble settings. The basic point is that a musical excerpt should be chosen to be representative but musically realistic and stimulating.

Taping Mechanics

This section considers the test maker who must record material for a particular test application. (Commercially produced tests generally have necessary stimulus recordings, although the principles are identical.) It presents several points for consideration; it is not a treatise on recording technology.

The two basic means of recording musical examples are line recording and live recording. Line recording generally is simpler because one goes directly via wires ("patchcords") from one device's electronic output to the recorder's electronic input. "Outside" sounds can not interfere, although various types of interference may occur. Signals may be taken from other tapes or phonograph records as well as electronic organs, synthesizers, or anything with an output jack. The new microprocessor-controlled synthesizer–cassette recorder combination may become valuable in test construction because one can quickly perform and record, and change if necessary, a variety of simple and complex musical excerpts.

Live recording requires using a microphone, or possibly two. While one often simply must use what is available, high quality microphones are an asset. A cardioid field pattern (i.e., area of maximum sensitivity adjacent to the microphone) may be advantageous in helping prevent lower level unwanted sounds from being recorded. The basic "heart shaped" pattern makes it less likely that the microphone will be sensitive to sounds that are not to the front or slightly to the sides of the microphone. In general, the microphone(s) should be located as close to the sound source, whether a speaking voice or a musical performance, as possible. Since in reality one records a room rather than only people in the room, echoes and resonating surfaces should be avoided. An overly "dead" room may produce a somewhat artificial sounding result.

A mixture of line and live recording may be necessary, as in producing a tape of numbered (speaker) musical excerpts (line-recorded). Separate line and microphone inputs are greatly desirable on the tape recorder, as is a pause control to engage when switching from one input mode to another. The pause control also will prevent the clicking sounds that result from starting or stopping a tape. If no pause control is available, one should turn the recording level controls to the lowest setting prior to starting or stopping the tape.

One should record at as high an intensity ("volume") level as possible without distortion, in accordance with the recorder's VU meter. It is easy to soften a "too loud" tape in playback, but a "too soft" tape can not be strengthened without adding hiss and/or distortion.

Phonograph records or prerecorded tapes should be monitored carefully for unacceptable extraneous sounds (as well as quality of musical performance) prior to recording. Phonograph records may be cleaned via a "washing" device, but cracks cannot be eliminated. Tapes that have been stored for a while may have "bled" or "printed through" so that one hears many extra sounds. While the modern noise reduction systems, which are integral parts of better quality recorders, may eliminate or reduce hissing and other sounds so that the new tape sounds better than the original, some recorded results simply will be too "noisy" to use.

Faster tape recording speeds (7.5 or 15 ips) generally yield a higher quality recording than slower speeds (3.75 or 1.875 ips). One must weigh the better quality against the greater amount of tape required for higher speed recording.

For most test construction, the choice of cassette or reel-to-reel tapes is largely a matter of convenience. High quality recordings suitable for virtually any music-testing purposes are possible on cassette tapes. In either case, one should avoid "bargain" tapes because they may stretch and/or tear easily. Reel-to-reel tapes are advantageous when one plans to splice in various sections. (Do *not* record on each side of the tape!)

Once test tapes are recorded it is prudent to create a backup copy or two. Tapes should be stored on end rather than on the side and should be stored in the rewind position to alleviate print through problems.

Sound Environment

Great care in producing a test tape may go for naught if the tape is played in an inappropriate environment. The testing room obviously should be reasonably free from outside noise, and the loudness level should be sufficient but not overpowering. In an unusually large room attention to people seated far from speakers or some other sound source may be necessary in order to verify that all test takers may hear.

When the testing task is relatively global, as in theme recognition, comfortable listening conditions, that is, music reasonably free of distracting noises at an obvious but not overly loud listening level, should suffice. However, in testing fine discrimination skills, such as detection of minute pitch or timbre differences, or judgment skills involving subtleties of phrasing, loudness, or tone quality, intraroom variables in acoustical properties may become important. Strictly speaking, everyone does not hear the same physical stimulus from place to place in a room because the combination of direct and reflected sound waves differs from place to place. Plomp and Steeneken (1973, p. 57) noted:

> The variability in the amplitude spectrum of a complex tone in a reverberant sound field defines the lower limit of a listener's ability to recognize tones. If their spectra do not diverge more than the differences introduced by reverberation, they cannot be labelled consistently by a listener; his responses would depend upon his location in the reverberant sound field. The amplitude spectra would have to be more different in order to obtain a reliable perceptual distinction.

When small discriminations are important the test administrator thus must try to equalize listening conditions among all test takers. Listening through earphones will prevent room acoustics from altering the stimulus, as will listening in a small sound-treated room. Sergeant (1973) demonstrated superior test performance in pitch discrimination when earphones were employed.

COPYRIGHT CLEARANCE

Using copyrighted musical works is potentially troublesome. The music and/or the recording may be subject to copyright protection, and a test maker can not naively rely on his or her lack of a profit motive in duplicating copyrighted printed music, phonograph recordings, and/or tapes.

Test makers may consider the doctrine of "fair use" in constructing classroom tests that involve musical excerpts. According to Public Law 94-553, enacted by the 94th U.S. Congress on October 19, 1976 as an extensive revision of existing copyright law, as it indicates in section 107,

the fair use of a copyrighted work, including such use by reproduction in copies or phonorecords [which includes discs and
tapes] or by any other means . . . for purposes such as criticism,
comment, news reporting, teaching (including multiple copies for
classroom use), scholarship, or research, is not an infringement of
copyright. In determining whether the use made of a work in any
particular case is a fair use the factors to be considered shall
include—

(1) the purpose and character of the use, including whether such
     use is of a commercial nature or is for nonprofit educational
     purposes;
(2) the nature of the copyrighted work;
(3) the amount and substantiality of the portion used in relation
     to the copyrighted work as a whole; and
(4) the effect of the use upon the potential market for or value of
     the copyrighted work.

Sound recordings made before February 15, 1972 are not subject
to copyright *as recordings,* according to section 301 of PL 94-553.
The music itself may be copyrighted; in general, copyrights do not
expire until 50 years after an author's death. Recordings made
since February 15, 1972 are subject to copyright in the same
manner as printed materials.

Copyright also is a consideration in using notated examples and
song lyrics. Even in seemingly "free domain" materials, the words
may be copyrighted, even though the music is not, or a particular
arrangement may be copyrighted. Most countries reciprocally recognize copyright.

Multiple copying of intact copyrighted music and recordings is
clearly illegal. Copying commercially published expendable materials, such as workbooks, is clearly illegal. Copying intact musical
scores, recordings, or textbooks (including this one!) solely to avoid
expenditures is clearly illegal. One-time copying or copying of brief
excerpts *may* be legal. If there are any questions regarding using a
particular work, the test maker should consult the copyright owner.

SUMMARY

This chapter's basic points are the following:

1. Objectives are more specific statements of intent than goals.

2. Behavioral objectives that indicate how test takers should
    demonstrate knowledge are valuable in test construction.

3. The test maker should decide what is important and ascertain that it is tested in proportion to its importance.

4. Taxonomies may be useful in indicating the relative objectivity, specificity, or comprehensive nature of potential test items.

5. Multiple-choice items that are written clearly, have one "best" answer, and avoid extraneous clues are very versatile and useful in building reliable and valid tests for many areas of musical knowledge.

6. Matching items must be manageable in length, relatively homogeneous, and avoid opportunity to answer one part by elimination.

7. True–false items must be highly specific and are open to considerable criticism.

8. Completion items are useful when one wishes the test taker to construct a response, but the test maker must be prepared for unexpected answers.

9. Short-answer items provide more opportunities for constructing responses and may be somewhat subjective.

10. Essay items stress writing skills and are subjective but may be the only way to have someone synthesize what he or she knows about a particular well-defined topic.

11. The basic statistics of item analysis are the difficulty index and the discrimination index; they may apply to items with no one correct answer as well as right-or-wrong dichotomous items.

12. Difficulty and discrimination indexes may be used to interpret strengths and weaknesses of particular items.

13. Recorded excerpts should be selected for the specific purpose, recorded as clearly as possible, and played in an appropriate environment.

14. One must heed copyright restrictions in selecting and recording music for tests.

Study Questions

1. Select an area of musical knowledge that interests you and construct five behavioral objectives pertinent to that area.

2. For each objective you wrote for number 1, write two test items, one of which is deliberately "bad" and one of which is deliberately "good." You may mix item types among the objectives, but be sure that each objective's corresponding "bad" and "good" item is of the same type. Explain *why* each item is "good" or "bad," or submit them to your classmates or colleagues to critique.

3. Select a chapter in this or some other textbook and list or outline the important points that you feel should be represented on a test of that chapter. Then describe how you would construct a test of those points. Be sure to consider item type and any need for recorded examples.

4. Consider the following scores (1 = right, 0 = wrong) earned by ten students on a ten-item test:

Student (Item)	1	2	3	4	5	6	7	8	9	10	Total
Arthur	1	0	1	0	1	1	1	0	0	1	6
Carol	1	0	1	0	1	1	1	1	1	1	8
Donna	1	0	1	0	1	1	0	1	1	1	7
Francois	1	0	1	1	1	1	1	1	1	1	9
Laura	1	0	1	1	0	0	1	0	0	0	4
Max	1	0	0	0	1	0	0	0	0	0	2
Olga	1	0	1	0	1	1	0	0	1	1	6
Ramon	1	0	1	0	1	1	0	1	0	1	6
Sylvia	1	1	0	0	0	0	1	0	0	0	3
Tyrone	0	1	0	0	0	0	0	0	0	0	1

Which, if any, items appear to be highly discriminating (in a negative as well as a positive direction) and which appear to be rather non-discriminating? Why? Now compute the item difficulty and discrimination index for each item. Explain any situation where items with identical difficulty indexes have different discrimination indexes.

REFERENCES

Asmus, E.P., Jr. *The effect of altering the number of distractors on test statistics: Is 3 better than 5?* Paper presented at the meeting of the Music Educators National Conference, Chicago, April, 1978.

Bloom, B. (Ed.). *Taxonomy of educational objectives: The classification of educational goals, handbook I: Cognitive domain.* New York: David McKay, 1956.

Boyle, J.D. (Comp.). *Instructional objectives in music.* Vienna, Va.: Music Educators National Conference, 1974.

Coffman, W.E. *Essay examinations.* In R.L. Thorndike (Ed.), *Educational measurement* (2nd ed.). Washington, D.C.: American Council on Higher Education, 1971.

Colwell, R. *The evaluation of music teaching and learning.* Englewood Cliffs, N.J.: Prentice-Hall, 1970.

Ebel, R.L. Expected reliability as a function of choices per item. *Educational and Psychological Measurement,* 1969, *24,* 565–570.

Gronlund, N.E. *Measurement in evaluation and teaching* (4th ed.). New York: Macmillan, 1981.

Harrow, A.J. *A taxonomy of the psychomotor domain.* New York: David McKay, 1972.

Krathwohl, D., Bloom, B.S., & Masia, B.B. *Taxonomy of educational objectives: The classification of educational goals, handbook II: Affective domain.* New York: David McKay, 1964.

Lehman, P.R. *Tests and measurements in music.* Englewood Cliffs, N.J.: Prentice-Hall, 1968.

Mager, R. *Preparing instructional objectives.* Palo Alto, Calif.: Fearon, 1962.

Plomp, R., & Steeneken, H.J.M. Place dependence of timbre in reverberant sound fields. *Acustica,* 1973, *28,* 50–59.

Sergeant, D. Measurement of pitch discrimination. *Journal of Research in Music Education,* 1973, *21,* 3–19.

Wesman, A.G. Writing the test item. In R.L. Thorndike (Ed.), *Educational measurement* (2nd ed.). Washington, D.C.: American Council on Higher Education, 1971.

6

Measuring Musical Aptitude and Ability

The measurement and prediction of musical ability is a time-honored topic in the psychology of music. A clear indication of what a prospective music student is likely to achieve has considerable practical significance for the student, parents, and music educators. Measuring musical aptitude and ability requires deciding what is important in light of the test user's conception of aptitude and ability. This chapter addresses that issue and reviews a few representative tests.

WHAT MIGHT BE TESTED?

"Aptitude" means potential or capacity for achievement (Lehman, 1968, p. 8). Radocy and Boyle (1979, p. 263) define aptitude as including the result of genetic endowment and maturation plus whatever musical skills may develop without formal musical education. Aptitude is a broader term than "capacity" and narrower than "ability." It usually excludes specific musical achievement. In principle, anything that one believes may predict future musical success, however one defines "success," is potential material for a music aptitude test, provided that the test does not require formal musical knowledge.

Since music is an aural art, a musician logically should be able to discriminate between sounds that vary in subtle ways. While ability to hear with great acuity per se apparently is of no musical advantage (Sherbon, 1975), aural discrimination of pitch, loudness, timbre, and duration is potentially fruitful as aptitude test material. Under optimal listening conditions, people can distinguish rather small pitch differences; in one study (Zwicker, Flottorp, & Stevens, 1957), listeners could detect frequency changes in a slowly resolving tone of as little as 0.5 percent. However, the just noticeable difference for pitch is not an unchanging value; it varies with frequency, intensity, duration, and rate of change (Roederer, 1975). Discrimination of rather small loudness differences is possible, but Western music has developed in such a way that the general artistic demand for a really wide dynamic range and subtle loudness differences is restricted (Patterson, 1974; Radocy & Boyle, 1979, p. 36). Timbre is highly multidimensional; people can compare tones for degrees of similarity in a global way (Grey, 1977). Differences in duration can be discriminated readily. The importance of paired comparisons of sensory properties is a subjective judgement for the investigator of musical aptitude.

Tonal memory, which also requires aural discrimination, is perhaps a more "musical" task than comparing individual sounds. Farnsworth (1969, p. 208) claims that test makers agree that "musical memory" requires careful attention. Tonal memory can mean rather specific recall for a sequence of pitches and/or durations, or it can mean a general recall of a melodic contour or form to the extent necessary for musical recognition. Curiously, specific tonal details may be less important than overall contour for recognition of familiar melodies (Dowling & Fujitani, 1971).

When exact recall of a tonal sequence is of concern, it is worth noting that research suggests that tonal melodies are easier to recall than atonal melodies (Long, 1976/1975). Ability to recall a certain tone from a prior sequence depends in part on the time interval before recall, position in the sequence, and the sequence length (Williams, 1975).

Naturally, in an aptitude test one would not expect melodic dictation or comparing an aural stimulus with printed notation because dictation and music reading are specific achievements. It is quite possible to make "same–different" comparisons between paired tonal sequences, or to indicate which of a set of short sequences matches a standard or which tone in a sequence is changed.

Musical form is based on patterns of unity, achieved through repetition, and variety. Identifying form depends on recognizing whether particular musical material is new, has been heard before, or is some alteration of what was heard before (Radocy, 1980, p. 100). While labeling specific musical forms and long-term identification of sections (as in sonata form) are achievement laden, aptitude measures could include contrasting paired examples that vary in their degrees of similarity. Differences could be rhythmic, as in altering a theme via augmentation or diminution, or melodic, as in retrograde or inversion. Research suggests that trained musicians are somewhat more sensitive to melodic than to rhythmic change, but that will vary greatly with individual listeners (Radocy, 1982). An effective contrasting technique is presenting a musical pattern followed by a pattern that is more ornate, but if mentally stripped of the ornamentation is either the same as or different from the initial pattern. This "imagery" technique is used in the *Musical Aptitude Profile* (Gordon, 1965), which we shall discuss shortly.

All the possibilities for assessing musical aptitude discussed thus far are essentially aural comparisons involving detecting some deviation from an initial standard. Audition skills logically *are* related to musical success, but musical ability, in a larger sense, is probably an interaction of audition, physical coordination, intelligence, and experience (Radocy & Boyle, 1979, p. 272).

So-called "nonmusical" or "extramusical" variables may bear strong relationships to eventual musical achievement, especially in specific instructional settings. Multiple regression analysis, an extension of correlation, can show the relationship of several predictors to a criterion variable. Using a criterion variable of apparent musical "talent" and "awareness," as rated by teachers of 291 students in a university laboratory school, Rainbow (1965) identified as significant predictors tonal memory, academic intelligence, musical achievement, interest in music, and socioeconomic background; academic achievement and socioeconomic background were significant while "musical" variables such as pitch discrimination, rhythm, and musical training were not. Particular combinations of significant and nonsignificant predictors varied among elementary, junior high, and senior high levels, but at least one "nonmusical" or "extramusical" variable was significant at each level. In a more recent study, Hedden (1982) used a music achievement test, presumably more reliable than teacher ratings, as a criterion variable. For 144 fifth- and sixth-grade students, the best single predictor variable was academic achievement; adding an attitude toward music or a musical self-concept measure modestly increased prediction power. A musical background measure as well as gender added nothing significant to the overall prediction ability.

Opinions differ regarding the relationship of intelligence to musical aptitude; some correlational studies (e.g., Gordon, 1968) suggest only a slight relationship. However, correlation techniques may show a spuriously low relation due to lack of reliability either of the aptitude or the intelligence measure. Sergeant and Thatcher (1974) conducted three experiments employing various measures of intellectual and musical abilities and analyzed their data via the statistical technique of analysis of variance. They concluded that all highly intelligent people are not necessarily musical, but all highly musical people are apparently highly intelligent. It is not surprising that academic intelligence in one form or another would be related to musical achievement, and therefore would be one indicator of musical aptitude, especially in a school setting. From a practical standpoint, one probably should consider intelligent children as potential musicians, particularly if they appear to have any musical interests.

"Intelligence" often refers to some sort of academic or linguistic ability, and such ability probably is assumed by most literature relating intellectual and musical abilities or aptitudes. In what may prove to be a highly influential book, Gardner (1983) presents a multiple intelligence theory, based on biological, neurological, clinical, and behavioral evidence, which encompasses separate linguistic, logical-mathematical, spatial, bodily kinesthetic, personal, *and musical* intelligences. While debate regarding the generality versus specificity of intelligence or musical ability is not new, theorizing a musical intelligence that is of equivalent stature to other forms of intelligence is new, and there may be future implications for those who wish to test musical aptitude. Certainly, more knowledge of musical development and anomalies therein are necessary.

Physical coordination obviously is relevant to playing certain instruments, but motor skill assessment is beyond the scope of this text.

What should a musical aptitude test test? That is a judgment based on what the test maker considers important. Aural skills frequently are tested, as the reviews of tests below indicate. Since success in school settings is linked to "nonmusical" variables, especially intelligence, an assessment of musical aptitude may include other variables.

REPRESENTATIVE EXAMPLES

There are or have been many tests of musical aptitude, as one might expect. According to Lehman (1968, p. 5), interest in creating musical aptitude tests grew between the two world wars and waned thereafter until the late 1960s. The tests selected for discussion here are representative of the approaches aptitude test constructors have taken, and, at least at the time of this writing, they are available commercially.

Seashore

The most widely known published standardized musical aptitude test battery may be the *Seashore Measures of Musical Talents* (Seashore et al., 1960). The Seashore battery is the oldest standardized music test available (it originally appeared in 1919); it has been researched and used extensively; it was a landmark work of a pioneering American music psychologist, and its validity is impeccable, mixed, or nonexistent, depending on the user's philosophy. A detailed discussion is justified here because of the battery's exemplary nature, positively and negatively.

The plurals "measures" and "talents" represent more than semantic nit-picking. Carl Seashore (1938) believed in a "theory of specifics," that is, musical ability is a set of loosely related basic sensory discrimination skills. One does not combine parts of the battery to obtain a total score; rather, one obtains a profile. Seashore further believed that a person's aural skills had a genetically determined capacity; battery scores would not change over time except to the extent that misunderstood directions and test-taking experience might affect the results. For Seashore, his tests were valid in and of themselves as measures of sensory skills important for musicians.

The present battery contains six sections: Pitch, Loudness, Rhythm, Time, Timbre, and Tonal Memory. The original 1919 version lacked a rhythm section; it was added in 1925. The original version also contained a consonance test, which was eliminated during an extensive 1939 revision. The basic task in each section is aural discrimination.

The pitch test requires the subject to indicate whether the second of 50 paired tones is higher or lower than the first tone, a standard of 500 Hz. The items become progressively more difficult; the frequency difference ranges from 17 to 2 Hz, which is about 59 to 9 cents (1 cent = 1/1200 of an octave, 100 cents = 1 semitone).

Fifty paired tones are judged regarding whether the second 440 Hz tone is stronger or weaker than the first in Seashore's loudness test. Decibel differences range from 4 to 0.5. As in the pitch test, the tones are "pure" tones, produced by an audio oscillator.

Pure tone patterns comprise the rhythm test. The subject listens to 30 paired patterns and indicates whether each pair's tones are the same or different. Patterns are five, six, or seven 500 Hz tones long; meters include $\frac{2}{4}$, $\frac{3}{4}$, and $\frac{4}{4}$.

The time test requires indicating whether the second 440 Hz tone is longer or shorter than the first in each of 50 pairs. The standard tone is 0.8 sec. The comparison tone varies from the standard by from 0.30 to 0.05 sec.

Complex tones (mixtures of frequencies) built on 180 Hz are used in Seashore's timbre test. For the 50 pairs, the subject indicates whether the two tones are the same or different. Differences are attained by varying the relative intensities of the third and fourth partials.

Sequences of electronic organ tones, grouped in 10 pairs each of three, four, or five tones, comprise the tonal memory test. One tone differs between the members of each pair; the smallest difference is a whole step. The subject's task is to identify the number of the tone that differs.

The tests' raw scores may be converted to percentiles in accordance with tables of norms for grades 4–16. The machine-scorable answer sheet provides space for drawing a "profile curve" that connects a subject's percentile location for each of the six tests.

The test manual claims reliabilities ranging from .55 to .85 for different sections at different grade levels. Lehman (1968, p. 40) reports that the pitch and tonal memory sections have been generally the most reliable while the timbre test is the weakest.

The Seashore battery's validity is open to question in accordance with one's views of musical aptitude and ability. There is little question regarding measurement of the particular skills; someone who scores well on the pitch test probably *is* good at making rapid minute pitch comparisons. Most validity studies were conducted with the 1919 version. Farnsworth (1969, p. 197) indicates that Seashore scores have more value for predicting success in music classes (e.g., harmony) of a tonal nature than they do for academic music classes (e.g., music history). This would be expected, due to the battery's content. Manor (1950) found a modest relation between the 1939 pitch and tonal memory tests and fourth-grade instrumental music success. Seashore's claim that the scores could be raised only as an artifact of testing is not valid. Subjects can improve their scores via relevant training procedures; for example, Wyatt (1945) showed average gains of 49 percent among adult musicians and 26 percent among nonmusicians.

Reliability and hence validity of a test requiring fine auditory discriminations will be influenced by the quality of recording and playback equipment and by listening conditions. Good listening conditions are crucial for Seashore administration; ideally, the battery should probably be administered via high quality headphones. Sound pressure level in a free reverberant field, such as most classroom test administration situations, will vary around the room, so the sound sensation experienced by a listener varies with where he or she is seated (Plomp & Steeneken, 1973). Sergeant (1973) documented significant differences in pure tone pitch discrimination scores, among musically skilled subjects, which depended on whether the test was administered under customary group-testing conditions, individually in a sound attenuation booth, or via headphones. Accuracy was greatest with headphones, least in the group condition.

Four of the six tests use dichotomous items. A completely random guess will have a fifty–fifty chance of being correct; consequently, the chance score is equal to half of the number of items.

Other criticisms of the battery include the lack of item numbers on the recording (answer columns are identified) and the "monster movie" voice that labels the columns and says things such as "Ready, . . . now, . . . for . . . the . . . PITCH . . . test!"

As a test of specific aural discrimination skills, Seashore's battery may be very appropriate. The person who earns a high score on all sections under good listening conditions likely will be an excellent auditory discriminator. The test user must decide whether such information is essential for his or her purposes. There certainly are musical tasks that require detecting subtle differences in tonal properties. Yet music is far more than "isolated" skills. To the extent that ability in those "isolated" skills is a valid indicator of musical ability as conceived by the test user, the Seashore battery is valid.

Wing

The *Standardised Tests of Musical Intelligence* (Wing, 1961) are in stark contrast to the Seashore battery. Wing, an eminent British music psychologist, believed in, and in an early factor analytic study (Wing, 1941), found a *general* factor of musical ability that should pervade all areas of musical learning. One legitimately can speak of the Wing *test* because there is a total score. The test may be considered more "musical" than Seashore because the stimuli are piano tones and are short melodies or chords. There are seven subtests.

Chord analysis is required in the first test, although some of the "chords" are two-tone simultaneous intervals. The subject indicates how many tones are presented in each of 20 stimuli. The answer sheet allows for up to six tones; no stimulus in fact contains more than four. "Hearing out" the number of tones in a simultaneous sound is not an easy task for an untrained ear; while intervals and chords generally do not merge into one sound, many people would have difficulty distinguishing beyond the fact that more than one sound is present.

The second test requires listening to paired chords for movement of one tone. The subject indicates whether the two chords remain the same, whether one tone moves down, or whether one tone moves up. The answer sheet requires only checking symbols for "up," "down," or "same."

Melodic alteration is the basis for the third test. Thirty paired melodies in which the second melody has one altered tone are presented; the subject indicates the number of the altered tone. Melodies range from 3 to 10 tones. The instructions invite the subject to write "S" for same if there is no alteration but in fact there are no unaltered melodies or places on the answer sheet to write "S." There are only dots corresponding to each tone.

The fourth test requires an evaluation of 14 paired performances regarding rhythmic accent. The subject indicates whether the "A" version or "B" version is "better" regarding the location of the "accentuated (more strongly played) notes" or if the two versions are the same, as three items are.

Another preference task comprises the fifth test; this time the subject must judge whether either version is "better" regarding appropriate harmonization or whether they are the same, as three are. The subject is told that the second version "Sometimes . . . has different notes below the tune (the notes played by the left hand may be different)." There are 14 items.

For test six the subject is told "Sometimes the louder and quieter portions are in different places when the tune is played the second time." The subject again indicates for 14 pairs whether they are the same, as three are, or, if they are different, whether version "A" or "B" is "better." The test basically requires judging the propriety of crescendo and diminuendo locations.

Phrasing sensitivity is tested in the last section. Fourteen paired melodies are judged for sameness (three are played the same) or, if different, for which version is "better." Pauses, legato, and staccato are employed. The subject is told "Sometimes the second playing has the notes differently grouped (different groups of notes may be played with short sharp strokes, or so that they follow on smoothly, etc.). The general effect may be compared to punctuation—that is, the use of commas, etc., in ordinary writing."

Wing claims a split-halves reliability of .90 for the entire test. He cautions that reliability will vary with testing conditions and subjects. Wing believes that the test is valid because test scores relate well to grades earned by children in musical training, as indicated by various studies. Much of Wing's own validity work is reported in an article (Wing, 1954) based on an earlier test version.

The tape frequently is a serious problem with administering the Wing test because (a) the technical quality is weak,* (b) the "same" performances were played twice rather than re-recorded, and (c) for American children, the characteristic British accent requires some acclimation.

The person who believes in a general factor of musical ability and a certain degree of "musicality" as characterizing the musically apt student may find the Wing test useful. The judgment of rhythmic accent, harmony, intensity, and phrasing may require a certain musical achievement, but conceivably a person can have developed the necessary sensitivity through immersion in Western, musical culture.

Bentley

The *Measures of Musical Abilities* (Bentley, 1966a), another British test, are based on the author's assumption that (a) the phrase or figure is music's most elemental form, (b) detailed recall of pitch and duration information is necessary for apprehension of melody (this may be questioned; see "what might be tested," above), (c) good intonation (except for fixed pitch instruments) requires discriminating tones less than a semitone apart, and (d)

---

*It is possible, when listening with headphones, to hear birds occasionally chirping in the background.

awareness of chords is necessary for evaluating one's contribution to an ensemble. The battery, intended mainly for children ages 7 to 12, consequently contains tests of pitch discrimination, tonal memory, chord analysis, and rhythm memory. A total score is possible. The test manual is rather sparse, but Bentley's (1966b) text, in a way, functions as a complete manual.

Bentley's pitch test is similar to Seashore's except that there is a "same" option (two pairs are comprised of identical tones) and the differences range from about 100 to 12 cents. There are 20 pairs of audio oscillator tones.

The second test, labeled "Tunes," requires another Seashore-like task: The subject listens to 10 paired organ melodies and indicates which tone has been altered.

A chord analysis test, similar to Wing's (again, some "chords" really are two-tone simultaneous intervals) is third. Organ tones are used for the 20 stimuli.

In the final test, involving rhythm memory, the subject indicates which beat in the second pair contains a difference from the first pair, or if both versions are the same, as are two of the 10 pairs.

Reliability is .84 by the test–retest method, and validity, as correlation with aural skill examination grades, is .94, according to Bentley. In a study with American junior high students, Young (1973) found a composite reliability of .83 and respective reliabilities for pitch discrimination, tonal memory, chord analysis, and rhythm memory of .65, .83, .74, and .61. Correlations of Bentley scores with Gordon *Musical Aptitude Profile* scores, a potential indicator of concurrent validity, varied from .26, between chord analysis and Gordon's musical sensitivity, to .58, between composite Bentley and Gordon scores. Bentley claims that the tests measure basic judgments which are a part of music making and therefore identify children who are likely to profit from formal music instruction.

As with Wing's test, the Bentley scores are grouped into the top 10 percent, the next 20 percent, the middle 40 percent, the next 20 percent, and the bottom 10 percent for norming purposes. Bentley argues (as does Wing) that finer discriminations are unnecessary; some may disagree.

For younger children, the test has the advantage of being relatively brief; perhaps it is too easy for older children. A person who wants an easy-to-use musical aptitude measure that combines some psychoacoustic and more "musical" tasks may be interested in Bentley's test.

Gordon MAP

Edwin Gordon (1965), a contemporary American music educator, created one of the most comprehensive measures of musical aptitude, the *Musical Aptitude Profile*. The test manual is extremely thorough; there are norms for grades 4 through 12, various combinations thereof, and musically select students. The manual includes extensive reliability and validity information and a detailed history of *MAP* development. The test has had considerable follow-up research, as examination of the *Journal of Research in Music Education* from the mid 1960s through mid 1970s indicates. The concepts of sensitivity to musical alteration and embellishment as well as preference underlie the battery. While the test taker must make many "musical" judgments, they are global enough that musical training is not necessary. It is enough to note similarity and difference or express a preference without giving details.

The *MAP* contains three major divisions: Tonal Imagery, Rhythm Imagery, and Musical Sensitivity. Tonal Imagery has subdivisions of Melody and Harmony. Tempo and Meter are subdivisions of Rhythm Imagery. Musical Sensitivity includes subdivisions of Phrasing, Balance, and Style. Scores are determined for the entire battery, each major division, and each subdivision. Orchestral string instruments produce the stimuli.

The Melody subtest requires indicating whether the second member of each of 40 pairs is an embellishment of the first or is basically a different phrase. The subject must decide whether removal of the added tones (paired phrases are of equivalent length) would leave a phrase like the first or different from it. The phrases include major and minor keys, mixed meter, various tempi, and syncopation. Gordon stresses that the meter remains unchanged within each pair; any rhythmic alterations are in melodic rhythm.

The Harmony subtest of the Tonal Imagery section also asks the subject for a same or different judgment in 40 items. Each item pair contains a melody line performed on violin, and a lower harmony line performed on cello. The task is to indicate whether the second lower line is the same as or different from the first lower line; the upper line always remains the same.

In the 40-pair Tempo subtest, played on violin, the subject is supposed to respond "different" if the second member has an ending in which the tempo increases or decreases. If tempo does not change, the subject should respond "same." When something is the "same," the second member is a re-recording of the first member's performance.

The Meter subtest requires another same or different judgment for 40 pairs; differences occur due to meter changes. The number of tones in paired examples remains the same. Changes in melodic rhythm occur only as necessitated by meter changes. Violin again is the performance medium.

The same selection is played twice in each of the 30 Phrasing items; violin and cello are performance media. The test taker indicates which version is "better."

The Musical Sensitivity section ends with violin performances of 30 items each in the Balance and Style subtests. Again, it is a matter of musical preference, presumably based on musical acculturation. The Balance test requires judging whether the first or second member of each pair has the "better" ending. In the Style test, the paired excerpts differ in tempo; the subject indicates preference for the first or second version.

Gordon reports numerous reliability figures. The entire *MAP* has a reliability ranging from a low of .90 for the fourth grade to a high of .96 for the eleventh grade. The respective lows and highs for the major sections are Tonal Imagery, .80 (fourth grade) and .92 (eleventh grade); Rhythm Imagery, .82 (fourth grade) and .91 (eleventh grade); Musical Sensitivity, .84 (fourth grade) and .90 (ninth and tenth grades). The lowest subtest reliability is .66, for fourth grade on the Harmony, Meter, Balance, and Style sections. Reliability estimates were computed via the split-halves procedure.

Validity, treated extensively in the manual, is based on correlations with teacher estimates of "musical talent," musical performance, and music achievement scores. Gordon also offers theoretical reasons for constructing the battery as he did.

All *MAP* items require a dichotomous decision: Something is the same or it is not; one or the other version is "better." The answer sheet, however, provides a "don't know" option. The taped instructions include an admonishment to avoid guessing. This presumably reduces the chance score and enhances reliability; in practice, of course, all guesses are not random (see Chapter 5).

Length of administration is one potential difficulty in some school situations. The manual recommends administering each major section on separate days. Each major section requires 50 minutes. Because of fatigue, it usually would be unwise to administer the entire battery in one day to any age group. Yet administration over three successive days may cause undue disruption in school situations where students must be excused from some academic activity. The test administrator could elect to administer only selected *MAP* portions, but then one is sacrificing aspects that the test author considers important. Scores and norms are available for all *MAP* divisions and subdivisions.

Few published music tests are more thorough than Gordon's *Musical Aptitude Profile*. The person who has the time to study the manual and administer the test, and who believes that musical aptitude is indicated by sensitivity to ornamentation and judgments that agree with customary practice in Western musical culture probably will find the *MAP* highly useful.

Gordon PMMA

The Seashore, Wing, and Gordon *MAP* measures basically are intended for grades 4–12; they could be used with adults. Bentley's battery provides norms for children as young as age 7. Gordon's (1979) *Primary Measures of Music Audiation* are for children in kindergarten through third grade. Gordon believes that musical aptitude does not "stabilize" until fourth grade, so a test of "immediate impressions" and "intuitive responses" is necessary. The controversial term "audiation" refers to recalling or creating musical sound without its physical presence. When one actually listens to music, one makes comparisons by "audiating" music heard previously. The *PMMA* are structured to require the child to react to immediate auditory impressions in accordance with his or her "audiation" abilities, which presumably depend on a combination of innate capacities and early informal musical experience. As a child normally has experienced music in some form since infancy, the basis for audiation exists; any new musical experience is similar or dissimilar to earlier experiences.

PMMA include a Tonal and a Rhythm test, each of which has 40 items. The Tonal test contains electronically synthesized tones of equal duration. The Rhythm test's electronically synthesized tones remain at one frequency. Tempo beats, at a low dynamic level, are included with the Rhythm stimuli. The basic task is a "same-different" comparison. Tonal items that differ do so because one or more tones change between the first and second members of an item pair; sequence length is from two to five tones. Differing rhythm items differ in meter or grouping of tones within one meter. Five seconds separate items; "first" and "second" are spoken to identify each pair member.

To simplify the response process, Gordon uses a pictographic scale and symbolic item identification. Each item is identified by a drawing of a common object with which most children would be familiar; objects include a spoon, car, sailboat, hat, and so on. The child answers by circling two smiling faces if the excerpts are the same, or circling one frowning and one smiling face if the excerpts are different.

Split-halves and test-retest reliability coefficients are reported in the manual for grades K–3. Respective composite split-halves reliabilities are .90, .92, .92, and .90; the respective test–retest reliabilities, which one normally would expect to be lower because of changes in the children between testing times, are .74, .75, .76, and .73. The lowest section reliability is a test–retest reliability of .60 for the Rhythm test at the kindergarten level.

Validity is claimed in the form of content validity, because of what Gordon believes to be "audiation's" nature, concurrent validity, because *PMMA* correlate low with academic achievement and intelligence tests and therefore presumably measure musical factors rather than general academic factors, and "congruent" (really also concurrent) validity, because of correlations of fourth grade students' *PMMA* scores with *MAP* scores. The content of the *PMMA*, in fact, requires immediate comparison of a short tonal sequence or rhythm pattern with a potential imitation. The ease with which a child can do this may be an outgrowth of "audiation." Low correlations with academic achievement and intelligence indeed do indicate that the test is measuring *something* else, and modest to high correlation with *MAP* probably would be expected.

As with the *MAP*, Gordon's *PMMA* manual provides a detailed rationale and presentation of technical information. Detailed percentile norms are available. The test appears well conceived and, even if one questions the concept of "audiation" (Gordon also discusses "keyality" as something different from tonality), the test does assess primary children's abilities to hear differences in short tonal and rhythmic patterns. The *PMMA* undoubtedly need further research, but they presently are a viable test for the person interested in children's aural discriminations of brief musical excerpts.

Gordon IMMA

Gordon's (1982) *Intermediate Measures of Music Audiation* are an advanced version of the *PMMA*. They are intended to discriminate among children who would obtain high (i.e., above the 80th percentile) *PMMA* composite or subtest scores. The *IMMA* are intended for grades 1–4 rather than K–3. The *IMMA* content is constructed to be more advanced than that of Gordon's *PMMA* but less advanced than that of his *MAP*.

The *IMMA* include a Tonal and a Rhythm test; each contains 40 items. The test taker indicates whether sets of paired tonal or rhythmic phrases are the same or different. The items are similar to *PMMA* items, but they are more difficult due to increased use of minor mode for tonal items, and, for both item types, the dispersion through the test section of six "very difficult questions."

Percentile rank norms are provided for each section and for the total *IMMA*. Gordon also provides section and total criterion scores for identifying in each grade children with "exceptionally high overall music aptitude." Split-halves and test–retest reliabilities are reported in the manual. Tonal section reliabilities range from .72 (fourth grade, split-halves method) to .88 (first-grade, test–retest method). Rhythm section reliabilities range from .70 (first and fourth grades, split-halves method) to .84 (same grades, test–retest method). The range of composite reliabilities is from .76 (fourth grade, test–retest) to .91 (first and second grades, test–retest). Validity is claimed on the basis of correlations with the *PMMA*, *MAP*, and teacher ratings on a five-point scale.

Strengths and weaknesses noted for the *PMMA* apply to the *IMMA*. The necessity for the pictographic scale becomes rather questionable for fourth graders, as indeed it may be for any child with the ability to recognize and order numbers.

Other Tests

Many tests have appeared and passed into history. In general, they no longer are available, although contact with the publisher or university testing centers might be fruitful. A listing of some tests appears in an appendix to this book.

"Promotional" tests occasionally appear, often with the cooperation of instrument manufacturers or music stores. They usually lack standardization; the lack of norms may leave the test administrator puzzled as to what the scores mean. Items generally are "easy" because differences between sounds are so obvious. Such tests are intended to recruit music students and should not be taken seriously as a means of assessing musical aptitude.

SUMMARY: WHICH TEST TO USE

There is no one criterion for selecting a measure of musical aptitude. Colwell (1970, pp. 26–42) discusses four criteria for selecting an appropriate test for a particular purpose. Two criteria are reliability and validity. Another criterion is *usability*, which refers to test administration and scoring. One must consider the time the test requires, necessary equipment and seating arrangements, cost, ease of scoring, applicability of the norms, and relation of the test to other aspects of evaluation. A fourth criterion is *usefulness*, which, for Colwell, refers to how well the test differentiates among those who take it. While an argument can be made for criterion-referenced achievement tests, aptitude testing implies selection or at least relative ordering of individuals.

The basic decision is a matter of whether a test will provide information that the user believes is important in evaluating aptitude. If one is particularly concerned with small differences in auditory signals, perhaps Seashore is appropriate. If one considers comparisons of alternate performance versions for some degree of similarity or adherence to cultural expectancy important, the Gordon *MAP* is a well-documented measure. If no published test is satisfactory because of one's philosophy or definition of aptitude, one must construct one's own measure. In many instances a test user really is interested in a student's ability to succeed in the context of formal music instruction with its requisite social and disciplinary aspects. The judicious blending of information about a student's intelligence, interests, resourcefulness, and self-discipline should be employed when a decision about a musical future is to be made, regardless of any aptitude test score.

Study Questions

1. State your own definition of musical aptitude.

2. Make a list of five or more observable behaviors that a person with a high degree of musical aptitude, in accordance with your definition, should be able to demonstrate proficiently.

3. Which one of the tests discussed in this chapter is the most satisfactory in accordance with your definition? Which is the least satisfactory? Why?

4. How should a measure of musical aptitude be validated in accordance with your definition? Why?

5. Examine your list of observable behaviors and indicate whether each is more nearly musical aptitude, musical achievement, or "nonmusical," and why.

REFERENCES

Bentley, A. *Measures of musical abilities.* London: George A. Harrap, 1966a.

Bentley, A. *Musical ability in children and its measurement.* New York: October House, 1966b.

Colwell, R. *The evaluation of music teaching and learning.* Englewood Cliffs, N.J.: Prentice-Hall, 1970.

Dowling, W.J., & Fujitani, D. S. Contour, interval, and pitch recognition in memory for short melodies. *Journal of the Acoustical Society of America,* 1971, *49,* 524–531.

Farnsworth, P. R. *The social psychology of music* (2nd ed.). Ames: Iowa State University Press, 1969.

Gardner, H. Frames of mind: The theory of multiple intelligences. New York: Basic Books, 1983.

Gordon, E. E. *Musical aptitude profile.* Boston: Houghton Mifflin, 1965.

Gordon, E. E. A study of the efficiency of general intelligence and musical aptitude tests in predicting achievement in music. *Council for Research in Music Education,* 1968, *13,* 40–45.

Gordon, E. E. *Primary measures of music audiation.* Chicago: G.I.A. Publications, 1979.

Gordon, E. E. *Intermediate measures of music audiation.* Chicago: G.I.A. Publications, 1982.

Grey, J. M. Multidimensional perceptual scaling of musical timbres. *Journal of the Acoustical Society of America,* 1977, *61,* 1270–1277.

Hedden, S. K. Prediction of music achievement in the elementary school. *Journal of Research in Music Education,* 1982, *30,* 61–68.

Lehman, P. R. *Tests and measurements in music.* Englewood Cliffs, N.J.: Prentice-Hall, 1968.

Long, P. A. Pitch recognition in short melodies (Doctoral dissertation, Florida State University, 1975). *Dissertation Abstracts International,* 1976, *36,* 4840A–4841A.

Manor, H. C. A study in prognosis. *Journal of Educational Psychology,* 1950, *41,* 31–50.

Patterson, B. Musical dynamics. *Scientific American,* 1974, *231*(5), 78–95.

Plomp, R., & Steenekén, H. J. M. Place dependence of timbre in reverberant sound fields. *Acustica,* 1973, *28,* 50–59.

Radocy, R. E. The perception of melody, harmony, rhythm, and form. In D. A. Hodges (Ed.), *Handbook of music psychology.* Lawrence, Kans.: National Association for Music Therapy, 1980.

Radocy, R. E. Magnitude estimation of melodic dissimilarity. *Psychology of Music,* 1982, *10*(1), 28–32.

Radocy, R. E., & Boyle, J. D. *Psychological foundations of musical behavior.* Springfield, Ill.: Charles C Thomas, 1979.

Rainbow, E. L. A pilot study to investigate the constructs of musical aptitude. *Journal of Research in Music Education*, 1965, *13*, 3–14.

Roederer, J. G. *Introduction to the physics and psychophysics of music* (2nd ed.). New York: Springer-Verlag, 1975.

Seashore, C. E. *Psychology of music*. New York: McGraw-Hill, 1938.

Seashore, C. E., Lewis, L., & Saetveit, J. G. *Seashore measures of musical talents*. New York: The Psychological Corporation, 1960.

Sergeant, D. Measurement of pitch discrimination. *Journal of Research in Music Education*, 1973, *21*, 3–19.

Sergeant, D., & Thatcher, G. Intelligence, social status, and musical abilities. *Psychology of Music*, 1974, *2*(2), 32–57.

Sherbon, J. W. The association of hearing acuity, displacusis, and discrimination with musical performances. *Journal of Research in Music Education*, 1975, *23*, 249–257.

Williams, D. B. Short-term retention of pitch sequence. *Journal of Research in Music Education*, 1975, *26*, 57–60.

Wing, H. D. A factorial study of musical tests. *British Journal of Psychology*, 1941, *31*, 341–355.

Wing, H. D. Some applications of test results to education in music. *British Journal of Educational Psychology*, 1954, *24*, 161–170.

Wing, H. D. *Standardised tests of musical intelligence*. The Mere, England: National Foundation for Educational Research, 1961.

Wyatt, R. F. Improvability of pitch discrimination. *Psychological Monographs*, 1945, *58*(2, Whole No. 267).

Young, W. T. The Bentley "measures of musical abilities": A congruent validity report. *Journal of Research in Music Education*, 1973, *21*, 74–79.

Zwicker, E., Flottorp, G., & Stevens, S. S. Critical band width in loudness summation. *Journal of the Acoustical Society of America*, 1957, *29*, 548–557.

7

Measuring Musical Achievement

What a person has *achieved* is what he or she has done or accomplished. Achievement is in the past and partly determines what a person can do in the present. Achievement measures assess specific musical knowledge and skills; aptitude measures generally do not. Prior achievement, of course, may be an indicator of likely future achievement because achievement is one indicator of ability. This chapter considers what might be measured as evidence of musical achievement and considers a few published standardized measures. Whereas Chapter 5 addressed specifics of item writing in relation to assessing instruction, this chapter looks more at what to test and less at how.

WHAT MIGHT BE MEASURED?

Musical achievement includes general musical knowledge, knowledge of notation, aural–visual skills, aural skills, and composition as well as performance. Consequently there are many potential sources of test items provided that the test user or writer believes that the underlying achievements are important in a particular context. Performance measurement is discussed in Chapter 8; the other areas are discussed here.

Unless one is testing the achievement of a specific class for which he or she has sole instructional responsibility, the test user or writer should function as part of some committee or other decision-making structure that determines what the desired achievements are. Curriculum planning in a particular school district or university department should include evaluation plans. At a state level, a state education department could arrange statewide representation on a planning committee. Developers of a nationally normed test should consider the beliefs of a nation-wide sample of music educators. At all educational and governmental levels it may be frustratingly difficult to obtain any consensus regarding what musical achievement should comprise, but some consensus is necessary if the resulting achievement test is intended for the products of more than one person's instruction.

General Musical Knowledge

"General musical knowledge" could include facts about music and musicians, aspects of music theory and history, musical acoustics, music "appreciation," and musical form. The person seeking or developing a test of general musical knowledge must evaluate and make decisions regarding the "generality" of "general" musical knowledge. Most music educators might agree that every high school graduate should be aware of a few "great" composers, the existence of common types of musical ensembles, and the usual form of a popular song. Most would agree that not every high school graduate needs to know how just intonation differs from equally tempered tuning, how to construct a French sixth chord, or different types of bowing (e.g., martele, jete, col legno, spiccato) available to an orchestrator. Music educators might agree less regarding the need for knowledge of basic harmonic progressions, existence of specific orchestras and opera companies, contemporary composers, arrangers, and performers, and sonata allegro and rondo forms.

When one is concerned for the general musical knowledge of music students there also could be disagreement. It is doubtful that college level music educators agree regarding the importance of all music education majors knowing details of the Orff, Kodály, Carabo-Cone, and Dalcroze approaches to music education; the need for all theory students to write counterpoint in a sixteenth-century style; or the importance of music history students being able to transcribe Gregorian chants from pneumatic to modern notation.

Once disagreements, if any, are resolved, objectives may be stated and item construction can proceed in accordance with Chapter 5. General musical knowledge lends itself well to all paper-and-pencil formats. If the achievement test is intended for a large group of examinees, the item formats in which the examinee constructs rather than selects a response may be impractical. The readability of items in terms of length and vocabulary may require extra concern when the test is intended for a relatively heterogeneous group of students. Consultation with different teachers and pilot testing items with small but representative student samples may alleviate readability problems.

Music Notation

Knowledge of music notation includes recognition skills and performance skills. Performance could include prepared singing, sightsinging, prepared instrumental performance or sightreading, clapping, chanting, or tapping rhythm patterns. Performances must be judged against some standard or against each other; subjective judgments are discussed in Chapter 8. Recognition skills include naming clefs, lines and spaces, notes and rests, meter and key signatures, metric structure, and possibly dynamic and tempo markings.

When the test group is of practical size, samples of notation can be labeled directly on the test paper. Multiple-choice items and matching tests can easily tap knowledge of symbols and lines and spaces when the test group is large.

There is more than symbol recognition involved in knowledge of music notation. Note equations, for example,

$$\tfrac{4}{4} \quad \quad \flat + \flat + \flat \; =$$

A. 4 beats.
B. $3\tfrac{1}{2}$ beats.
C. 3 beats.

may indicate students' abilities to read and combine note values, as can instructions to mark measures that are incorrect in accordance with the meter signature. The type of multiple-choice item represented by

Which of the following will sound least like the others when all are performed correctly?

can also be used effectively. Students can locate downbeats and upbeats on printed music to show understanding of metric sub-division. Students can be asked to "compose" music in designated meters and/or using designated pitches and clefs; while imprac-tical with a large group in a paper-and-pencil format, new microcomputer and software combinations that allow composi-tion at the computer terminal will likely become cheaper, easier to use, and adaptable to testing applications.

Aural-Visual Skills

Aural–visual musical skills require an interaction of hearing and sight. Common examples include error detection while following printed music, and melodic and harmonic dictation.* The degree to which one sensory mode or the other is more important may vary from moment to moment, especially with dictation, but both are essential.

Testing detection of aural–visual discrepancies requires playing music (which should be recorded for consistency) to go with notated examples. The test maker must consider the following questions in constructing such a test: How sophisticated should the test takers' skills be? Should the test takers detect pitch errors, rhythm errors, or both in any item? How long should the item be? How many times should each item be played? Should more than

---

*Strictly speaking, dictation involves hearing, holding what is heard in memory, and writing it in notation. Visually impaired persons may not write notation in the customary way but they certainly can indicate what they hear. Dictation is considered an aural–visual skill here because a person produces tangible, usually *visible* evidence of what he or she hears.

one error occur in a measure? Is it enough to indicate where an error occurs? Should the test taker rewrite the printed music to show what in fact was played? Conceptually, should the notation or the performance be "wrong"? Should errors be limited to pitch and rhythm or should interpretative "errors" regarding tempo, dynamics, and phrasing be included? The answers to these questions depend on the test writer's objectives and the learning experiences of the test takers.

A type of "reverse discrepancy" item might be a multiple-choice item in which the examinee indicates which one of a set of examples is in fact performed. When there is but one line of notation and the test taker is supposed to indicate where and/or what the errors are, boxes can be provided under each measure for indicating presence of an error and/or error type when correction is not expected, as in

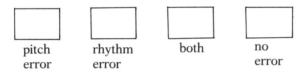

| pitch | rhythm | both | no |
| error | error | | error |

These can be transferred to a machine scorable answer sheet as ABCD answers.

Aural–visual discrepancy detection is not limited to "serious" music students. Kindergarten and first grade students may be tested for accuracy of representing melodic contour in iconic notation. ("If the music goes *up,* draw a circle around the train going *up;* if the music goes down. . . .") Young children can recognize and show through body movements correct and incorrect representations of melodic contour. Older students can use more abstract lines and shapes to represent contour.

Dictation is a traditional activity in music theory classes and has some practical use. Dictation items do not necessarily have to require the examinee to write each note of an extensive four-part excerpt or a melody. The test writer must decide just how much to require and how many times the examinee will listen to each excerpt.

In melodic or harmonic dictation multiple-choice items can request examinees to indicate which of an array of notes is in fact the missing note. As a simplistic example, a descending F major scale could be played as examinees look at the corresponding notation, which has a question mark substituted for the sixth note. Then the examinees must choose C, A, or F to substitute for the question mark. Examples could be far more complex, and answer choices could be different versions of an entire measure. Some of the newly available microcomputer-controlled software packages may enable testing more lengthy dictation processes and still offer rapid scoring.

There is no one answer to the question of how many times an excerpt should be performed in a dictation test. Some instructors prefer several playings, possibly with instructions to concentrate on pitch, rhythm, or one of four voice lines; others prefer just one playing. If the achievement test is for a particular class, the instructor's advice should be followed; when the test is intended for a larger group, committee decisions are necessary.

Another aural–visual skill is silent thematic recognition or reproduction, which requires a type of long-term tonal memory. A list of printed excerpts may be presented in multiple-choice, matching, or short-answer format; the test taker's task is to indicate what the excerpt is, probably by composer and title, and possibly by movement and/or theme number. In the reproduction format, a list of titles is provided, and the test taker must select or write the theme in correct notation. Writing the theme is an especially demanding task and can be tedious to score. Furthermore, the examiner–scorer must decide whether the excerpt (as a right–wrong dichotomy) or each individual note is the scoring unit. The excerpt could also be judged (e.g., on a 1-5 scale) for "degree of correctness" without attempting to score each note.

Aural Skills

Aural skills refer to certain recognition and discrimination abilities. While the ability to detect "same or different" or "higher or lower," count the tones in a chord, or imagine whether an ornamental melody basically is changed or not may be deemed appropriate as an indicator of aptitude, attaching specific labels to musical structures and changes is clearly achievement.

Recognizing particular musical works while hearing them, clearly an achievement skill, easily fits a multiple-choice, matching, or short-answer format. The particular recognition task can be rather simple, as in playing part of Beethoven's *Fifth Symphony* and providing choral music or popular songs as foils—or rather demanding, as in playing part of one of the lesser known Mozart symphonies and providing a Mozart instrumental work for each answer choice. Interesting essay questions can ask students to identify an excerpt's composer and explain *why* they believe that composer is a viable choice; this could be a relatively sophisticated way of testing knowledge of style and compositional devices.

Any recognizable musical structure can be test material. Chord classification, interval recognition, tonality, form, chord progression, and meter recognition may be tested easily via multiple choice. Other material for recognition includes instruments, voices, likely national origins of ethnic music, historical era, performance medium, and any musical property about which people may verbalize.

Aural discrimination skills might include intonation judgments, indicating which of a set of excerpts contains modulation, telling which phrase ending is more artistic in accordance with common performance standards, or any musical examples in which two or more performed versions are compared. Whereas the authors consider recognition to be labeling (or selecting a label for) one example, they consider discrimination to be selecting among examples that which best exemplifies a label. When the discrimination task involves just two versions of a performance, a "don't know" or "unsure" answer option *may* reduce the likelihood of guessing.

Composition

An exercise in musical composition may be compared with a comprehensive essay item. Composition is an opportunity to synthesize aural and aural–visual skills and notation as well as a creative act. Music students at virtually any age and degree of sophistication may be asked to order and arrange sounds in some meaningful way; composition need not be limited to music majors enrolled in theory classes. Instructions to compose may be well-structured or vague, just like essay instructions. There may be certain specifications regarding form, performance medium, style, tonality, or other musical characteristics, or, analogous to the "Discuss . . ." type of essay item, the student simply may be told to "compose something." It is easier to evaluate reliably a specified composition. While the marketplace or music history ultimately may evaluate a composition intended for a public audience, composition exercises can provide clear opportunities for a teacher to evaluate knowledge of musical structures and styles. Scoring an intact composition is similar to scoring an essay;

the evaluator makes a subjective decision regarding the extent to which criteria are met. Both Chapter 5's discussion of essay items and Chapter 8's discussion of performance evaluation techniques are relevant to evaluating musical compositions.

REPRESENTATIVE TESTS

Numerous published music achievement tests have appeared; many passed into obscurity. To illustrate particular testing tasks, the Colwell *Music Achievement Tests*, the *Iowa Tests of Music Literacy*, and the *Silver Burdett Music Competency Tests* are reviewed here because they are comprehensive and available. Other tests are cited in an appendix to this volume.

Music Achievement Tests

Colwell's (1969, 1970b) *Music Achievement Tests* include four separate tests, all of which assess aural or aural–visual skills that presumably are related to important music education objectives, as indicated by music series textbooks and a group of experienced music educators. Respective Kuder–Richardson reliabilities for the four tests are .88, .94, .90, and .90. Reliabilities of individual sections vary, with the least reliable being the *Cadence Recognition* section of Test 4 (.39) and the most reliable being the *Auditory–Visual Discrimination* section of Test 2 (.91). Content validity is based on songbook objectives and teacher judgments; criterion-related validity is based on a correlation of .92 between the top and bottom 20 percent of selected classes and test scores. Raw score, standard score, and percentile norms exist for grades 4, 5, 6, 7, 8, 4–8 combined, 9–12 combined, and 4–12 combined for Tests 1 and 2. Tests 3 and 4 provide norms for individual grades 4 or 5 through 12 and 4–6, 7–9, and 10–12 combinations; there also are norms for students with piano and instrumental experience. Thus the battery is a reasonably reliable and valid means for making norm-referenced comparisons regarding the designated aural and aural-visual skills.

Test 1 includes *Pitch Discrimination, Interval Discrimination,* and *Meter Discrimination. Pitch Discrimination* has two subtests: In one part, the student indicates which of two tones is higher or the same for 15 items; in the other part there are 10 three-tone items, and the student indicates which tone is lowest. (The half step is the smallest interval; it is interesting that this achievement test requires nothing less than a half step while Seashore, an aptitude test, requires discrimination among very small intervals.) In the *Interval Discrimination* section the task is to classify musical excerpts as scalewise or "leaping." The first part contains 10 three-tone patterns. The second contains 18 intact phrases of the sort commonly found in elementary song series. *Meter Discrimination* requires classifying 15 items as moving in twos or threes. To break the dichotomy, an "in doubt" response is provided for *Interval Discrimination* and *Meter Discrimination*.

Test 2, more advanced than Test 1, contains three sections, all of which have two subtests. The *Major–Minor Mode Discrimination* section has one subtest in which the student hears 15 pairs of piano chords; both members of any pair are major or minor. The student indicates the mode for each item. The second subtest contains 13 harmonized phrases; the student must indicate whether each phrase is major, minor, or changing in mode. In the *Feeling for Tonal Center* section, the first subtest requires hearing 10 four-chord major cadences, each of which ends with the tonic in the soprano and bass lines, and selecting which of three following tones is the key tone (there also is a "none" response). Ten phrases form the second subtest; again, the student selects the key tone from three choices (or indicates "none"). The final section, *Auditory–Visual Discrimination*, has two 12-item subtests. The student compares a printed four-measure phrase with what he or she hears and indicates any measure containing a discrepancy. The first section contains pitch errors; the second contains rhythm errors.

Test 3, more difficult yet, contains four sections. The first is *Tonal Memory*, in which 20 four-note block chords are followed by arpeggiated versions. The student indicates whether each arpeggio is the same as or different from the corresponding chord, and, if different, which of the four tones is altered. In the 20 *Melody Recognition* items, a piano melody is followed by a three-part (violin, viola, cello) performance; the student indicates whether the high, middle, or low voice contains the melody. *Pitch Recognition* requires the student to follow 20 two-note items on an answer sheet. The first tone is played, then three more are played; the student indicates which of those three tones (or none) is the second notated tone. The final section, *Instrument Recognition*, contains a 10-item "solo" subtest and a 5-item "accompanied" subtest. The student must select the solo or prominent instrument from an array of four; "none" is also a possible answer.

Test 4 contains four major sections, the first of which is *Musical Style*. In a subtest on composers, 20 orchestral excerpts are played and, for each, the student selects which of four composers is most likely the excerpt's composer. In a texture subtest, the task is to indicate whether each of 20 piano excerpts is monophonic, homophonic, or polyphonic; an "in doubt" response also is allowed. *Auditory–Musical Discrimination*, the second section, includes 14 four-measure phrases. The student follows the notation and indicates each measure that contains a rhythmic discrepancy between sound stimulus and notation. *Chord Recognition* requires listening to 15 block piano chords and indicating which of three following chords sounds like the first; "none" and "in doubt" responses are possible. *Cadence Recognition*, the final section, requires indicating whether each of 15 phrase endings is a full, half, or deceptive cadence; "in doubt" responses are possible.

The *Music Achievement Tests* were carefully developed and have extensive informative manuals. They represent a comprehensive attempt at evaluating certain aural skills. The test user who decides that those skills are important thus has a well-standardized, easy to administer, and easy to score (machine or hand) evaluative instrument.

Iowa Tests of Music Literacy

The *Iowa Tests of Music Literacy* (Gordon, 1970) are a comprehensive sequential series of measures. There are six *ITML* levels, with an identical set of subtests at each level. The levels are in terms of difficulty, not academic grade, although the first three levels are intended for grades 4–12 and the next three levels are intended for grades 7–12. Composite split-halves reliabilities range from .87 (level 3, grades 4–6) to .94 (level 1, grades 10–12). Individual subtest reliabilities are all at least .70. Content validity is based on Edwin Gordon's belief that aural perception and a tonal–rhythmic "literacy" are basic to music achievement. George (1980) indicates (p. 329) "the ultimate judgment about content validity [of the ITML] must be made by the test user in terms of the test's appropriateness for one's particular instructional program in music."

The *ITML*'s two major sections are *Tonal Concepts* and *Rhythmic Concepts*. Each section contains three identically titled subtests: *Aural Perception, Reading Recognition,* and *Notational Understanding*. Nine scores are possible: one for each subtest, one for each major section, and one for the total battery. Within each subtest area the tests are sequential across the six levels.

Within the *Aural Perception* subtest for *Tonal Concepts*, the student must listen to melodies and make modal judgments. At levels 1 and 2 the task is to classify each melody as major or minor. Levels 3 and 4 require classification of each melody as "usual" or "unusual"; "usual" melodies are major or minor, "unusual" melodies are modal (e.g., Dorian) or, in level 4, atonal. Level 5 has two-part melodies and level 6 has chordal accompaniments; for each level the melodies must be classified as major or minor. As with the entire *ITML*, an "in doubt" response is available to discourage guessing.

The *Reading Recognition* part of *Tonal Concepts* requires detecting discrepancies between an aural melody and printed notation. The response possibilities are "yes" (for same), "no" (for different), and "in doubt." Level 6 requires chord symbols rather than note-for-note notation. Bass clef is added to treble for levels 4 and 5. With succeeding levels, the melodies become more intricate.

The *Notational Understanding* part of *Tonal Concepts* requires completing printed notation. Four notes of a nine-note pattern are printed; for the remaining five notes, the student selects one of two alternatives. C major or A minor are used for the first four levels; level 5 adds one sharp or flat. Level 6 has no key signatures and includes two-part excerpts.

In the *Rhythmic Concepts* section the *Aural Perception* part requires meter discrimination. At the first two levels, the students supposedly classify patterns as duple or triple meter; in fact they classify patterns as duplets or triplets. (Gordon considers $\frac{6}{8}$ meter as triple meter!) At levels 3 and 4 one discriminates between "usual" meters (duple or triple patterns) and "mixed" meters (mixtures of duplets and triplets that have a duple or triple meter signature) for level 3 or "unusual" meters (e.g. $\frac{5}{8}$) for level 4. Levels 5 and 6 require classifying rhythms as "mixed" or "unusual," with "uncommon" patterns added for level 6. As with *Aural Perception* in the *Tonal Concepts* section, the terminology may be confusing. Is "usual" a synonym for common or simple? Is "unusual" a synonym for rare or compound? Perhaps this portion is really a measure of sensitivity to subdivision of the beat.

The *Reading Recognition* subtest (of *Rhythmic Concepts*) requires detecting aural–visual rhythmic discrepancies in a manner similar to *Reading Recognition* in the *Tonal Concepts* section. *Notational Understanding* is similar also; the student makes appropriate notes, flags, beams, rests, and ties. The stimulus patterns become more complex with increasing levels as more "uncommon" patterns (i.e., "uncommon" in the sense that they are seldom encountered in music) are employed.

The *ITML* are extensively normed and relatively easy to administer and score. If a test user can accept the concept of usual and unusual rather than more traditional musical dichotomies or trichotomies (e.g., major–minor–modal, simple–compound) and labeling beat subdivisions rather than metric accent patterns as duple or triple, the *ITML* may be a useful tool for measuring a certain musical auditory awareness as a series of specific achievements.

Silver Burdett Music Competency Tests

These 18 tests (six levels, three tests per level) are an attempt to operationalize a concept of criterion-referenced testing (see Chapters 2 and 3) by keying the tests to the objectives of a 1–6 graded music series. The tests, created by Richard Colwell (1979), are very comprehensive, especially regarding perception of melody, rhythm, timbre, texture, form, tonality, and dynamics. ("Competency" connotes more than superficial learning; each test supposedly requires a thorough understanding of the particular book to which it is keyed.) Obviously, the tests may be inappropriate for students whose schools do not use the elementary music series to which the tests are referenced. The tests are standardized; they are not simply a bonus for purchasing the series! Test–retest reliabilities run from .69 to .94. Validity is in terms of the content of the Silver Burdett music series and in terms of relations of test scores and teacher ratings. The concept of developing a test to go with a set of curricular materials is not new, but the preparation of such a detailed evaluation instrument marketed as an integral part of a music curriculum is rare.

SUMMARY: WHICH TEST TO USE?

The teacher-made achievement test can be keyed to the specific objectives of an instructional sequence, so, in principle, it probably is the best measure of achievement for a particular class at any educational level. If the tester's goal is to obtain information about a group of classes, the persons responsible for the instruction in each class must agree on common objectives which will be the basis for testing. If the goal becomes comparing products of a particular school with a national sample, a published standardized measure is required. Colwell's (1970a) four criteria for selecting an appropriate test—reliability, validity, usability, and usefulness—are relevant. In the end, as has been suggested before, a responsible person ultimately must decide what is important for students to know and how they may demonstrate that knowledge satisfactorily.

Study Questions

1. Make a list of at least 10 specific musical achievements that, in your opinion, are reasonable for normal first graders, fourth graders, eighth grade general music students, high school band members, nonmusic majors enrolled in a university music appreciation class, *or* music majors who have completed a theory sequence. Be sure that your list includes general musical knowledge, knowledge of musical notation, aural–visual skills, aural skills, and composition.

2. For each achievement you listed, describe (or actually construct) an appropriate type of test item.

3. Consider Colwell's four criteria for selecting an appropriate test. On the basis of the reviews, evaluate each of the three tests discussed above, in accordance with those criteria, regarding the test's suitability for any three of the areas mentioned in number one.

REFERENCES

Colwell, R. *Music achievement tests 1 and 2.* Chicago: Follett Educational Corporation, 1969.

Colwell, R. *The evaluation of music teaching and learning.* Englewood Cliffs, N.J.: Prentice-Hall, 1970a.

Colwell, R. *Music achievement tests 3 and 4.* Chicago: Follett Educational Corporation, 1970b.

Colwell, R. *Silver Burdett music competency tests.* Morristown, N.J.: Silver Burdett, 1979.

George, W. E. Measurement and evaluation of musical behavior. In D.E. Hodges (Ed.), *Handbook of music psychology.* Lawrence, Kans.: National Association for Music Therapy, 1980.

Gordon, E. E. *Iowa tests of music literacy.* Iowa City: Bureau of Educational Research and Service, University of Iowa, 1970.

8

Measuring Musical Performance

The measurement of musical performance is inherently subjective. Music consists of sequential aural sensations; any judgment of a musical performance is based on those sensations as they are processed by the judge's brain. While many listeners may agree regarding particular judgments, especially if they involve "right" notes, decisions involving correct tempi, phrasing nuances, execution of ornamentation, and tone quality are the decisions of individuals functioning as *subjects,* hence the decisions are *subjective.** While one may structure a performance measurement process to enhance objectivity and minimize nonmusical aspects, it never can be as objective as a multiple-choice test.

This chapter addresses the "What might be measured?" question and reviews the limited published performance measures. It concludes with the authors' discussion of several particular performance evaluation techniques, adapted from psychology and psychophysics.

---

*Certain *aspects* of music can be measured objectively. Stroboscopic devices can indicate frequency deviations. Modern spectral analysis systems can show a complex tone's frequency components, their relative strengths, and changes across time. But the total musical experience based on the physical aspects remains subjective.

WHAT MIGHT BE MEASURED?

Given the subjective nature of musical performance, what should be measured in its evaluation? One needs to consider the relative merits of evaluating the performances on an overall or global basis versus evaluating specific aspects. There are reasons for using sight-reading as well as prepared performances. The "nonmusical" aspects of performance may be considered as something to control or as part of the total performance situation.

A musical performance, especially of one distinct work in a given style, may be judged as an entity. It may be classified in one of several categories ("pass–fail," "1-2-3-4-5," etc.), assigned a score, or be ranked in relation to other works. If what counts is the judge's overall impression, whatever its basis, the judge may be said to be employing a *global* approach.

When the global approach is employed, one may explain the judgment in terms of detailed criteria. Two judges may use the same personal criteria and arrive at rather different decisions or they may use rather divergent criteria and arrive at an identical decision. Several performances of a particular work may be heard with differing evaluative emphases given to rhythm, intonation, tone quality, and other aspects.

An approach based on itemized details or *specifics* of performance contrasts with a global approach. A judge can follow a checklist and assign a score or give a comment for each of several performance aspects, such as articulation, rhythm, intonation, style, dynamics, and so on. Likely specific aspects will vary with the performance medium and the musical style. Bowing is crucial with orchestral strings; improvisation is critical in jazz. The overall performance can be assigned a score that is a sum of scores on the several identified aspects. Judges may disagree about the relative importance that should be attached to particular aspects.

A balance of a global and a specifics approach is possible where the particular performance aspects function as guidance but not necessarily as specific categories that must be quantified. This is somewhat analogous to a good essay question. The global versus specifics issue probably reduces to a matter of how much structure is desired in the performance measure.

A mixture of prepared performance and sight-reading is advisable in those styles where one normally is expected to adhere to printed music. Sight-reading may control for excessive practice of one or two selections. Prepared performance may control for excessive reliance on reading skills developed at the expense of tone quality and musical nuance. In most settings, the judge should know whether the performer is sight-reading or presenting a rehearsed performance.

Are "nonmusical" or "extramusical" performance aspects something to eliminate as evaluative criteria or are they integral aspects, particularly when one is using a global approach? The answer depends on one's priorities and beliefs.

Music is an aural phenomenon; strictly visual aspects should have nothing to do with performance quality. Wearing formal attire does nothing for phrasing or tone quality. A choir's blend does not suffer because a few singers wear colored shirts or blouses while most singers wear white. Except to the extent that music memorization is a desideratum, whether or not a soloist uses music is not likely to affect performance quality. Whether or not one can see a pianist's hands is irrelevant to the pianist's musical interpretation. What a solo singer does or does not do with the hands has no influence on what is or is not done with the vocal tract.

Yet an audience may consider a musical performance as more than the sounds. Audiences do react to the lack of formal attire when such attire is customary, as in a symphony concert. Some people insist that certain performer mannerisms, which may involve the hands, are "distracting," or that a music stand "gets in the way." Lights, costumes, and special effects are integral parts of many performances of rock music as well as of opera.

Knowledge of who is performing inevitably arouses certain expectancies. The phenomenon in which experienced musicians differentially evaluate physically identical performances (as in the same recording played twice) on the basis of how the alleged performers are labeled is well documented (Duerksen, 1972; Radocy, 1976). School performing groups as well as concert artists build reputations that sell tickets as well as create anticipation of what will be heard.

Performer anonymity and suppression of visual influences may be attained easily through tape recording. With modern recording and playback equipment, there is no justification for declining to base evaluation on recorded performances because of poor recording quality. The tape can be heard as many times as necessary; as long as someone who coordinates the evaluation knows who the performers are, there is no need for judges to know who is performing. The concert- or recital-like aspects may be preserved by recording a public performance. However, evaluation decisions are delayed, and, in a larger sense, some people may feel that "extramusical" aspects such as eye contact and stage presence are important.

What should be measured? It depends on whether one wants to analyze the performance into specific constituent parts, and decide the relative importance of each part, or evaluate the performance as a global impression. It also depends on the extent to which one wants to limit non-auditory aspects.

PUBLISHED MEASURES

The only readily available published performance measures are the *Watkins–Farnum Performance Scale* (Watkins & Farnum, 1954; 1962), for wind instruments and snare drum, and the *Farnum String Scale* (Farnum, 1969), for orchestral strings. Both tests require performance of printed music, progressively increasing in difficulty. The subject's basic task is to play as far as he or she can without making excessive errors. The tests may be used as measures of prepared performance or sight-reading.

The *WFPS* is an outgrowth of a cornet performance measure; it contained melodic exercises based on 23 cornet methods (Watkins, 1942). Sets of 14 exercises exist for cornet and treble clef baritone; B flat, alto, and bass clarinet; saxophone and oboe; flute; horn; trombone, bass clef baritone, and bassoon; and tuba. Twelve snare drum exercises are included.

The test must be administered individually. The student begins with the first exercise, with the aid of a metronome, and plays until he or she scores zero in two consecutive exercises. Each exercise has a possible score that is indicated on the scoring sheet. The scoring unit is the metric measure, and the examiner subtracts one from the possible score for each measure containing an error. Only one error is subtracted from any measure. The examiner is given detailed explanations of what constitutes errors; indicating the type of error via a code letter is optional. A detailed consideration of *WFPS* error types illustrates the need to make arbitrary decisions about what is an error, which necessarily is a part of any specific performance measure.

"Pitch" errors are additional tones, omitted tones, or incorrect tones. The examiner is instructed specifically that a "fuzzy" attack or deviation in pitch during a sustained tone that began on correct pitch are not errors. Initially playing an incorrect pitch but immediately changing it to the correct one is *not* an error if a lip adjustment is made without retonguing but *is* an error if a fingering adjustment is made. Temporary overblowing or squeaks thus are not errors, but suddenly switching from (written) F sharp to F natural on clarinet is.

A "time" error results when a tone is not sustained within plus or minus one full count. The tolerance allowed may seem questionable to many musicians. In $\frac{4}{4}$ meter a dotted half note played as a whole or half note is a time error. However, if it is played for two-and-a-small-fraction counts or for just under four counts it is not an error. An omitted or improperly sustained rest also is considered a time error.

A "change of time" error is a "marked" tempo change or a measure played in an incorrect tempo. The examiner is urged to practice with a metronome prior to giving the test so that he or she may become sensitive to a tempo change of 12 beats per minute in either direction during an exercise. (Plus or minus 12 beats per minute is the criterion for a "marked" change.) The measure in which a tempo increase occurs is an error. A decrease is more complicated; all measures played at the slower tempo are errors, up to four measures. Then the player is supposed to be stopped, told he or she is playing too slowly, and restarted at correct tempo. Another tempo decrease is allowed to continue, but all of the measures are errors.

"Expression" errors are failure to observe dynamic markings and terms, such as ritard, a tempo, and crescendo. The *amount* of response is not a criterion; if a $f > p$ dynamic contrast is indicated and the examiner feels that the change is only $f > mf$, that is not an error. Failure to make *any* change in accordance with a marking is an error.

Failure to observe correct articulation is a "slur" error. The examiner is instructed that students who have been taught to play with an especially legato tongue stroke should be cautioned and then held to a strict standard.

Failure to observe a fermata is considered and coded as a "time" or rhythm error, but it is evaluated in accordance with "expression" error criteria. Pauses are another type of rhythm error if they occur within a measure but not if they occur between measures. (The examiner is told that the student should not be informed that a pause on a bar line will not be considered an error!)

Failure to observe a repeat sign is an error. However, if the player stops to ask if he or she should observe a repeat, the examiner is supposed to say "yes" and not score an error.

The snare drum exercises call for particular rudiments by name, but scoring directions make no mention of what to do if a player does not execute the sticking for a requested rudiment but nevertheless plays with accurate rhythm.

The *Farnum String Scale* is very similar regarding types of errors and scoring rules. A quarter-tone error is the minimum criterion for a "pitch" error. The instructions in the *WFPS* regarding a tempo decrease also are applied to a tempo increase.

The *FSS* substitutes "bowing" errors for "slur" errors. Incorrect bowing in any measure is an error; inept bowing is not, although the examiner is told to comment that bowing should be improved.

No reliability or validity information is reported in the *FSS* manual. The *WFPS* manual reports correlations between a Form A and a Form B which range from .87 to .94. Correlations of students' *WFPS* scores and instructors' rankings of those students' performing abilities range from .68 for drum to .87 for cornet and trumpet.

The *FSS* manual does not indicate what to do with the scores, although "grading charts" appear on the individual sheets. The *WFPS* manual provides minimal scores for grades of A, B, C, and D at particular points of time in years of instruction. Strictly speaking, these are not norms. There is a grading chart showing an "average" curve across time that is based on "thousands of scores from the schools in one city." There are not separate data for the different instruments.

The musical examples generally increase in difficulty consistently. One might question the extent to which particular examples are idiomatic for various instruments. Some dynamic indications appear contrived. There is no consideration of what generally are accepted as correct woodwind fingerings in technical passages. Tone quality, extremely important and obvious in instrumental performances, is completely irrelevant in the scoring.

Despite the criticisms that may be levelled against the *WFPS* and the *FSS*, the tests do attain a certain relative amount of objectivity by providing highly specific directions for scoring performance aspects about which most experienced teachers could agree regarding correctness. If criteria seem too lenient, the examiner might experiment with more rigorous criteria for a particular application. Pauses between measures could be an additional error, credited to the measure immediately prior or following; the tolerance for "time" errors could be more discriminating. The very existence of the scales provides a ready-made tool for assessing players in different programs with a common measure.

SELECTED TECHNIQUES

Given divergent performance criteria, demands for performance measures that are more than "I like it and never mind why," and the lack of published measures, the person concerned with assessing musical performances often should construct his or her own measure. There are various techniques with origins in psychophysics or psychology that the authors believe are applicable to the measurement of musical performance.

In evaluating a musical performance, the evaluator is conceivably making some *judgment* about the performance in relation to some standard and/or to other performances, or making a *choice* regarding where the performance stands with consideration of its characteristics. Dunn-Rankin (1983, p. 5) distinguishes between judgments of similarity, which he believes are necessary to construct a psychological scale, and preferences among objects, which provide a description of the objects. Whether one conceives of the performance evaluation task as measuring judges or measuring the performance may make some theoretical difference in the chosen measurement procedures.

Dunn-Rankin (p. 9) identifies five types of judgment or choice tasks, which are quasi-taxonomic in nature. One task is *placing* or *grouping*, as in clustering similar objects; grouping performances roughly on the basis of some characteristic such as tone quality might exemplify placing. The second type is *naming* or categorizing, which Dunn-Rankin exemplifies by opinion polls and could be exemplified musically by an audition procedure conducted on an in–out (pass–fail) basis. Dunn-Rankin's third type is *ordering*, as in judging a contest to determine a winner. *Quantifying* is the fourth type; a judge places a number on some stimulus aspect. The final type is *combination* in which one sorts stimuli into ordered categories running from "good" to "bad." As with the well-known Bloom and Krathwohl taxonomies (see Chapter 5), a person could waste considerable time trying to place a task into one and only one category, but the task types do provide some suggestions for judges' tasks.

Likert Scales

According to Nunnally (1970, p. 435), the most generally useful model for scaling people regarding psychological traits is the *sum-*

mative model, so-called because one obtains a total score by adding individual item scores. The model, which underlies most paper-and-pencil achievement measures, assumes that each item is monotonically related to some underlying psychological trait and that the total score is approximately linearly related to that trait.[*] Summative scales often are called *Likert scales*, named for the researcher who especially advocated their use as measures of attitudes (Likert, 1932). While intended as attitude measures, one can justify Likert scales in measuring musical performance if one views performance assessment as scaling peoples' attitudes toward what they are hearing. If one insists that performance judges are functioning as observers in a psychophysical task similar to judging apparent weight or loudness, that is, where "things" rather than people are scaled, a Likert scale is theoretically inappropriate.

The Likert scale assumes an underlying continuum running between two extremes. The respondent indicates a position along that continuum by circling a number or letter or checking a location along a line. Usually there is a particular statement to focus each response. In a global approach to measuring performance, a Likert item might be:

I think this performance is of high musical quality.
SA   A   N   D   SD

The letters stand for strongly agree, agree, neutral or uncertain, disagree, and strongly disagree. Numbers or spaces to check also could be used. In a more specifics-oriented approach there might be a list of statements about particular performance aspects:

The rhythm was accurate.   SA   A   N   D   SD
The tempo was appropriate.   SA   A   N   D   SD
The phrasing was tasteful.   SA   A   N   D   SD

Opinions differ regarding the optimal number of categories. Nunnally (1970, p. 427) recommends at least 10 categories if only one scale is employed, otherwise fewer categories are necessary. In

---

[*]In a monotonic relationship, A increases as B increases, although it may not increase at a consistent rate. In a linear relationship, A increases as B increases and does so at a constant rate that, when graphed, looks like a straight line. All linear relations are monotonic, but not all monotonic relations are linear.

general, greater numbers of categories will increase reliability, but the increase becomes negligible with still further categories. In the authors' opinion five categories are quite sufficient for most purposes; beyond 11 categories it becomes rather difficult to discriminate between adjacent categories.

Opinions also differ regarding the desirability of a middle neutral or uncertain category. It may be desirable to force respondents to agree or disagree, to like or dislike at least a little. On the other hand, if there is room for a genuine uncertainty that is not simply avoiding an issue, a neutral category is desirable. The authors lean toward having a middle step.

Reliability can be assessed via coefficient alpha, as described in Chapter 3. Item selection should be based on how well each item correlates with the total test, that is, item discrimination. With just one item, using many judges is necessary to assess reliability. Given the merits of having a relatively large number of items (perhaps around 30) for reliability, the Likert scale probably is more appropriate for a specifics than for a global approach.

Semantic Differential

A type of scale that is anchored by explicit antonyms is the semantic differential, an outgrowth of work in the measurement of meaning (Osgood, Suci, & Tannenbaum, 1957). In performance assessment, possible scales might include "bright–dark," "in tune–out of tune," "artistic–insensitive," and "balanced–unbalanced." A set of opposite meaning adjectives could be constructed for various judges to use in describing a musical performance; the judges' ratings could be averaged and a profile curve drawn for each performance:

	1	*2*	*3*	*4*	*5*	
melodious	—	—	—	—	—	cacophonous
exciting	—	—	—	—	—	depressing
rhythmic	—	—	—	—	—	arhythmic
accurate	—	—	—	—	—	inaccurate
sonorous	—	—	—	—	—	harsh
blended	—	—	—	—	—	unblended
sensitive	—	—	—	—	—	insensitive
in tune	—	—	—	—	—	out of tune

Since the terms may be interpreted in various ways, serious use of the semantic differential should include a factor analysis to discover underlying "super scales," dimensions, or factors to which the antonymic scales may be related. A correlation matrix consisting of all possible pairwise correlations (36 in the above example) of the scores from a set of judges is submitted to a series of mathematical processes to extract the common factors or "core variables" that "explain" scores on the various scales. Factor analysis, which is partly an art as well as a scientific research tool, is beyond the scope of this text, but, in simple applications, profile curves for a set of performances may be useful in making gross classifications.

Paired Comparisons

Paired comparisons is a technique for discriminating among similar performances when rankings are desired. While time consuming and requiring recorded examples when used in music, paired comparisons can resolve ambiguities by making fine discriminations. The simple technique discussed here is based on a discussion by Hays (1967); the classical exhaustive treatments are in Thurstone (1927), Guilford (1954), and Torgerson (1958).

Certain conditions are necessary for successful use of paired comparisons. The number of stimuli must not be excessively large. There must not be any pairwise comparisons consistently heard as favoring the same performance. Several judges must be employed. One must have access to a normal curve table and make a certain assumption.

The assumption is that there is a "true" difference between two ambiguous stimuli but that over an extended period of time, or among many individuals, judgments of the difference will vary in accordance with a normal distribution, centered on the "true" difference. The normal distribution is found in many naturally varying phenomena and is assumed for many psychological and educational variables. It is the so-called "bell-shaped" curve of a distribution of occurrences that theoretically is unbounded, has a coinciding mean, median, and mode, and has the proportion of occurrences of the variable distributed in accordance with the normal curve table. There are more occurrences closer to the central tendency values than to the extremes. For any particular z-score value along the bottom of the curve, the proportion of total occurrences included under the curve to that point can be read from a normal curve table, which appears in many statistics texts.

For example, consider the normal curve

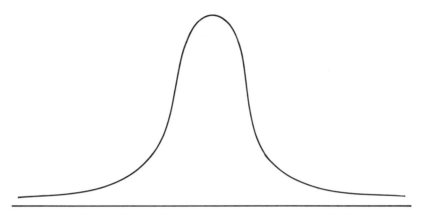

z: −3.00 −2.00 −1.00 0.00 1.00 2.00 3.00

If one starts from the left, .001 of the occurrences under the curve lie to the left of a z-score of −3.00. The proportion of curve area to the left of −2.00 is .023. At −1.00 the proportion is .159. For 0.00, 1.00, 2.00 and 3.00, the respective proportions of all occurrences under the curve are .500, .841, .977, and .999.

Consider a specific example. Suppose that six flute players, all of whom are excellent flautists who can produce a virtually flawless performance of a designated major work, are to be ranked; the highest-ranked performer will be awarded a cash prize. To apply paired comparisons, one would record the performers on separate cassettes under identical conditions. The only performance identification on the tape would be by code letter or number. The tapes might be played in all possible pairwise combinations* of different performances (15) for a panel of ten judges who are qualified to evaluate flute performance. Each judge presumably would function as a microcosm of the large scale judging of ambiguous differences; his or her judgments would have places on a normal curve. The basic input is the proportion of times any performance is preferred over any other. The raw data can be tabled as the proportion

*The number of possible pairwise combinations of n objects or events is given by $\frac{n(n-1)}{2}$.

of times the column stimulus is preferred over the row stimulus: (Comparisons of a performance with itself are assumed to be .50.)

	A	B	C	D	E	F
A	.50	.70	.90	.60	.90	.80
B	.30	.50	.70	.40	.70	.50
C	.10	.30	.50	.20	.80	.40
D	.40	.60	.80	.50	.60	.80
E	.10	.30	.20	.40	.50	.40
F	.20	.50	.60	.20	.60	.50

The A performance was preferred over B by three judges, B was preferred over A by seven, C was preferred over D by eight, and so on—for whatever reasons. Presumably, the reasons are musical.

The next step is to convert the proportions to z-scores in accordance with a normal curve table. The format of individual tables varies, but essentially they show the area under a curve between the mean (z = 0.00) and any particular z value. The proportions below .50 will have a negative z value. The table of z-scores that matches the above matrix is:

	A	B	C	D	E	F
A	0.00	0.52	1.28	0.25	1.28	0.84
B	−0.52	0.00	0.52	−0.25	0.52	0.00
C	−1.28	−0.52	0.00	−0.84	0.84	−0.25
D	−0.25	0.25	0.84	0.00	0.25	0.84
E	−1.28	−0.52	−0.84	−0.25	0.00	−0.25
F	−0.84	0.00	0.25	−0.84	0.25	0.00

The scale values now are obtained by summing the z-scores in each column and dividing by 6, in other words, finding the means. The scale values for the six flute performances, based on ten judges' comparisons of all pairs, thus are A, −0.70; B, −0.04; C, 0.34; D, −0.32; E, 0.52; F, 0.20. Performance E is the "winner." If the scale values "look" strange, one may apply a T-score conversion, as discussed in Chapter 3, and round to the nearest whole number to give respective scores of 43, 50, 53, 47, 55, and 52. In fact, the z-scores may be converted to T-scores prior to summing and dividing if the evaluator is more comfortable with T-scores.

In order to employ paired comparisons, one must "buy" the theoretical assumption that many people making many judgments of differences between similar stimuli will make judgments that err sometimes one way, sometimes the other, with the distribution of judgments centering on a "true" difference in accordance with the normal distribution. As a means of combatting the psychophysical time error, in which the second of a set of paired highly similar events is somehow judged as having more of some property than the first event,* one could record each possible pair in both directions and randomly assign half the judges to listen in one order and half in the other order. One must have the necessary time and resources. If theoretical and practical demands are met and the stimuli are sufficiently similar, the technique is a viable way to order performances that are otherwise difficult to order.

Successive Intervals

When paired comparisons are impractical because there are too many performances, a method of *successive intervals* may be employed. This method is based on a law of categorical judgment, which essentially says that category boundaries fluctuate in accordance with the normal distribution, just as stimulus differences fluctuate normally according to a law of comparative judgment. The judges' task is categorization of all stimuli rather than ranking each member within each possible pair (Ghiselli, Campbell, & Zedeck, 1981, pp 404–408).

As an example of using successive intervals to evaluate performances, consider a task in which 10 judges rate 10 band performances by assigning each band to a I, II, III, IV, or V category (similar to many rated festivals) in this way:

Performance	V	IV	III	II	I
A	1	1	5	2	1
B	3	2	3	1	1
C	1	1	4	3	1
D	1	1	1	2	5
E	1	1	3	4	1
F	1	1	3	3	2
G	1	1	2	4	2
H	2	3	3	1	1
I	1	1	5	2	1
J	1	1	4	2	2

The first step is to convert the raw number of assignments of

---

*For examples in the evaluation of musical performance, consult the previously cited Duerksen (1972) and Radocy (1976) studies in which listeners judged the second of two identical performances as better when they had no information about the alleged performers.

each band to each category to the proportion of judges who assigned each performance to each category. This yields:

Performance	V	IV	III	II	I
A	.10	.10	.50	.20	.10
B	.30	.20	.30	.10	.10
C	.10	.10	.40	.30	.10
D	.10	.10	.10	.20	.50
E	.10	.10	.30	.40	.10
F	.10	.10	.30	.30	.20
G	.10	.10	.20	.40	.20
H	.20	.30	.30	.10	.10
I	.10	.10	.50	.20	.10
J	.10	.10	.40	.20	.20

This table is now converted to a table of cumulative proportions; the proportions are added successively to the right. (Of necessity, the "I" column will be 1.00.)

Performance	V	IV	III	II	I
A	.10	.20	.70	.90	1.00
B	.30	.50	.80	.90	1.00
C	.10	.20	.60	.90	1.00
D	.10	.20	.30	.50	1.00
E	.10	.20	.50	.90	1.00
F	.10	.20	.50	.80	1.00
G	.10	.20	.40	.80	1.00
H	.20	.50	.80	.90	1.00
I	.10	.20	.70	.90	1.00
J	.10	.20	.60	.80	1.00

Now the z-score for each cell entry is found from a normal curve table: (Since there are four boundary points between five categories, the "I" column is dropped from consideration. Each z-score may be interpreted as the z-score for the upper boundary of a lower category.)

Performance	V	IV	III	II
A	−1.28	−0.84	0.52	1.28
B	−0.52	0.00	0.84	1.28
C	−1.28	−0.84	0.25	1.28
D	−1.28	−0.84	−0.52	0.00
E	−1.28	−0.84	0.00	1.28
F	−1.28	−0.84	0.00	0.84
G	−1.28	−0.84	−0.25	0.84
H	−0.84	0.00	0.84	1.28
I	−1.28	−0.84	0.52	1.28
J	−1.28	−0.84	0.25	0.84

The "true" category boundaries are found by finding the mean value of each column. Respectively, these are V = −1.16, IV = −0.67, III = 0.24, and II = 1.02. Then the mean of the "true" category boundaries is computed; this is −0.57.

Now to find the performance values, the mean z-value of each row is obtained and is subtracted from the mean category boundary of −0.57. The resulting values for each performance are

A	−0.49
B	−0.97
C	−0.42
D	0.90
E	−0.36
F	−0.25
G	−0.19
H	−0.89
I	−0.49
J	−0.29

As with paired comparisons, there are difficulties if a performance is not categorized at least once into each category. The z-score to assign a proportion of 1.00 is theoretically uncertain because the normal curve is unbounded. Yet the method of successive intervals is viable for those situations where relatively similar performances must be sorted and ranked.

Magnitude Estimation

Using magnitude estimation to assess musical performance is comparatively rare, but, especially when a global-type evaluation is desired, it is possible. It exemplifies the task that Dunn-Rankin calls quantifying. Much of this section is based on the work of S. S. Stevens, the Harvard psychophysicist who set forth the theory and summarized many of his applications and those of his students in his text (1975), posthumously completed and published by his wife, Geraldine.

Essentially *magnitude estimation* is matching one sensory continuum to another. Stevens was interested in measuring sensations such as loudness, taste, pitch, brightness, shock, and warmth. He believed that measurement, as the assignment of numerals to objects or events in accordance with rules, can be a *matching* operation; it is not limited to counting units. People generally do not match values from diverse sensory continua in everyday life, but most people are quite willing to attempt magnitude estimation, despite the seemingly unusual nature of the task (Baird & Noma, 1978, p. 73).

Although many magnitude estimation applications are to measuring sensation, the technique can be used to assess more global cognitive phenomena. Examples of magnitude estimation usage include measuring apparent severity of crimes (Ekman, 1962), musical preferences among "normal" and "abnormal" subjects (Koh, 1965), apparent sizes of musical intervals (Radocy, 1978), and apparent dissimilarity between paired melodic performances (Radocy, 1982). It is not necessary to extend the results to psychophysical relationships in order to measure via magnitude estimation.

The most frequent applications probably involve matching numbers to stimuli. The "more" of some property—loudness, musical preference, musical performance quality—that a stimulus has, the larger the number it suggests. The judge is told to assign any positive number to represent the perceived amount of the stimulus property. Fractions and decimals are acceptable. The judge is encouraged to double or halve a number if the property apparently changes by twice or by half as much. Theoretically, one is matching the continuum of *numerosity* (apparent number) to the stimulus continuum.

Opinions differ regarding whether the subjects should receive a common standard, as in being instructed to call the first stimulus "10" or "100." Stevens recommended not providing a common standard and, instead, converting the original numbers to a *common modulus*, in accordance with a procedure that we shall explain later. Lack of a common standard does not reduce reliability. When 51 subjects rated the perceived tone quality of recorded trumpet performances, Figgs (1981) allowed them to set their own standards; she obtained coefficient alpha reliabilities of .980 and .997 for magnitude estimations of isolated tones and melodic excerpts respectively.

Any measurement procedure involving subjective judgments may be questioned; using magnitude estimation, in particular, requires a belief that reliable measurement can result from assessment of phenomena through sensory impression. If this concept is too incredible for the reader, he or she may choose to omit the detailed illustration of a magnitude estimation procedure immediately following.

Consider a situation in which five judges evaluate ten performances. The judges assign numbers on the basis of their perceptions of performance quality. In this instance, they perform a global evaluation; some react especially to tone quality; others admire technical virtuosity. Suppose that the following performer-by-judge matrix results:

Performance	J1	J2	J3	J4	J5
A	94	10	12	5	25
B	76	5	7	4	18
C	32	2	4	1	8
D	53	4	5	2	12
E	46	3	2	2	10
F	51	5	6	3	11
G	128	15	18	10	50
H	70	9	10	6	30
I	37	4	8	3	10
J	75	10	14	6	40

There are, of course, inconsistencies among the judges. Magnitude estimation characteristically shows large amounts of variation. Some variation may be due to judges' sensory differences; some may be due to particular numerical biases (Baird & Noma, 1978, pp. 101–102).

The first step is to select a *common modulus,* that is, the person in charge of the evaluation selects a common standard to impose on the original estimations. To select a common modulus one arbitrarily designates a number for a selected stimulus and then converts each judge's estimation to reflect a proportionate relationship of his or her estimation to the arbitrary selection. The authors recommend selecting a stimulus that receives a median or near median value from most judges. Performance B seems near the middle for four of the five judges, so it is selected, although, in principle, any performance would work. Any number could be designated, but 5 is selected as the common modulus. Now, all the original estimations are converted to be in the same proportional relationship to 5 as they are to whatever value was assigned originally to performance B. Judge 1 called performance B a 76; $5 \div 76 = .07$. Consequently, all of Judge 1's original estimations are multiplied by .07. Judge 2 called B a 5, so Judge 2's estimations remain as is. Judge 3 called B a 7; $5 \div 7 = .71$, so all of Judge 3's original estimations are multiplied by .71. Similarly, Judge 4's original estimations are multiplied by 1.25 ($5 \div 4$) and Judge 5's by .28 ($5 \div 18$). The magnitude estimation table in accordance with the common modulus of 5 is then:

Performance	J1	J2	J3	J4	J5
A	6.18	10.00	8.57	6.25	6.94
B	5.00	5.00	5.00	5.00	5.00
C	2.11	2.00	2.86	1.25	2.22
D	3.49	4.00	3.57	2.50	3.33
E	3.03	3.00	1.43	2.50	2.78
F	3.36	5.00	4.29	3.75	3.06
G	8.42	15.00	12.86	12.50	13.89
H	4.61	9.00	7.14	7.50	8.33
I	2.43	4.00	5.71	3.75	2.78
J	4.93	10.00	10.00	7.50	11.11

Because of the assumed proportionate relations among the estimations, Stevens recommended using the geometric mean,

$$\overline{X}_G = \sqrt[n]{(X_1)\,(X_2)\,(...)\,(X_n)},$$

as an average stimulus value.* The median is also permissible. In the above example, the respective geometric means, and hence "values" of the performances on a scale that theoretically has no upper limits, are:

A	7.45	F	3.83
B	5.00	G	12.30
C	2.02	H	7.14
D	3.34	I	3.57
E	2.46	J	8.37

The reliability of the above illustration, found via coefficient alpha with each judge considered an item and the sums of the converted estimations for each performance considered the source of overall score variance, is .97.

Magnitude estimations may not work well if judges listen to different performances on different occasions, as if performers A–D were heard on Friday and the remainder on Saturday, or as if Judges 1 and 2 listened on Friday and the remainder listened on Saturday. The performances should be ordered randomly and, as with other procedures, the number of stimuli can not be so great as to fatigue the judges. If stimuli are very similar there may be diffi-

---

*In other words, for each stimulus, one multiplies the n converted estimations together and finds the nth root of the product. Such a root is found by dividing the *logarithm* of the product by n and then finding the *antilog* of that result. This is a simple operation on many modern calculators.

culty in obtaining estimations that consistently and clearly differ. The judges may require some practice if they never have made magnitude estimations.

Since magnitude estimation is matching one continuum, such as apparent performance quality, with another, numerosity is not the only possible matching continuum. One could adjust lights, draw lines, squeeze a hand grip, or, theoretically, do anything that enables varying the apparent magnitude of one thing to show variation in apparent magnitude of something else.

Magnitude estimation probably is most useful in situations where one must obtain rather global (or general) evaluations of diverse amounts of homogeneous stimuli in a rather short amount of time. It is a controversial technique, and the user must be prepared to defend its use.

Rank Orders

There is a very simple way to evaluate performances if one does not care how different the performances are or how they compare with any absolute standard; the performances simply can be ranked. Seating arrangements in band and orchestra sections often are made this way. When more than one judge is employed, the ranks may be averaged, and those averages ranked in turn. Of course, the basis for rankings may be from paired comparisons, magnitude estimation, or some detailed procedure as well as rapid informal judgments.

Contest-Festival

Many a music educator has a collection of contest or rated festival stories; some have joyful endings, some have woeful endings. Despite justifiable criticism of music programs that may overemphasize a once-a-year performance rating at the expense of comprehensive music education, rated festivals are likely to be around for some time because they are a tradition, a powerful motivator, and a potential source of pride in a job well done.

The concertlike aspects of festivals mean that nonmusical or extramusical criteria may affect evaluation. Ideally, evaluation should be of anonymous (to the judges) recordings of the public performances. Rank order techniques, magnitude estimations, or Likert-like checklists of specific attributes could be employed. If time permitted, paired comparisons, particularly when there is to be a "winner," might be useful.

The conventional festival evaluation form is a mixture of qualitative commentary and categorization. Specific performance aspects are listed and the judge is invited to make a plus or minus sign or comment about particular areas. For example, on the 1983 Kansas music festival forms (KSHSAA, 1982) a band judge is to comment on tone, intonation, technique, balance, interpretation, musical effect, and "other factors." Space is provided for private comments to the director. The vocal solo form requests a + or − on 33 specific attributes, grouped in categories of tone, intonation, diction, breath control, musicianship, and literature. The judge is supposed to assign in all cases a I, II, III, IV, or V final rating.

The "official" descriptions of what the ratings mean (KSHSAA, 1982, p. 8) are:

Rating I—An outstanding performance, with very few technical errors and exemplifying a truly musical expression. *This rating should be reserved for the truly outstanding performance.*

Rating II—An unusual performance in many aspects but not worthy of the highest rating due to minor defects in performance, ineffective interpretation or improper instrumentation.

Rating III—An acceptable performance but not outstanding. Showing accomplishment and marked promise, but lacking one or more essential qualities, i.e., interpretation, intonation, instrumentation.

Rating IV—A poor performance showing many technical errors, poor musical conception, lack of interpretation, incomplete instrumentation or lacking in any of the other essential qualities.

Rating V—An ineffective performance indicating deficiencies in most of the essential factors and indicating that much careful attention should be given to the fundamentals of good performance. This rating should be used sparingly and only when it is possible to cite major faults.

These are *categories* (just as are the numbers or spaces in a Likert scale), and the judge must decide where the category boundaries are. What is "outstanding," "unusual," "acceptable," "poor," or "ineffective" will vary with time, place, and person. Some adjudicators may apply college music major standards to high school festivals and give very few Is. Other judges may give almost everyone a

I because "they all try so hard." As they go through the day, many judges try to attain a certain balance among the upper three ratings, with IIs predominating. One thing that significantly could improve festival adjudication in the present common format is to provide judges in advance with a firm idea of where the local standards are through "anchors" or model performances.

ANCHORS

This section concludes with a brief recommendation for the use of anchors or models because they can apply to many measurement techniques as well as help establish category boundaries. Recorded performances of what a festival manager, scholarship committee, or other policymaker(s) consider outstanding, mediocre, or poor can help "anchor" a judge's standards. Demonstraton of a bright and dark or thick and thin tone can help make explicit what the terms mean.

Naturally, the anchors will reflect what someone or some group believes is representative of a category or term. This is inevitable. Except for certain aspects that have a close physical parallel, such as correct fingerings and time values, music performance evaluation is inherently subjective. Psychological principles need to be applied that recognize the fact and make performance evaluation as realistic, practical, and "human" as possible.

Study Questions

1. Would you use the *Watkins-Farnum Performance Scale* or the *Farnum String Scale?* Why or why not? In what situation would you use it or particularly avoid using it?

2. Make a list of the characteristics that would describe an excellent performance on your major performance medium in a particular musical style. Then, determine whether such a performance should be evaluated on the basis of each specific characteristic or in a global manner, with the characteristics functioning as guidelines.

3. What evaluation procedure would you recommend and *why* for each of the following situations?

   A. Seating a concert band's 15 clarinet players in order of ability.
   B. Selecting one of 100 applicants for the position of principal bassoon in a major orchestra.

    C. Choosing the winner from among six finalists in a piano competition.

    D. Selecting 40 of the 120 voices in a high school chorus for a select concert chorale.

    E. Ranking 10 bands in a marching competition.

    F. Assigning a grade to each of 35 fifth-grade instrumentalists after their first semester of study.

4. Five judges used magnitude estimation to score eight alto saxophone performances. The resulting performer-by-judge matrix is:

Performer	J1	J2	J3	J4	J5
Andy	3	10	5	7	4
Claudia	16	22	20	21	15
Denise	18	20	25	24	20
Henry	4	6	5	9	7
Jay	7	12	10	15	11
Margot	26	37	40	30	32
Ralph	20	30	30	28	24
Valerie	10	18	15	16	17

    A. Which performer and what number will you designate as the common modulus and why?

    B. Using your selected common modulus, convert each judge's values in accordance with it.

    C. Compute the geometric mean for each performer. (Results will vary with different common moduli, *but* the *relative* results will be the same, i.e., the "best" performer will have the highest mean, the "second best" the next highest, etc.)

REFERENCES

Baird, J.C., & Noma, E. *Fundamentals of scaling and psychophysics.* New York: Wiley, 1978.

Duerksen, G. L. Some effects of expectation on evaluation of recorded musical performances. *Journal of Research in Music Education,* 1972, *20,* 268–272.

Dunn-Rankin, P. *Scaling methods.* Hillsdale, N.J.: Lawrence Erlbaum Associates, 1983.

Ekman, G. Measurement of moral judgment: A comparison of scaling methods. *Perceptual and Motor Skills,* 1962, *15,* 3–9.

Farnum, S. E. *Farnum string scale.* Winona, Minn.: Hal Leonard, 1969.

Figgs, L. D. Qualitative differences in trumpet tones as perceived by listeners and by acoustical analysis. *Psychology of Music,* 1981, *9* (2), 54–62.

Ghiselli, E.E., Campbell, J.P., & Zedeck, S. *Measurement theory for the behavioral sciences.* San Francisco, Calif.: W.H. Freeman and Co., 1981.

Guilford, J. P. *Psychometric methods* (2nd ed.). New York: McGraw-Hill, 1954.

Hays, W. L. *Quantification in psychology.* Belmont, Calif.: Brooks/Cole, 1967.

KSHSAA music manual. Topeka, Kans.: Kansas State High School Activities Association, 1982.

Koh, S. D. Scaling musical preferences. *Journal of Experimental Psychology,* 1965, *70,* 79–82.

Likert, R. A technique for the measurement of attitudes. *Archives of Psychology,* 1932, No. 140, 5–53.

Nunnally, J. E., Jr. *Introduction to psychological measurement.* New York: McGraw-Hill, 1970.

Osgood, C. E., Suci, G. J., & Tannenbaum, P. H. *The measurement of meaning.* Urbana, Ill.: University of Illinois Press, 1957.

Radocy, R. E. Effects of authority figure biases on changing judgments of musical events. *Journal of Research in Music Education,* 1976, *24,* 119–128.

Radocy, R. E. The influence of selected variables on the apparent size of successive pitch intervals. *Psychology of Music,* 1978, *6* (2), 21–29.

Radocy, R. E. Magnitude estimation of melodic dissimilarity. *Psychology of Music,* 1982, *10* (1), 28–32.

Stevens, S. S. *Psychophysics.* New York: Wiley, 1975.

Thurstone, L. L. The method of paired comparisons for social values. *Journal of Abnormal Social Psychology,* 1927, *21,* 384–400.

Torgerson, W. S. *Theory and methods of scaling.* New York: Wiley, 1958.

Watkins, J. G. Objective measurement of instrumental performance. New York: Teachers' College Bureau of Publications, Columbia University, 1942.

Watkins, J. G., & Farnum, S. E. *The Watkins-Farnum performance scale: Form a.* Winona, Minn.: Hal Leonard, 1954.

Watkins, J. G., & Farnum, S. E. *The Watkins-Farnum performance scale: Form b.* Winona, Minn.: Hal Leonard, 1962.

9

Measuring Attitudes and Other Affective Variables

WHAT MIGHT BE TESTED?

Affective behaviors, along with cognitive and psychomotor behaviors, comprise three broad categories of human psychological behaviors. The categories are not discrete; an individual's thinking, feelings, and actions often are interrelated, although in varying degrees dependent upon the primary nature of the psychological activity. Affective behaviors include a significant feeling component, and a variety of terms are used to label the psychological constructs that appear to have significant feeling components: attitude, interest, preference, opinion, value, and appreciation. Perhaps the most common of these is attitude.

An attitude is a psychological construct that can not be observed; rather it must be inferred from behavior. There is not complete agreement regarding the extent to which an attitude involves cognition, affect, and psychomotor activity, although Cook and Selltiz (1964) maintain that the affective dimension of attitude is its central aspect.

Attitude measurement is fraught with many problems, a number of which appear to be related to definition. Other issues in attitude measurement concern the intensity of attitudes and the extent to which attitudes underlie, influence, and/or interact with other psychological behaviors. To demarcate attitude from simple feeling, interest, opinion, value, appreciation, and preference clearly is a task that experts in the field have yet to do with complete satisfaction, and any claim to do so here would be presumptuous. Readers concerned with the historical, theoretical, and philosophical underpinnings for differentiating among the terms are encouraged to examine Allport (1935), Edwards (1957), Fishbein (1967), and Kiesler, Collins, and Miller (1969).

The present discussion necessarily is limited to examining the types of affective behaviors that are relevant to musicians. Besides the need to examine general attitudes toward music, musicians often are concerned with examining musical taste, preference, interest, appreciation, sensitivity, and aesthetic response. As might be expected, authors differ considerably in their definitions for and use of these terms. For example, Roeckle (1968) notes that taste, appreciation, and preference all imply making judgments and considers them to be equivalent terms, whereas Kuhn (1979) provides separate definitions for attitude, taste, and preference.

Whatever terms are used to describe the varying affective responses to music, persons concerned with assessing the constructs implied by the terms have two primary responsibilities: (a) providing clear working definitions of the terms and what they imply and (b) selecting or devising tests that require behaviors from which one may infer these implied affective states. Furthermore, it must be recognized that the various affective states, which individuals develop as a result of experience, are internalized neuropsychic states reflecting positive or negative predispositions toward music and music-related objects, events, or phenomena. They provide an individual's primary means for guiding his or her approach/avoidance behaviors to music and music-related objects, events, or phenomena.

Krathwohl, Bloom, and Masia (1964) developed a continuum for classifying educational objectives in the affective domain and in the process attempted to relate attitude, appreciation, interest, and value to the levels of the continuum. The continuum represents a range of stages in an "internalization" process, the levels of acceptance an individual has regarding social and psychological phenomena. The stages range from "awareness" of a phenomenon to the "characterization" level at which an individual develops a consistent response pattern reflective of an integrated value complex with respect to the phenomenon. They suggest that "interest" is typically used to describe behaviors toward the lower level of the continuum. They also suggest that "appreciation" overlaps with many "interest" behaviors, but generally does not extend as low on the continuum as some interest behaviors. "Value" and "attitude" are viewed as covering the same mid-level range on the continuum and also overlap with some appreciation and interest behaviors. While the continuum has been useful in calling attention to levels of affect, it has not clearly differentiated among the more commonly used terms for affect.

To facilitate the present discussion, some working definitions for the various terms are necessary. While they are neither discrete nor exhaustive, the definitions do reflect the general meanings as defined by measurement specialists. The respective definitions may be used variously regarding music, musical styles, and music-related objects, events, or other phenomena.

Attitude, the most general term, connotes a predisposition toward mental or psychomotor activity with respect to a social or psychological object, event, or phenomenon. The predisposition may be either positive or negative, that is, reflecting either approach or avoidance activity. An attitude is not directly observable, but must be inferred from an individual's reactions to an object, event, or phenomenon. Kuhn (1979) notes that an attitude is relatively stable and enduring and that any real change in attitude is probably long-term in nature. Kerlinger (1973) even suggests that attitudes may be considered an integral part of personality.

Interest connotes feelings of concern, involvement, and curiosity (Halsey, 1979, p. 593). Just like attitude, interest is inferred from an individual's behavior regarding objects, events, and phenomena. A clear demarcation between "attitude toward something" and "interest in something" is difficult to make, but it appears that in common usage interest more often is manifested through active participation or involvement with the object, event, or phenomenon, whereas attitude is considered more covert, more of a value judgment.

Taste, as applied to music, usually implies an element of connoisseurship, reflecting some agreement with the "experts" regarding quality and excellence. Kuhn considers taste to be similar to attitude: Both imply essentially covert predispositions, both are developed as a result of experience, and both appear to be long-term in nature.

Preference generally is considered more overt, or behavioral, than taste or attitude in that a preference usually involves the individual in the act of making choices. Indicating a preference involves choosing, esteeming, or giving advantage to one thing over another through a verbal statement or some other behavioral manifestation. Abeles (1980) suggests that preference and taste actually represent a continuum from a short-term (preference) to a long-term (taste) commitment. In most preference studies, preferences are expressed in relation to a stimulus object in a given context.

Appreciation, perhaps the most abused term of all, apparently is used with respect to music in both a broad and narrow sense.

> In the broadest sense music appreciation includes knowledge about music and musicians; familiarity with notation, instruments, and musical literature; and acquaintance with historical and technical facts. In a narrower sense, however, music appreciation refers to sensitivity to the aesthetic values of music, and in this sense it is extremely difficult to measure. (Lehman, 1968, p. 25)

The broader definition appears to reflect considerable emphasis on knowledge, whereas the narrower definition places greater emphasis on feeling response to aesthetic qualities of music.

Sensitivity implies perception of and responsiveness to sensory stimuli and reflects both cognitive and affective dimensions. In common usage it appears to imply making both subtle discriminations and subtle feeling responses. In these respects it is more akin to taste than to the other terms considered here.

Aesthetic response is usually the term given to feeling response to beauty or the aesthetic qualities of an object, event, or phenomenon. It involves perception and cognition of the artistic qualities of an object or event (usually an artwork but possibly the beauty or artistic qualities of other objects or events) and the feelingful response to these qualities. There must be a stimulus object, and the aesthetic response generally is considered to be short-term but intense in nature and in respect to a particular stimulus.

To summarize, a variety of neuropsychic constructs used to infer various affective states have been reviewed. While some behavioral psychologists might question using the terms attitude, interest, taste, appreciation, sensitivity, preference, and aesthetic response to describe affective response, other psychologists agree that the terms are indeed meaningful and useful. The neuropsychic constructs that these terms imply necessarily are inferred from behavior. Once the constructs are defined, persons concerned with measurement of them must (a) select or devise tests (behavioral samples) that are acceptable as a basis for making inferences regarding the construct, (b) collect samples of behavior, and (c) quantify the behavioral samples into meaningful data appropriate to making the desired decisions.

SPECIFIC TESTS

Only three currently available published standardized tests purport to measure aspects of musical behavior related to attitude: (a) *The Standardised Tests of Musical Intelligence* (Wing, 1961), (b) the *Musical Aptitude Profile* (Gordon, 1965), and (c) the *Indiana–Oregon Music Discrimination Test* (Long, 1965). While the Wing and Gordon tests are designed as aptitude tests, they both include sections that ask respondents to select the "better" of two renditions of an excerpt; such a task is essentially an expression of preference, although Wing refers to these portions of his test as "appreciation" subtests, and Gordon labels the preference portion of the *MAP* as a measure of "musical sensitivity." The *I–OMDT* also requires respondents to express preferences for one of two renditions of a musical excerpt.

Wing "Appreciation" Subtests

Subtests 4 through 7 were designed as tests of appreciation (Wing, 1968). The four subtests, which are labeled respectively as tests of rhythmic accent, harmony, intensity, and phrasing appreciation, were designed to measure "sensitivity to performance" (Wing, 1968, p. 83). Descriptions of the four subtests appear in Chapter 6.

While a number of researchers have reported reliabilities for the total Wing battery, most of which are above .80, only Wing and Heller have reported reliability coefficients for the appreciation subtests. Wing reported a coefficient of .84 based on the test–retest responses of a group of 15-year-old boys. Heller (1962/1963), using college students for subjects, reported coefficients that were much lower; test–retest coefficients were .28 and .50, and a split-halves coefficient was .42.

The extent to which the four appreciation subtests comprise a valid measure of "appreciation" or "sensitivity to performance" is questionable. Wing's validity work was in relation to the total *STMI* rather than just the four appreciation subtests, and Heller (1962/1963) questions whether the four appreciation subtests contribute significantly to the validity of the total test. Two recent studies (Sampsell, 1980; Boyle, 1982) that examined correlations among the four appreciation subtests, the *I–OMDT,* and the sensitivity portion of Gordon's *MAP* reported correlation coefficients that were low or negligible (and statistically nonsignificant). Questions remain regarding the validity of the appreciation portions of the Wing test as a measure of "appreciation" or "sensitivity to performance."

MAP "Musical Sensitivity" Subtest

The musical sensitivity portion of the *Musical Aptitude Profile* has three subtests: phrasing, balance, and style. Descriptions of the subtests and reliability data appear in Chapter 6.

Just as for the *STMI,* the preference portion of the *MAP* generally has been validated as part of the broader construct of musical aptitude. However, the test manual provides validity estimates for the sensitivity subtests based on correlations between test scores and teachers' estimates of musical talent. Reported correlation coefficients between teachers' estimates of musical talent and the total sensitivity portion of the *MAP* range from .48 to .85; coefficients for the subtests were somewhat lower, ranging from .19 to .87. Additional information regarding the validity of the sensitivity subtests is provided in Gordon's (1967) three-year study of the test's predictive validity for elementary school instrumentalists. Generally, correlations between the sensitivity subtests and the instrumental performance evaluations and music achievement test scores yielded validity coefficients ranging in the .40s.

Also, as noted previously, correlation coefficients between the sensitivity portion of the *MAP* and the appreciation portion of the Wing test were low (.38 and .39) and not statistically significant. Furthermore, the correlations between the *MAP* sensitivity test and the *I–OMDT* were even lower: .28, .34, and −.02 (Gallagher, 1971; Sampsell, 1980; Boyle, 1982).

Whether correlations with teachers' ratings of talent or performance ability and ratings provide an adequate basis for substantiating the validity of the *MAP* sensitivity test as a measure of sensitivity in its own right is doubtful. Hopefully researchers can develop stronger bases for establishing empirical validity of the *MAP* sensitivity test.

Indiana–Oregon Music Discrimination Test

The *Indiana–Oregon Music Discrimination Test* is a revision of Hevner's *Oregon Music Discrimination Test* (Hevner & Landsbury, 1934). The test contains 43 pairs of musical excerpts; however, the author recommends that only the first 30 pairs be used for testing elementary school children and that the first 37 pairs be used for testing junior high school students. Each pair contains two examples of the same musical excerpt; they may be exactly the same, or, as in 38 cases, one example may be changed from what the composer had intended. If changed, either the rhythm, harmony, or melody is changed. The respondent must indicate which of the two examples he or she prefers or whether there is no difference between them; in addition, he or she must indicate whether the change in the alternate version is in rhythm, harmony, or melody. Split-half reliability coefficients for the 43-item test are .88 for students in grades 10 through 12 and .82 for college students.

As evidence of validity, the manual for the *I–OMDT* reports correlation coefficients between test scores and (a) responses on a questionnaire regarding musical experience, (b) Gordon's *MAP* total test and sensitivity test, and (c) Colwell's *Music Achievement Tests.* Correlation coefficients between the *I–OMDT* and the experience variables reported via the questionnaire were generally quite low. Correlation coefficients with the *MAT* and *MAP* respectively were .46 and .38; the correlation with the sensitivity portion of the *MAP* was even lower: .28. Sampsell (1980) and Boyle (1982) reported correlation coefficients with the Wing appreciation subtests of .17 and .14 and with the *MAP* sensitivity test of .34 and −.02.

The tests discussed above seem to raise more questions than they answer regarding the measurement of preference. Although all require respondents to express preference, the lack of significant correlation coefficients among the tests suggests that they may be measuring different constructs.[*] Persons concerned with under-

---

[*] The *I—OMDT* may not be a "preference" measure at all in the sense of expressing a choice between two authentic musical works. Basically it requires detecting whether a change exists and which, if either, version is a "better" performance. Making a choice among different rhythms, harmonies, and melodies is a somewhat different task than evaluating the phrasing contrasts that appear in Wing and *MAP*. All of the "preference-sensitivity" measures may have a familiarity component: Someone acquainted with the art music or quasi-art music styles used in the tests should have an advantage.

standing and measuring music appreciation, taste, attitude, and so on, obviously need to consider other alternatives, such as those that follow.

SELECTED TECHNIQUES

Kiesler, Collins, and Miller (1969) recognize five general categories of attitude measures: Measures in which inferences are drawn from (a) self-reports of beliefs, behaviors, and so on, (b) observations of ongoing overt behavior in a natural setting, (c) individuals' reactions to or interpretations of partially structured stimuli, (d) performance of given "objective" tasks, and (e) physiological reactions to an attitudinal object or representations of it. By far the most commonly used techniques are those involving self-reports. Various types of self-reports using rating scales (discussion follows) appear to be the most accepted means for gathering attitudinal data. Measures in the other four categories are used less for a variety of reasons.

Difficulties in observing overt behaviors in a natural setting are many of those reasons, not the least of which are economy of time, cost, and effort in obtaining data for many individuals. Also, interpretation of behavioral data from natural settings often must be limited to the given individual being observed and the particular situation.

The common technique used to elicit individuals' reactions to partially structured stimuli is essentially a projective technique in which an individual is asked to describe a scene, characterization, or other behavior of a third person in a given situation. According to Kiesler, Collins, and Miller, this approach is seldom used for testing theories of attitude.

Drawing inferences regarding attitude from the performance of objective tasks involves presenting individuals with tests of information or ability. The approach assumes that performance is influenced by attitude. The approach, which involves considerable judgment on the part of the evaluator, has been little used in measuring attitudes toward music and music-related objects, events, and phenomena.

Much research has been conducted using physiological reactions as a basis for inferring affective response. A variety of physiological measures have been used as the dependent variable: heart rate, respiration rate, systolic and diastolic blood pressure, electrodermal response (galvanic skin response), electroencephalography (brain wave response), electromyography (muscle tension), pilometer response (movement of hairs on the skin), pupil (eye) dilation, and even gastric motility. The various studies employing these measures are beset with many methodological problems, both in research design and measurement procedures (Dainow, 1977). Dainow and other reviewers of such research acknowledge that musical stimuli appear to have a generalized arousal effect on many of these functions; however, data are so inconsistent that making predictions or generalizing about attitudes or any type of affective response on the basis of physiological responses is questionable. Technological developments and refinements are enhancing the reliability of physiological measures, and more consistent data should become available (see Chapter 10).

Because of the inherent problems in using the four approaches discussed, most of the discussion that follows is devoted to techniques of the self-reported type. Further, Kuhn (1979) has noted that when one is concerned with examining the attitudes of groups of people, self-reported measures (a) are in all likelihood quite adequate, (b) are the most efficient type of measure, and (c) are really the only practical type of measure.

Self-report Techniques

Before discussing what have come to be the "classic" techniques for measuring attitudes, it should be noted that attitudes may be solicited with respect to (a) a given stimulus that is present in the testing situation or (b) a symbolic representation of a given object, event, or idea that is not present. While Kuhn would argue that the former is a preference and the latter is an opinion, the authors view the classic measurement techniques as generally applicable to both situations; the real difference appears to be in the inferences drawn. Persons with a more behavioristic perspective would be more predisposed to eliciting responses to stimuli present in the testing situation and to being quite conservative in drawing inferences. Persons more predisposed to speaking in terms of neuropsychic constructs (attitudes, feelings, musical taste, etc.) would be more willing to make inferences based upon self-reports in response to symbolic representations of objects, events, or ideas.

Confounding the inference-drawing process from self-reports is the axion that "What people say and what people do are not always the same." Kuhn (1979), however, notes that it normally can be assumed that attitudes reflected by people in nonthreatening situations accurately show their underlying predispositions.

Adams (1982) recognizes three classic techniques for eliciting self-reports regarding attitudes: (a) consensual-location scaling, (b) summated ratings, and (c) cumulative scaling. All essentially involve the development of scales—systems for assigning symbols or quantitative values to individuals or their behaviors according to rules.

The most common consensual-location technique is the equal-appearing-intervals method (Thurstone & Chave, 1929). The procedures are cumbersome and involve (a) developing and refining a number of statements toward a given phenomenon (e.g., musical style), (b) submitting these statements to a large number of "judges" who are asked to sort them into 11 groups on a continuum from least to most favorable, (c) calculating a scale value for each statement, (d) eliminating items on which judges' ratings vary widely, and finally, (e) selecting 20 items (10 positive and 10 negative) evenly graduated along the continuum. The 20-item scale, often called a "Thurstone" scale, then is administered to the group whose attitudes are to be measured, and the respondents then are simply asked to check the statements with which they agree. Each item has a particular numeric value based on the consensus of the judges. While this method has been much used, it generally is viewed as too time consuming for most situations.

Perhaps the most commonly used self-report scale is the summated rating scale, better known as a Likert (1932) or Likert-type scale. Essentially, a summated rating scale contains items (statements) that are considered approximately equal in attitude or value loading. The respondent is asked to indicate a degree of intensity of feeling between two extremes such as agree–disagree, like–dislike, or accept–reject.* The scores, usually from 1 to 5 or 1 to 7, are summed, or, as in most cases, summed and averaged, to obtain an individual's attitude score with respect to whatever object, event, or situation is under consideration. To avoid response bias, a balanced number of positive and negative statements are included, and the scale values are reversed for negative statements.

While such scales generally are easy to develop, true Likert scales require careful review and piloting of the statements as well as final

---

*Likert scales may be applied to evaluation of any homogeneous phenomena that can be placed on a continuum. Chapter 8 examined Likert scales in the context of performance evaluation.

selection of items based on item discrimination indexes that indicate which items discriminate best between overall high-scoring (most favorable response) and low-scoring (least favorable response) groups in the pilot sample. Failure to follow this procedure may result in a lack of scale homogeneity; scales using items not selected via item discrimination indexes usually are referred to as Likert-type scales rather than true Likert scales.

Formats for Likert scales may vary. For example, a person interested in evaluating students' attitudes toward "classical" music might record ten representative excerpts, ask students to listen to them, and indicate on a 5-point scale the degree to which they like them. The response forms could look like any of the following:

	strongly like	like	undecided	dislike	strongly dislike
EXAMPLE NO.					
(respondents check the appropriate blank)					
1.	——	——	——	——	——
2.	——	——	——	——	——
etc.					

OR

(respondents circle the appropriate letters)

1.	SL	L	U	D	SD
2.	SL	L	U	D	SD
etc.					

OR

(respondents circle the appropriate numbers)

1.	5	4	3	2	1
2.	5	4	3	2	1
etc.					

To determine a student's attitude toward classical music, one would simply assign a value of 5 to the "strongly like" column and 4 through 1 to the other columns, sum the values a student assigned to each excerpt, and divide by the number of excerpts. One might infer that the higher a student's mean score or rating for the excerpts, the more he or she likes classical music or the more positive his or her attitude toward classical music.

The same technique might be used in measuring students' responses to statements about music, musical styles, musical performances, composers, or even activities in the general music classroom. Student attitudinal data can be invaluable to teachers as a basis for planning instructional activities.

Scalogram techniques developed by Guttman (1944, 1947, 1950) have come to be known as the cumulative scaling technique. A cumulative scale ("Guttman" scale) includes a relatively small number of homogeneous items that are assumed to be unidimensional, that is, measuring response toward only one object, event, or phenomenon.* There is a cumulative relationship between items; the items are ordered according to a value scale (from low to high) with respect to approval of, agreement with, or acceptance of all preceding items on the scale; similarly, to disapprove, disagree with, or reject an item implies such on all subsequent items. Guttman's original standards for item sequencing were such that when a respondent endorsed an item, the probability was .90 or higher that he or she would endorse all preceding items on the scale.

Ordinarily, cumulative scales should have 8 to 10 items, although many scales include fewer. Adams (1982) notes the problems of using scales with small numbers of items. Also, because items are selected empirically, the ones meeting the standards for reproducibility (reliability) may not be representative of the attitude domain under consideration. Although this is a concern with all methods of attitude scaling, the risk is compounded because of the small number of items.

Cumulative scales have limited application, but they can be useful in assessing a group's attitudes toward a single well-defined object, event, or situation. For example, a person might be interested in examining high school choral directors' attitudes about the importance of sight-reading skills. To assess these attitudes by means of a cumulative scale would involve developing a number of statements, arranging them along a continuum, and then having choral directors respond to them. The choral directors would be asked to answer each question "yes" or "no." A continuum of questions such as the following might be used:

1.   Are sight-reading skills useful for high school choral students?

2.   Should high school choir members be required to develop some skills in sight-reading?

3.   Are sight-reading skills important enough that teachers in the

---

*Guttman scales theoretically may be used in achievement measures if there is a logical hierarchy of difficulty among test items. In practice, they are difficult to attain.

elementary grades and junior high school should devote class time toward helping students develop them?

4. Should high school choral directors devote rehearsal time to helping students develop sight-reading skills?

5. Is the development of students' sight-reading skills sufficiently important that choral directors should systematically seek new information from research and other professional sources on how to teach sight-reading?

6. Should the development of sight-reading skills be as important in a high school choir as preparing for high-quality public performances?

Presumably anyone who responds "yes" to question 6 would respond "yes" to all the others. Anyone responding "yes" to 3 and "no" to 4 should respond "yes" to 1 and 2 and "no" to 5 and 6 because of his or her location on the cumulative scale. A "no" response that occurs earlier than the highest "yes" response on the scale or a "yes" response that occurs later than the lowest "no" response could be considered an "error." The proportion of errors determines the coefficient of reproducibility,

$$R = 1 - \frac{e}{nk},$$

where

$$e = \text{number of errors}$$
$$n = \text{number of respondents}$$

and

$$k = \text{number of scale items.}$$

The coefficient of reproducibility is a principal statistic for determining the "goodness" of a Guttman scale. According to Lemon (1973, pp. 163–167), acceptable minima are .85 or .90, and the coefficient can differ with different interpretations of what constitutes an "error."

Suppose that 15 choral directors respond to the above scale in the following manner:

Director	1	2	3	4	5	6	Errors, HY Criterion	Errors, LN Criterion
D1	Y	Y	Y	Y	Y	N	0	0
D2	Y	Y	Y	Y	Y	Y	0	0
D3	Y	Y	Y	Y	N	Y	1	1
D4	Y	Y	N	Y	N	Y	2	2
D5	Y	Y	N	Y	N	N	1	1
D6	Y	N	N	N	Y	N	3	1
D7	Y	N	N	N	N	N	0	0
D8	Y	Y	N	Y	N	N	1	1
D9	Y	Y	Y	Y	N	N	0	0
D10	N	N	Y	N	N	N	2	1
D11	Y	Y	Y	Y	Y	N	0	0
D12	Y	Y	N	Y	Y	N	1	2
D13	Y	Y	Y	Y	Y	Y	0	0
D14	N	N	Y	N	Y	N	3	2
D15	Y	Y	Y	Y	N	Y	1	1
							15	12

A "highest yes" criterion, that is, errors being "no" answers to items lower in the scale than the highest item receiving a "yes" response, yields a different result than a "lowest no" criterion, that is, errors being "yes" answers to items higher in the scale than the lowest item receiving a "no" response, for D6, D10, D12, and D14. With $n = 15$ respondents, $k = 6$ items, and $e =$ either 15 or 12 errors, the respective R values for the "highest yes" and "lowest no" criteria are .83 and .87. One is below the "liberal" minimum of .85, the other above.

The coefficient of reproducibility is not the only criterion for an acceptable Guttman scale. Ford (1950) indicated that in addition to a coefficient of reproducibility $> .90$, a scale should have (a) errors for no more than 5 percent of the test population, (b) a frequency of error resulting from a given response ("yes" or "no," agreement or disagreement) that is less than half the frequency of that response, and (c) no item providing more than 15 percent of the total errors.

In addition to the techniques described above, there is a variety of other somewhat less formal techniques that are useful in eliciting self-report attitudinal data. The appropriateness of a particular technique depends on the type of data sought and the necessity for subsequent formal quantitative analysis of the data. The need for sophisticated statistical analysis might be necessary when attitude data are used as a dependent variable in a research design; a classroom teacher, however, might only be interested in obtaining some general, yet representative and reliable indication of a group's attitudes toward certain types of instructional activities.

The open-ended question is an often-used technique, both in research and teaching. Open-ended questions often elicit much useful information, but a problem with information elicited by such means is that its relative lack of structure often causes difficulty in reducing the answers for manageable data analysis. Careful analysis of open-ended questions requires a coding system for categorizing responses. While open-ended questions can be easily developed, coding and interpreting responses usually are time-consuming and require considerable judgment on the part of the evaluator. Unless one has a particular need for open-ended responses, persons contemplating using self-report attitudinal measures should consider alternative techniques that are more structured and hence require much less subjective judgment in the data analysis process.

Another consideration in favor of structured techniques may be especially important when the evaluator does not have a "captive" group that *must* respond. For example, surveys are important in assessing attitudes of teachers. Teachers usually are not compelled to respond, and a survey form that requires what the respondent may consider excessive amounts of writing may be ignored, while a form requiring little more than checking or circling would be completed.

The paired-comparison or two-alternative forced choice technique,* which is used by Gordon (1965), Wing (1961), and Long (1965), is perhaps the most common technique for music preference tests. Essentially the technique presents two renditions of an excerpt, or two different excerpts, and the respondent is asked to indicate which he or she prefers, likes better, or thinks is the better of the two. Sometimes an additional choice must be made: "Are the two excerpts the same or equally liked or preferred?" Adding this possibility makes the respondent's task more difficult.

Similar to the paired-comparison technique but involving from three to five options (excerpts or activities) is the multiple-choice technique. This technique works well when one is interested in determining a particular preference from among several listed alternatives, but problems arise when the respondent is asked to indicate a preference from among several recorded excerpts. The use of recorded excerpts places a heavy burden on the listener's memory for the excerpts. Also, the order in which the excerpts are heard may influence responses.

---

*This should not be confused with the paired-comparison *scaling* technique, discussed in Chapter 8 in relation to performance evaluation.

Usually intended for use with young children, pictographic scales, or multiple choice with pictures, using a smiling, neutral, or frowning face, facilitate responses without involving a verbal response. Respondents are instructed to circle the face that best represents their feelings toward a piece of music, an activity, or an idea.

The Q-sort technique involves a set of statements, each on an individual card, about some specific variable toward which attitudes are to be assessed. In the typical unstructured Q-sort, the statements are assumed to be relevant to the variable under consideration (Kerlinger, 1973, p. 587). (In a structured Q-sort, the statements are selected on the basis of their reflection of an underlying theoretical principle and thus are more useful for testing hypotheses.) Respondents are asked to sort the cards according to some like–dislike, agree–disagree, or accept–reject continuum. Kerlinger recommends that the number of cards be between 60 and 90; the number of categories into which the cards are sorted range from two to as many as 15, depending on the type of gradations to be made. Specification of how many cards to allocate to each category standardizes the mean and variance of the Q-sort, so two respondents who may differ greatly in the extent to which they endorse the statements nevertheless may produce identical Q-sorts. The variations in Q-sort technique are many, but it appears to be a useful and convenient way for eliciting preference responses. The subsequent statistical analysis of data also varies, depending on the purpose of the Q-sort and whether a single group or more than one group is being studied. In general, a Q-sort may be appropriate for clustering people according to their attitudes; it may not be appropriate for comparing "average" group responses (Lemon, 1973, pp. 93–100).

Originally designed to provide an objective method for measuring properties of words and concepts, the semantic differential has been adapted for a variety of uses, including musical performance (discussed previously) and assessing attitudes toward music and music-related activities. When used to describe performance or the music being performed, the bipolar adjectives (antonyms) usually are descriptive or evaluative in nature. They provide continua, normally either 5 or 7 point, between adjectives that describe the performance in various ways, both analytically and aesthetically. When used to measure attitudes, the bipolar adjectives included in the semantic differential focus on the feeling response to the music or musical activity. A particular type of response frequently studied via this method is mood response to music. For example, an excerpt is played and the respondent is asked to check on each continuum his or her feeling of the mood reflected by the music. Some typical pairs of adjectives:

happy	___	___	___	___	___	sad
humorous	___	___	___	___	___	gloomy
cheerful	___	___	___	___	___	depressing
restless	___	___	___	___	___	calm

Of course, there are problems in using the semantic differential. One must be sure to select vocabulary appropriate for the respondents; the adjectives must hold some general meaning for them. Also, the vocabulary necessarily would be much more limited for elementary or junior high school students than for college students. For administration, just as for the Likert-type scales, some of the adjective pairs must be randomly reversed to avoid response bias and then reversed again for data analysis and reporting. Some other adjective pairs useful for evaluating attitudinal response are:

interesting	–	boring
beautiful	–	ugly
enjoyable	–	not enjoyable
good	–	bad
pleasurable	–	painful
fun	–	work
acceptable	–	unacceptable
valuable	–	worthless

For evaluating an individual's or a group's response to the music or musical activity, the simplest method for analyzing semantic differential data is to list the adjectives and plot a profile of the mean responses; if comparisons are to be made, for example, of a group's responses to "classical" and some current rock excerpts, the mean responses along the continuum for each pair of adjectives could be plotted and the profiles compared visually. For further analysis, an evaluator could quantify the categories between each adjective pair and apply appropriate statistical tests, but for many purposes the visual comparison is adequate. More sophisticated analyses of semantic differential data are possible using factor analysis procedures to uncover underlying scales that can be grouped together for scoring.

Perhaps the most common tool for examining mood response to music is the adjective check list, the best known of which is Hevner's adjective circle. (See Figure 9.1.) Farnsworth's (1954) revi-

6
bright
cheerful
gay
happy
joyous
merry

7
agitated
dramatic
exciting
exhilarated
impetuous
passionate
restless
sensational
soaring
triumphant

5
delicate
fanciful
graceful
humorous
light
playful
quaint
sprightly
whimsical

8
emphatic
exalting
majestic
martial
ponderous
robust
vigorous

4
calm
leisurely
lyrical
quiet
serene
soothing
tranquil

1
awe-inspiring
dignified
lofty
sacred
serious
sober
solemn
spiritual

3
dreamy
longing
plaintive
pleading
sentimental
tender
yearning
yielding

2
dark
depressing
doleful
frustrated
gloomy
heavy
melancholy
mournful
pathetic
sad
tragic

Figure 9.1: **Hevner Adjective Circle**

sion of the circle also has received considerable use. (See Figure 9.2.) Hevner's original circle consists of eight categories of mood terms, each category just slightly different from the category on either side. The respondent listens to a musical excerpt and selects the category in which he or she finds a word describing the mood of the excerpt. The authors find it easy to elicit rather consistent results on the Hevner adjective circle, perhaps reflecting some commonalities among respondents' learning with respect to mood and music's narrative qualities during the general acculturation process with music in the Western world. However, sophisticated analysis techniques for the adjective circles have yet to be developed; by and large, data analyses involve only descriptive statistics. One useful technique is to express the spread or average deviation of responses around the circle. The authors view the semantic differential technique as potentially more useful than adjective checklists for providing data based on adjective descriptors.

A more recent adjective scale (Asmus, 1979/1980) employs one to four Likert-type scales. The listener indicates his or her degree of agreement that the music makes him or her "feel" as each of 41 words suggests. The 41 terms are organized into nine factors, which in turn are organized into three "super" factors. Definitive research is necessary, but the Asmus 9-AD measure may be a promising

A	B	C	D	E
cheerful	fanciful	delicate	dreamy	longing
gay	light	graceful	leisurely	pathetic
happy	quaint	lyrical	sentimental	plaintive
joyous	whimsical		serene	pleading
bright			soothing	yearning
merry			tender	
playful			tranquil	
sprightly			quiet	

F	G	H	I	J
dark	sacred	dramatic	agitated	frustrated
depressing	spiritual	emphatic	exalting	
doleful		majestic	exciting	
gloomy		triumphant	exhilarated	
melancholic			impetuous	
mournful			vigorous	
pathetic				
sad				
serious				
sober				
solemn				
tragic				

Figure 9.2: **Farnsworth's Modification of the Hevner Adjective Circle**

affective measure because of its administrative, scoring, and analytical ease.

The variety of possible paper-and-pencil self-report forms eliciting information regarding attitudes is great. Persons devising such scales, however, must consider carefully a number of factors when selecting, or, as in most cases, devising testing instruments. The following guidelines should be helpful:

1. The test should be designed to elicit specific feelings, attitudes, etc. regarding particular music, musical styles, or music related activities.

2. Attitude measures should be nonthreatening. In most cases the anonymity of the individual respondent should be preserved. The testing situation should be such that respondents feel free to answer in an honest and forthright manner. This requires the development of items that will not arouse defense mechanisms.

3. Attitude measures should never be used as a basis for evaluation of student achievement. Attitude and achievement are entirely different matters.

4. Attitude measures, as with all tests, should be purposeful. The testmaker's and the respondents' time should not be wasted gathering data that will serve no purpose.

5. In analyzing data from attitude measures, the analysis should be as sophisticated as the purpose of the situation appears to warrant. Often mere knowledge of a group's preferences or likes and dislikes is sufficient. In certain research situations where an attitude measure serves as a dependent variable, considerably more sophisticated analyses may be warranted.

Other Measures of Attitude

While self-report measures clearly are the most common measures of attitude, several other techniques are useful and should be mentioned.

Observational techniques require using trained observers to record into discrete categories the behavior of individuals under study. The behaviors are recorded during specific timed intervals, and inferences about attitude are made after the behaviors are categorized. Ideally, the observations should be made unobtrusively, in other words, in such a way that the individuals being observed will not react to the observers. Persons trained to use carefully structured observation instruments can develop high inter-observer agreement, thus providing a measure of reliability for classifying behaviors into categories. However, drawing inferences regarding attitudes from such classification schemes still is a subjective task, and adequate evidence of the reliability of such inferences is not readily available.

Wapnick (1976) notes that a recent trend has focused on behavioral assessment of preference. A common procedure is to monitor listening time. The evaluator stages a situation in which the respondent has time to select, by some dial or push-button mechanism, the music to which he or she wishes to listen. The observer records, or has electronic devices to record, the amount of time the respondent spends listening to the various musical alternatives available. If the respondent spends the most time listening to an excerpt of rock music, the investigator may infer that rock is the preferred musical style.

Many other behavioral measures are potentially available to assess attitudes toward music: the number and type of records purchased, the number and type of concerts attended, the preferred radio stations, and so on. However, many other variables (e.g., cost, time, practicality) may influence the validity of such measures. Although Kuhn (1979) suggests that behavioral measures may offer added precision in measuring attitudes, he notes the need for studies on the relationship between self-report and behavioral measures and recommends that, when groups of subjects are to be tested, the only practical measures are of the self-report variety. The authors concur.

SUMMARY

Several neuropsychic constructs, each of which appears to reflect a significant affective component, are *attitude, interest, taste, preference, appreciation, sensitivity,* and *aesthetic response.*

Three published, standardized music tests include preference portions. A variety of self-report techniques for assessing attitudes exist. Besides the three "classic" techniques of consensual-location scaling, summated ratings, and cumulative scaling, other less formal self-report techniques include open-ended questions, paired comparisons, Q-sort, pictographic scales, semantic differential, adjective check lists, and Asmus's 9-AD technique. Other measures include observation of behaviors, for example, listening time, concert attendance, and record purchases.

Study Questions

1. Compare the descriptions of and/or listen to the Wing "appreciation" subtests, the *MAP* "musical sensitivity" subtest, and the *Indiana-Oregon Music Discrimination Test* and discuss the extent to which you think the respective test titles (appreciation, sensitivity, and discrimination) are appropriate for each of the tests. Are there other titles that might be appropriate for such tests?

2. Construct, administer, and analyze three attitude measures exemplifying the techniques suggested in the chapter and compare the problems in construction, administration, and analysis of data from the three measures.

3. Devise mood response tests for 10 musical excerpts using (a) the semantic differential technique and (b) Farnsworth's revision of the Hevner adjective circle. Administer the tests to a group of high school or college students and compare the data from the two tests in terms of usefulness with respect to understanding the group's mood responses to music.

REFERENCES

Abeles, H.F. Responses to music. In D.A. Hodges (Ed.), *Handbook of music psychology*. Lawrence, Kans.: National Association for Music Therapy, 1980.

Adams, G.S. Attitude Measurement. In H.E. Mitzel (Ed.), *Encyclopedia of educational research* (5th ed.) (Vol. 1). New York: Free Press, 1982.

Allport, G.W. Attitudes. In C. Murchison (Ed.), *Handbook of social psychology*. Worchester, Mass.: Clark University Press, 1935.

Asmus, E.P., Jr. The operational characteristics of adjectives as descriptors of musical affect (Doctoral dissertation, University of Kansas, 1979). *Dissertation Abstracts International*, 1980, *40*, 4289A–4290A.

Boyle, J.D. A study of the comparative validity of three published, standardised measures of music preference. *Psychology of Music*, 1982, Special Issue, 11–16.

Cook, S.W., & Selltiz, C. A multiple-indicator approach to attitude measurement. *Psychological Bulletin*, 1964, *62*, 36–55.

Dainow, E. Physical effects and motor response to music. *Journal of Research in Music Education*, 1977, *25*, 211–221.

Edwards, A.L. *Techniques of attitude scale construction*. New York: Appleton-Century-Crofts, 1957.

Farnsworth, P.R. A study of the Hevner Adjective Circle. *Journal of Aesthetics and Art Criticism*, 1954, *13*, 97–103.

Fishbein, M. Attitude and the prediction of behavior. In M. Fishbein (Ed.), *Readings in attitude theory and measurement*. New York: Wiley, 1967.

Ford, R.N. A rapid scoring procedure for scaling attitude questions. *Public Opinion Quarterly,* 1950, *14,* 507–532.

Gallagher, F.D. A study of the relationships between the Gordon Musical Aptitude Profile, the Colwell Music Achievement Tests, and the Indiana-Oregon Music Discrimination Test (Doctoral dissertation, Indiana University, 1971). *Dissertation Abstracts,* 1971, *32,* 2729A. (Order No. LC 71-26, 927).

Gordon, E. *Musical aptitude profile.* Boston: Houghton Mifflin, 1965.

Gordon, E. A three-year longitudinal predictive validity study of the Music Aptitude Profile. *Studies in the psychology of music* (Vol. 5). Iowa City: University of Iowa Press, 1967.

Guttman, L. A basis for scaling qualitative data. *American Sociological Review,* 1944, *9,* 139–150.

Guttman, L. The Cornell technique for scale and intensity analysis. *Educational and Psychological Measurement,* 1947, *7,* 247–280.

Guttman, L. The problem of attitude and opinion measurement. In S.A. Stouffer et al. (Eds.), *Measurement and prediction.* Princeton, N.J.: Princeton University Press, 1950.

Halsey, W.D. (Ed.). *Macmillan contemporary dictionary.* New York: Macmillan, 1979.

Heller, J.J. The effects of formal music training on the Wing musical intelligence scores (Doctoral dissertation, State University of Iowa, 1962). *Dissertation Abstracts,* 1963, *23,* 2936. (Order No. 63-927)

Hevner, K., & Landsbury, J. *Oregon Music Discrimination Test.* Chicago: C.H. Stoelting, 1934.

Kerlinger, F.N. *Foundations of behavioral research* (2nd ed.). New York: Holt, Rinehart & Winston, 1973.

Kiesler, C.A., Collins, E.E., & Miller, N. *Attitude change: Critical analysis of theoretical approaches.* New York: Wiley, 1969.

Krathwohl, D.R., Bloom, B.S., & Masia, B.B. *Taxonomy of educational objectives, handbook II: Affective domain.* New York: David McKay, 1964.

Kuhn, T.L. *Instrumentation for the measurement of attitudes.* Paper presented at the meeting of the College Music Society, San Antonio, October 1979.

Lemon, N. *Attitudes and their measurement.* New York: Wiley, 1973.

Lehman, P.R. *Tests and measurements in music.* Englewood Cliffs, N.J.: Prentice-Hall, 1968.

Likert, R. A technique for the measurement of attitudes. *Archives of Psychology,* 1932, No. 140, 5–53.

Long, N.H. *Indiana-Oregon music discrimination test.* Bloomington, Ind.: Midwest Music Tests, 1965.

Roeckle, C.A. Notes on music taste. *Missouri Journal of Research in Music Education,* 1968, *2* (2), 5–16.

Sampsell, S.A. *A study of the comparative validity of three measures of music sensitivity.* Unpublished master's thesis, Pennsylvania State University, 1980.

Thurstone, L.L., & Chave, E.J. *The measurement of attitudes.* Chicago: University of Chicago Press, 1929.

Wapnick, J. A review of research on attitude and preference. *Council for Research in Music Education,* 1976, *48,* 1–20.

Wing, H.D. *Standardised tests of musical intelligence,* (5th ed.). Windsor, England: National Foundation for Educational Research, 1961.

Wing, H.D. *Tests of musical ability and appreciation* (2nd ed.). *British Journal of Psychological Monograph Supplements* (Vol. 27). London: Cambridge University Press, 1968.

10

Other Useful Measurement Tools

In addition to measuring aptitude, ability, achievement, performance, and attitude, evaluators often desire other kinds of information, some of which do not require response to or production of musical stimuli. At other times they may be interested in obtaining information regarding students' musical behaviors without the students knowing that they are being observed or tested. Procedures for obtaining such evaluative data do not fit conveniently into any of the preceding chapters, although many evaluators find these types of data useful. The purpose of this chapter, therefore, is to examine these and some other data gathering tools and techniques.

WHAT MIGHT BE MEASURED?

Experience has shown that it is often useful for teachers and other evaluators to have some knowledge of students' general background regarding educational and musical opportunities. The authors have noted elsewhere that *opportunity* for experience with music is an important variable underlying musical ability and achievement (Radocy & Boyle, 1979, p. 280). Rainbow (1965), Phillips (1976), and Sergeant and Thatcher (1974) all have provided data to support the contention that an individual's home environment and general socioeconomic status have a strong relationship to an individual's success in music. Information regarding students' educational opportunities is relatively easy to obtain and may provide important input for educational decision making.

Another potentially useful type of information includes those nonmusical behaviors related to *general academic achievement.* The results of Rainbow's (1965), Whellams' (1970), and Hedden's (1982) studies of variables related to musical success revealed that general academic success was a significant predictor of musical success. A former colleague of one of the authors developed a highly successful string program in a public school district by recruiting high general academic achievers as string players. General academic achievement data usually are available in a variety of forms, both formal and informal, in many schools.

Besides knowledge of students' opportunities for general educational and musical experiences and their general academic achievement, a teacher or other evaluator can often avail him- or herself of other informal knowledge about students that may be useful. Knowledge of work habits, general motivation to succeed, and other less well-defined traits may be useful in understanding students' achievement or nonachievement. All music teachers at one time or another have students who appear to possess great potential for high level achievement yet who do not begin to "work up to their potential." Perhaps some understanding of the variables underlying the students' apparent lack of motivation could facilitate better guidance and motivation.

Another useful type of information is that gained from *observation. Systematic observation,* the purpose of which is to obtain objective data relevant to teacher and student activities and interactions in a learning environment, has become a major movement in education. Proponents of systematic observation argue that it is a relatively economical means for collecting accurate, objective, and quantifiable records of actual classroom behavior (Medley, 1982).

Techniques of *unobtrusive measurement,* developed by social scientists (Webb et al., 1966), also have potential use in education. The purpose of unobtrusive measurement is to avoid the problems of reactions to evaluators and/or testing instruments.

Systematic observation and unobtrusive measurement techniques have potential for gaining a wealth of information about students, teachers, and the general learning environment. However, both require trained observers and knowledge of procedures for structuring the observational data, but the potential of both techniques for understanding musical behavior warrants the time and effort expended in learning to use them.

Technology offers a variety of potential tools for evaluating musical behavior. Measures of psychophysiological responses to musical stimuli have met with varying interest and success. Criticisms of such measures have been harsh, particularly regarding methodology, reliability, and validity of many measures (Dainow, 1977), but there appears to be a renewed interest in psychophysiological data, particularly with the availability of computer data analysis. A number of other technological devices offer potential for measuring musical behaviors, and it appears that the technology has developed sufficiently to make the use of these tools economically and methodologically feasible. Certainly, the computer has great potential for measurement and evaluation of musical behaviors.

Another type of measurement especially important for music education evaluators concerns professional development. With the increasing concern for quality education in schools, there has been a growing need to identify quality teachers.

While many other variables possibly could be examined in a chapter labeled "other useful measurement tools," the above concerns warrant primary consideration, and the balance of the chapter examines their uses in the measurement and evaluation of musical behaviors. Specific topics include assessment of background, measures of nonmusical variables, unobtrusive measurement, systematic observation, electronic measures, and measurement of professional development.

BACKGROUND ASSESSMENT

"Background" is a catchall term that is much used in educational and other social science research. The most common procedure for obtaining background data on students has been by some type of self-report tool, usually a questionnaire. As noted in Chapter 9, self-report data are subject to certain limitations, but if the data sought are relevant to an educational function and are nonthreatening to the students, the self-report questionnaire is probably the most satisfactory method for gathering such data. Also, if the information is to be used for decisions regarding groups rather than individuals, it may be more appropriate to have the respondents answer the questionnaire anonymously, thus further reducing any potential threat to the individual respondents.

The need for teachers and other evaluators to solicit this information on their own, however, is decreasing, because many schools have data banks from which such data are readily accessible to qualified personnel having need for it. Before undertaking to develop a questionnaire to elicit background information, teachers or other evaluators should first consult their school records and, if the needed data are included, determine whether they may have access to them. Federal law states that information from school records is to be released only to qualified personnel who need it for use in counseling, and interpretations of "qualified personnel" may vary from one school district to another.

Whether a person undertakes to gather background data from existing school records or from an evaluator-developed questionnaire, there is the possibility that educators' unrestricted access to and use of certain data might be construed as an "invasion of privacy." If there is any question that the data might constitute an invasion of privacy, *informed consent* should be obtained from students and/or their parents. Informed consent involves making them aware of the "purpose for which the information is being obtained, the nature of the information sought, and the ways in which the information might be used" (Gronlund, 1981, p. 426).

When an evaluator must develop his or her own data-gathering instrument, the primary consideration should be the purpose for which the data are to be used. Data should be used only for the specific function for which they are gathered. Although the accessibility to machine-scored response sheets and computer analyses of data may tempt some evaluators and/or researchers to elicit more background data than are necessary for their primary purpose, only relevant and necessary data should be solicited.

The particular data to be gathered via a background questionnaire or "inventory" will vary with the purpose for which it is sought, but usually will include certain basic demographic data such as age, sex, and racial or ethnic group; however, if one has no need for those data, they should not be sought. A background inventory used by persons concerned with music education more likely will be designed to elicit information about musical experiences in the home, musical instruments available, listening opportunities, musical participation of parents and siblings, and listening habits of the various family members. Sometimes evaluators will be concerned with relative time spent in musical activities and other leisure time activities. Often background measures include sections designed to elicit the respondents' opinions regarding various types of music. The possible types of information that may be obtained via a background questionnaire are many, but relatively simple, single focus questionnaires appear to be more appropriate for most purposes.

Another consideration in the development of a background questionnaire is the age level of the students who are to answer it. Certainly questions must be written at a reading level that is appropriate to the respondents' age; furthermore, the questions must be limited to types of information that they are likely to have. Fourth-grade children are unlikely to know all of their parents' musical interests, experiences, or listening habits.

Finally, the background questionnaire must be designed with consideration of administrative efficiency and data analysis. Often this is a matter of selecting a closed structure or open structure format. The closed structure format usually involves having the respondent check the appropriate response from a list of alternatives included with the question. While this is a quick and convenient format, it sometimes forces the respondent to choose an answer that is not quite accurate. On the other hand, the open structure format takes more time to administer and sometimes may be subject to the limitations of a respondent's ability to state an answer clearly and accurately. Also, data from open structure questionnaires are more time-consuming and difficult to score and analyze. Perhaps the best solution is to use a closed structure format and allow space for qualification and/or explanation, if necessary. However, because a closed structure format often tends to suggest responses, the designer of the instrument must be particularly careful that the response alternatives for a given question include virtually all of the possible responses to a question. For questions for which this can not be ascertained, it may be necessary to use open structure responses.

The bottom line regarding the use of background questionnaires or inventories is that they have an educationally valid purpose. Unless this criterion is met, they are a waste of everyone's time.

ASSESSMENT OF RELEVANT NONMUSICAL BEHAVIORS

The primary concern here often is a matter of *what* to measure and the *uses* to be made of the data rather than *how* to measure. Specifically, which behaviors should be assessed and how will the data relevant to those behaviors facilitate making decisions regarding educational experiences and musical opportunities?

Besides general academic intelligence, Rainbow (1965) noted that three other nonmusical variables were significant predictors of musical success: home enrichment, interest in music, and socioeconomic background. A recent five-year study (Bloom, 1985) of some 120 "superstars," including Olympic swimmers, concert pianists, sculptors, tennis players, and world-class mathematicians and scientists, affirmed the strong influence of home and parents on the development of talent, irrespective of the particular activity or field of study. Finkelstein's (1982) review and synthesis of the literature related to family studies, socioeconomic status, and school achievement also lend support to Rainbow's, Phillips's (1976), and Sergeant and Thatcher's (1974) conclusions regarding the influence of home and socioeconomic status on musical ability.

Although many other nonmusical variables may be of interest to individual evaluators and researchers, it appears that the nonmusical variables of greatest potential use to individuals concerned with the development and evaluation of musical behaviors are those related to the home environment and experiences, general academic intelligence and achievement, socioeconomic status, and interest in music. As discussed above, information regarding home environment and experiences often is most easily obtained by means of a background questionnaire, and academic intelligence and/or achievement data usually are available through existing school records.

While some general information regarding socioeconomic status may be inferred from school records, several relatively easy to use indexes that provide more reliable and valid assessments have been devised. According to Hopkins and Stanley (1981, p. 454), the most widely used index of socioeconomic status is Warner, Meeker, and Eells's (1949) *Index of Status Characteristics*. It uses four factors—occupation, source of income, housing, and dwelling area—as bases for arriving at an index score. Each factor has seven levels and the rating on each factor is multiplied by a given weighting for that factor. The resulting index score is then converted into one of five social classes: upper, upper-middle, lower-middle, upper-lower, and lower-lower. Surprisingly, amount of education and amount of income are not factors in the scale; they are believed to be redundant with the other factors.

The other commonly used socioeconomic status measure is

Hollingshead's (Hollingshead & Redlich, 1957) *Two-factor Index of Social Position.* This index is particularly easy to use because it only requires information regarding occupation and education. These factors also have seven levels each and are multiplied by weighting constants to arrive at the index score. Occupational data are weighted almost twice as heavily as educational data: seven to four. Just as for the *Index of Status Characteristics,* the resultant index score is converted into one of five social class categories.

Although interest inventories can be constructed regarding virtually any aspect of music, music teachers often want to obtain some measure of students' interests in music vis-à-vis other activities or vocations. Relatively simple inventories can be constructed using Likert-type scales to obtain data regarding a *group's* relative interest in music and nonmusical activities. Usually data analyses from such inventories involve only descriptions of a group's mean ratings for the respective activities, although much more sophisticated analyses are possible if one has need for them. However, if one is concerned with obtaining some measure of an individual's interest in music vis-à-vis other activities or vocations, some particular standardized measures would be more useful, for example, *The Strong-Campbell Interest Inventory* (Campbell, 1974; Campbell, et al., 1974) and Kuder's (1966) three inventories, the *Kuder Preference Record-Vocational,* the *Kuder Occupational Interest Survey,* and the *Kuder General Interest Survey.*

The Strong–Campbell Interest Inventory was designed to distinguish individuals who were successful in a given occupation group from individuals in general, based on the assumption that interests typical of a given occupational group would differ from those of people in general and at least from those of any other occupational group. The inventory has 124 occupational scales that were empirically derived from actual scores for individuals from different occupations. Most of the inventory's items ask the respondent to indicate his or her preference for a listed activity by indicating whether he or she dislikes it, is indifferent to it, or likes it. The responses then are compared with norms for the responses of individuals in the respective occupation under consideration. Because an individual's responses to the inventory must be scored separately for each occupation, hand scoring is impractical. The manual provides normative scales for both male and female musicians.

The *Kuder Preference Record–Vocational* was Kuder's original measure; the *Kuder Occupational Interest Survey* appears to be an update of the original version, and the *Kuder General Interest Survey* was designed as a downward extension of the original instrument through sixth grade. Essentially the same procedures are used in all three instruments. The respondent selects the most liked and least liked of three activities listed in each item, thereby ranking the three activities. The Kuder inventories are designed to assess general areas of interest, and the scoring system determines the respondent's relative preference strengths on 10 distinct scales: outdoor, mechanical, computational, scientific, persuasive, artistic, literary, musical, social-service, and clerical. The Kuder scales may be hand-scored and are viewed by Hopkins and Stanley (1981, p. 430) as more useful at the high school level than at the college level.

UNOBTRUSIVE MEASUREMENT

The intent of unobtrusive measurement is to assess situations and/or individuals without the risk of evoking responses that may be characteristic only in an assessment situation. Anderson et al. (1975, p. 454) note that traditional evaluative measures (usually tests) used to assess instructional and research programs may distort the characteristic behavior that students would ordinarily display in the learning situation. Webb et al. (1966, pp. 13–21) cite four types of reactions that may be reduced or avoided by use of unobtrusive measures: (a) the guinea pig effect—awareness of being tested, (b) role selection on the part of the test taker, (c) measurement itself as a change agent, and (d) response sets or biases of test takers.

There are three general types of unobtrusive measures: (a) physical traces, (b) archival records, and (c) observations. All essentially involve observation, but the first two types do not involve direct observation of human subjects; rather, they are concerned with examining evidence of human subjects' past activities. Unobtrusive measurement by means of physical traces literally involves examination of wear and tear on materials used or other physical objects. Counting the number of instruments left overnight in a school instrument storage room may provide some indication of how much home practice students are doing. Archival records are particularly useful in program evaluation, but they also are useful in evaluating individuals' behaviors.

Records of class attendance, completed assignments, books or other materials checked out, and records of extra rehearsals attended are examples of records that may be useful in evaluating individuals. Records of materials requisitioned by teachers, lesson plan notebooks, copies and recordings of concert programs, enrollments in elective music courses, and enrollment trends in elective music courses vis-à-vis other elective courses may be useful to program evaluators.

For observations to be unobtrusive, the individuals being observed either must be unaware that they are being observed, or, if an observer or observing instrument such as a video monitor is apparent to those being observed, they must be unaware that the intent of the observer or observing instrument is to evaluate them. Both situations obviously involve a certain amount of deception, thus possibly creating both moral and ethical problems. Few teachers welcome a principal's unobtrusive monitoring of their classroom through a school's intercom system!

Nevertheless, there may be times when evaluators do not wish to risk creating reactive effects to evaluation, and in these instances unobtrusive measurement techniques may be warranted. At most, in summative evaluation procedures, unobtrusive measurement only should be used to supplement more traditional evaluative measures, and, "as with more conventional measures, a good case must be made for the relevance and relative unambiguity of meaning of any unobtrusive measures used" (Anderson et al., 1975, p. 455). Of course, sensitive educators constantly are aware of students' expressions and body language, which may provide evaluative clues, even though the students are not especially aware that such behaviors may be serving an evaluative function.

SYSTEMATIC OBSERVATION

"Systematic observation" refers to "observations of classroom behavior made by a trained observer who records the behaviors according to an observation system. An 'observation system,' in turn, is a scheme that specifies both the events that the observer is to record and the procedure to be used in recording them" (Medley, 1982, p. 1842). Medley is one of the foremost authorities on systematic observation, and much of the following discussion is based on his excellent article. Readers interested in overviews of most of the better known observation systems should also see Medley and Mitzel (1963), Simon and Boyer (1967; 1970), and Stallings (1977).

Medley clearly demarcates between systematic observation and three other methodologies used in observation of classroom behavior: ecological observations, ethnographic observations, and observation systems for rating teacher effectiveness. A basic distinction between systematic observation and ecological observation is that the categories of behavior to be observed in systematic observation are specified a priori, whereas those for the ecological observer are defined a posteriori; that is, after the records have been made. A priori categories tend to limit and focus observations, while the ecological observer attempts to make a complete and detailed record of everything that happens during a visit. Medley argues that ecological observation seems most useful as a research tool seeking to discover new knowledge rather than for verifying knowledge previously discovered.

Ethnographic observation tends to focus on unique aspects of the classroom, whereas systematic observation tends to ignore the unique and focus on commonalities among classrooms. Ethnographic observation also tries to capitalize on the observer's unique sensitivities; in contrast, systematic observation considers objectivity and interchangeability of observers essential. Ethnographic observation also is viewed as a research tool for use in the context of discovery as opposed to systematic observation, which is used primarily in the context of verification.

A basic difference between a systematic observation system and a teacher rating system is that the former yields a record of *behavior* while the latter produces a record of the rater's *judgments* regarding the degree to which each of a set number of teacher behaviors or other characteristics was manifest during the observation period. "Characteristics" often are highly inferential psychological constructs that are difficult to define precisely; behaviors recorded by means of a systematic observation procedure are clearly observable, thus requiring low inference interpretation by the observer. Medley argues that teacher rating scales also should be low inference, but it appears that in reality many are not. Perhaps this is one reason why teacher evaluation is beset by so many difficulties.

There are three basic types of systematic observation systems in general use: sign systems, category systems, and multiple-coding systems. "A sign system is in essence a list of events or kinds of events selected because the occurrence of any one of them in a classroom is considered relevant or significant (hence the term 'sign')" (Medley, p. 1842). Each event in the list is a "sign," and the recorder must record which of the signs he or she sees during a "period,"—a brief, specified (usually three to five minute) time interval. During a single visit to the classroom, a recorder may record for several periods. Each sign or event refers to a single event, which may be either teacher or student behavior.

A category system "consists of a mutually exclusive, all-inclusive set of categories for classifying classroom events" (Medley, p. 1844). A category system allows the observer to record events only in a certain domain, for example, verbal behavior, nonverbal behavior, or musical performance behavior. A simple and somewhat typical verbal category system is one devised by Withall (1949). Each verbal event in a classroom must be classified into one of five categories: (a) *pupil-supportive*—expressions of positive affect or considerations for pupils; (b) *problem-structuring*—utterances having to do with the substantive content of instruction; (c) *neutral*—utterances unclassified in any other category; (d) *directing*—orders, commands, and so on; and (e) *reproving*—expressions of negative affect or disapproval.

A multiple-coding system allows the recording of a single event in two or more categories. Medley notes that multiple coding may involve so many discriminations that the recorder will be unable to record every event that occurs during a given observation period; however, he suggests that the loss in terms of sampling of events may be compensated for by the better description of the events observed.

Medley views three basic problems in the use of systematic observation methods: (a) collecting accurate records of behavior, (b) ensuring that the behavioral samples are representative of what happens in the classroom at other times, and (c) deriving measurements from the record that faithfully describe the behaviors recorded. The primary means by which data are collected is to send an observer into a classroom with a paper-and-pencil form called an "observation schedule" to record the behaviors as they occur. Other procedures involve an indirect approach, that is, an audio or video tape is made of the classroom for coding later by either a trained observer or some mechanical recorder. Medley suggests that the direct approach is the more reliable.

Problems related to ensuring a representative behavioral sample essentially are matters of having adequate samples of behavior and valid recordings of the behaviors. Different types of systems (signs, category, and multiple coding) have different coding problems; the amount of training required to use a system varies both with the system's type and complexity.

The simplest and most commonly used procedure for quantifying records is to determine the total frequency of occurrence of each event in a record together with a grand total frequency of all events recorded. Each individual frequency is then converted to a proportion (or percent) of the total. The resultant proportions reflect the relative rate of each occurrence in a given classroom.

The earliest applications of systematic observation to music classrooms initially were limited to recording verbal behaviors, but subsequent researchers and evaluators either adapted existing observation systems or developed their own for use in various music-learning settings, for example, rehearsal situations (Erbes, 1972/1973; Ervin, 1975/1976), instrumental classes (Snapp, 1967; Reynolds, 1974), and the applied music studio (Gipson, 1978). Perhaps the most extensive and significant applications, however, have been made by Clifford Madsen, Professor of Music Education at Florida State University, and his students, colleagues, and former students. His guidelines for use of systematic observation are set forth in two sources, Madsen and Madsen (1974) and Madsen and Yarbrough (1980). Both are essential reading for individuals concerned with applying systematic observation procedures to the music classroom or rehearsal.

"Through systematic observation of music classes and rehearsals one may begin to understand the relationships between characteristics of teacher/conductor behavior and student attentiveness, performance, and attitude" (Madsen & Yarbrough, 1980, p. 41). Madsen and Yarbrough view systematic observation as a basic tool for understanding and improving instruction. For their purposes, observations in music classrooms should focus on teacher approval/disapproval behavior, mistakes of reinforcement, magnitude or intensity of reinforcement, and student appropriate/inappropriate behavior. In performance situations, they recommend that observation systems focus on teacher approval/disapproval, mistakes of reinforcement, performance time versus nonperformance time, conductor overt behaviors, and student attentiveness. In addition, they summarize guidelines for using systematic observation procedures and provide examples of observation schedules for observing and recording (a) student behavior in a regular classroom, (b) teacher behavior in a regular classroom, (c) teacher and student behaviors in an elementary music class, (d) teacher and student behaviors in a choral rehearsal, (e) teacher and student behaviors in an instrumental rehearsal, and (f) music conductor behavior.

ELECTRONIC MEASURES

"Electronic" is used here in a broad sense to include any measurement tool that uses electrical energy in recording human behavior for testing, measurement, or evaluation purposes. In this sense, a tape recorder may be considered an electronic measuring instrument if it is used to record musical behaviors for evaluative purposes.

Two basic types of electronic measurement tools are examined: (a) bioelectrical measures of various physiological rates in response to musical stimuli and (b) equipment used to record musical performance and other cognitive and psychomotor responses to musical stimuli. The bioelectrical measures are of particular interest to music psychologists concerned with *understanding* musical response and have little or no utilitarian value for evaluation of educational programs. The equipment used to record musical performance and other cognitive and psychomotor responses, however, has particular potential for evaluation of musical behaviors in academic settings.

Bioelectrical Measurement

Electronic measurement of response to music is not new. Researchers have measured a variety of bioelectrical responses to music for nearly 100 years,[*] but as noted previously, the reliability and validity of many of the measurements (and the research based on these measurements) have been questionable. However, with what Stern, Ray, and Davis (1980, p. 10) view as a "revolution in instrumentation," it appears that tools capable of providing reliable and valid measurements of many physiological variables are now available.

Bioelectrical measurement is useful in psychophysiological research, the purpose of which is to examine interactions between physiological responses and psychological responses. The underlying hypothesis of many of the music studies using such

---

[*]See Radocy and Boyle (1979, pp. 190–195) for a brief chronology of such research.

measurements is that the frequency and/or amplitudes of various bodily processes controlled by the autonomic nervous system reflect affective response to music. However, as noted above, Dainow (1977) criticizes much of the research because of measurement and other methodological problems. Perhaps the quality of research will improve with improved measurement techniques.

Stern, Ray, and Davis (1980) attribute the "revolution in instrumentation" to the introduction of the *integrated circuit* and the digital computer designed for research in small laboratories. They maintain that inexpensive biofeedback equipment is available today that performs integrations and filtering functions which, as recently as 1970, would have cost 10 to 20 times the price. They also state that today's commercially available equipment is excellent and reliable, thus allowing the researcher to worry less about electronic problems and to devote more time to theoretical and empirical work related to the interaction of psychological and physiological factors.

A brief overview of the types of physiological measures that might be useful to a researcher interested in the interactions of physiological and psychological response to music follows. Music psychologists interested in pursuing research of this nature, however, should read Stern, Ray, and Davis's excellent and very readable textbook (1980), particularly because of its clear discussions of (a) principles of psychophysiology, (b) safety and ethics in psychophysiological measurement, and (c) the equipment and procedures used in psychophysiological recording.

The primary data-gathering procedure used in psychophysiological measurement entails using a polygraph, most of which are capable of recording the rates of several physiological events simultaneously. Electrodes are attached to the subject's skin in the appropriate places for the specific variables being measured; the physiological energy is converted to electrical potential by means of transducers and is then transmitted to the polygraph, where the signal goes through a coupler or signal conditioner, a preamplifier, and a main or power amplifier before output to graphic representation.

Besides the various physiological rates under control of the autonomic nervous system,* a commonly used psychophysiologi-

---

*The autonomic nervous system includes those "ganglia, nerves, and plexuses which regulate activities of the viscera, heart, blood vessels, smooth muscle, and glands" (Stern, Ray, & Davis, 1980, p. 227).

cal measure is *electroencephalography* (EEG), a technique for recording variations in brain wave rhythms. Five brain wave rhythms have been identified, primarily on the basis of frequency and amplitude, and are labeled alpha (8–13 Hz), beta (14–30 Hz), gamma (31–50 Hz), delta (0.5–4 Hz), and theta (5–7 Hz). Although EEG data are useful to neurologists for a variety of purposes, the waves of most interest in psychophysiological research are beta waves, which generally are considered measures of cortical activity, and alpha waves, which may indicate a relatively relaxed state.*

Electromyography (EMG) is a measure of muscle tension, and it has been demonstrated that muscle tension can be altered by music (Sears, 1960).

Two techniques for measuring eye response are *pupillography*, which measures pupil size, and *electrooculography*, which measures eye movement. The former is used as an indication of arousal, while eye movements are studied in relation to reading behaviors.

Some common psychophysiological measures are those related to the cardiovascular system: *heart rate, blood pressure,* and *plethysomography*, a measure of blood volume. As with other psychophysiological measures, musical stimuli can easily evoke changes in the rates or amplitudes of these measures, but what these changes mean is not clear.

Other physiological measures of interest in psychophysiological research include *respiratory* (breathing rate and amplitude), *electrogastrographic* (gastrointestinal responses), and *electrodermic* activity (skin responses, formerly called psychogalvanic reflex or galvanic skin response).

Uses of psychophysiological measures are not for the amateur, and music psychologists interested in their use would be wise to engage the assistance of trained technicians. Nevertheless, with technological advances of the past decade, they offer other potentially valuable tools for measuring and understanding response to music.

Other Electronic Measures

In contrast to the bioelectrical measures, which by and large record *covert* behaviors that might otherwise be difficult (or in

---

*Readers interested in a review of EEG research and music should consult Wagner's (1975) review of the literature.

some cases impossible) to record and quantify, the other electronic measures record *overt* behaviors. Virtually all of these behaviors are observable without the aid of the electronic devices, but the electronic devices essentially provide means for improving the accuracy of observation and, in many cases, a permanent record of the behavior so that it may be examined and analyzed further. In addition, some of the electronic devices do much more than record responses: they analyze, interpret in relation to norms, and provide feedback or reports of the analysis and interpretation.

At best, the present discussion provides only a cursory examination of selected tools; nevertheless, it is included as a reminder of some obvious and under-used tools and in the hope that it may pique interest in further exploration by others.

Perhaps the most basic electronic tool for evaluation of musical behavior is the tape recorder. Although it may be (at least, should be) a common teaching and evaluation tool in every music classroom and rehearsal hall today, it is a relatively new aid, especially when considered in relation to the history of music. It can provide teachers and students an opportunity to hear, critique, and evaluate their performances. It can provide supervisors and evaluators with a record of performance and classroom activities. It is a useful tool for both unobtrusive and systematic observations, at least for the audible activities of a classroom or other learning environment. Further, it may be used to record performances or other audible responses for subsequent and repeated analyses. In short, the tape recorder is one of the most useful tools available to individuals concerned with evaluation of musical behaviors.

Video tape recorders also have proven to be extremely valuable. They have become a standard tool for evaluating conducting and instructional behaviors in teacher education programs. They also are useful for indirect unobtrusive and systematic observations, and many marching band directors regularly videotape their students' performances. Just as tape recorders, video tape recorders are readily available in most schools, and the combined aural and visual feedback they provide constitutes one of the most valuable devices for improvement of instruction that is available today.

Electronic tuners with built-in pitchmeters constitute another useful measurement tool. They are available from several different manufacturers. Besides providing a standard reference frequency, most can indicate in cents how far a performed frequency deviates from the standard. Their uses in measurement are limited to isolated sustained tones, but this type of information can be useful, especially in developing intonation for instrumentalists.

Several electronic measuring tools used in speech analysis also may be useful in analyzing musical sounds. Hollien (1981) describes several such instruments, including the oscilloscope, a fundamental frequency analysis system, "instantaneous" spectrometers, long-term spectral analysis equipment, and sound level meters. The potential uses of these tools appear to be most appropriate for psychophysiological research, but each of the tools could be useful in providing specialized evaluative feedback in certain instructional situations.

Another recently developed tool for measuring pitch responses is the *Pitch Master* developed by Temporal Acuity Products, Inc. Designed primarily as a teaching tool, it provides a singer or instrumentalist with visual, aural, and quantitative feedback regarding the accuracy of a melody in relation to a prerecorded model. The score essentially is based on one point for every .25 second that the performance is in tune, that is, within preset tolerance limits. The *Pitch Master* appears to have great potential both as a teaching tool and as a tool for melodic pitch assessment in a "real time" performance situation.

The *Tap Master* is another teaching machine with potential as a measurement tool. Designed as an individualized instructional tool for teaching rhythm reading, it provides a score for the number of notes tapped correctly in a rhythm exercise performed by tapping a response button on the machine. Its use in evaluation is limited to measurement of notated rhythm pattern performance, but it does provide objective and reliable data.

The electronic tool that is potentially most useful for measurement and evaluation of musical behaviors is the computer, but to date its primary use has been for scoring and analyzing test data. Gronlund (1981, p. 417) maintains that "the type of feedback made possible by the computer has been a major factor in the trend toward using test results to improve learning and instruction."

Grayson (1982) notes that computer-aided testing is now possible with personal, mini, and central or mainframe computers. Three particular uses have been made of computers in test construction and administration: (a) test construction from computer-based item pools, (b) administration of individual tests, and (c) tailoring of tests to match the abilities of individual test takers.

Although the pitch subtest of the *Seashore Measures of Musical Talents* (McCarthy, 1984) and the *Drake Musical Aptitude Tests* (Robinson, 1985) have been adapted for administration on an Apple personal computer, computers have yet to be used for general aptitude or achievement testing; rather, their use other than for data analysis and management has been almost exclusively in conjunction with computer-based instruction where knowledge of results is an integral part of the instructional program. Since sound generation capabilities have been incorporated into computer systems, the potential for individualized training in aural and aural–visual skills has been greatly increased. Computers now can provide musical sound, visual graphics (musical notation), and visual–verbal stimuli for use in instruction and testing. A cursory review of available software suggests that many ear-training and aural–visual discrimination programs are presently available for personal computers as well as the larger systems, and ongoing testing and evaluation is an integral part of most programs. What makes the computer so valuable in such programs is the immediacy of feedback it provides and the records of responses it makes and uses in guiding subsequent learning experiences.

Another use of computers has been in the evaluation of performance. Although some of the technical problems related to error tolerances need refining, Peters' (1974) feasibility study revealed that "presenting and judging an instrumental performance for pitch and rhythm accuracy is feasible for computer-assisted instruction" (p. 160). Some of Peters' subsequent work in the computer-based laboratory at the University of Illinois, in cooperation with the Center for Music Research at Florida State University, has resulted in the development of a "pitch extractor" that will enable the computer to analyze musical performance input for pitch accuracy. Not yet commercially available, the pitch extractor has the potential of rendering objective measurements of performances heretofore possible only through subjective means. Even without the availability of pitch extractors, the computer is a powerful tool for many testing purposes, including (a) test scoring, data analysis, and data interpretation relative to programmed norms, (b) test item analysis, (c) test item pool generation, (d) administration of individual tests, (e) tailoring tests to match individual test takers' abilities, and (f) providing immediate evaluative feedback in computer-based instructional programs. It can present and score immediately most traditional verbal objective test item types. In addition, it can provide aural, notational, and combined aural–notational stimuli for assessment of responses in a wide variety of formats.

In conclusion, the computer and other electronic devices already have become useful tools in the measurement and evaluation of musical behaviors, but their full potential is yet to be realized.

MEASURES OF PROFESSIONAL DEVELOPMENT

Two final measurement tools will be mentioned because they serve important functions related to the professional development of music educators: the *Graduate Record Examination, Subject Test—Music* (Educational Testing Service, 1951-) and the *National Teacher Examinations, Specialty Area—Music Education* (Educational Testing Service, 1979; 1985).

The GRE advanced music test is used primarily as a tool for making admission and placement decisions relative to graduate study in music. Primary emphasis is on music history and literature, although there are also a number of theory-related questions concerning music fundamentals, instrumentation, and orchestration. The tests must be scored by the Educational Testing Service and the results are made available to the institutions and students involved. Lehman (1968, p. 64) claims that as a measure of the scholarly aspects of music and, to a limited extent, the aural aspects of music theory, the GRE music test is unequalled. When used as an admissions tool, scores on the GRE music test usually are considered along with several other measures of potential for graduate study, including the GRE aptitude measure, undergraduate grade-point averages, auditions, and letters of reference.

The music education examination of the *National Teacher Examination* is designed to assess prospective teachers' knowledge of all phases of music teaching from the elementary school through the high school. It includes questions about general music instruction, orchestra, band, and choir, and Lehman (1968, p. 67) maintains that its breadth is its greatest limitation. He questions the reality of expecting all teachers to be competent in all phases of music instruction and argues that questions regarding the instrumentation of a high school band contribute little to assessing the qualifications of an elementary general music teacher. Lehman maintains that a test of this nature can be valid only to the extent that prospective teachers are expected to teach all phases of music at all levels. Lehman also questions the "correct" response for several items, suggesting that there are other "correct" ways of accomplishing the same task. While Lehman's criticisms were based on an earlier edition of the test, one author's recent examination of the current edition of the test revealed that Lehman's views are still valid. Even with these shortcomings, the test may provide useful information for those states and school districts that have not developed their own teacher competency tests for specialized subject areas such as music. However, to use the test as the sole means for evaluating music teacher knowledge and skills appears unwarranted.

SUMMARY

A variety of measurement tools have potential for evaluation of musical behaviors. Measures of student background are useful for eliciting information regarding students' home musical environment and opportunities for musical experience outside of school. Selected nonmusical variables such as general academic achievement, socioeconomic status, home environment, and interest in music also may be useful in predicting success in music.

Unobtrusive measurement and systematic observation techniques have respective potentials as a nonreactive measurement tool and method for objectively recording actual student and teacher behaviors in a classroom and rehearsal situation.

Various types of electronic measures, including bioelectrical measures of covert physiological rates, the tape recorder, the videotape recorder, the *Pitch Master*, the *Tap Master*, and the computer (with its many applications), have potential utilities that are only beginning to be realized.

Two measures of professional development, the *GRE, Subject Test—Music* and the music education section of the *NTE*, may have high technical quality, but should be used with caution and in conjunction with other measures.

Study Questions

1. Design an instrument for assessing the musical background of (a) beginning instrumental music students, (b) secondary school music appreciation students, and (c) adult musicians interested in singing in a university/community choir.

2. List the nonmusical variables which might be useful as adjuncts to auditions in selecting students for a highly selective high school choral group. Compare the types of information that each variable will provide and the usefulness of the information to the conductor of the group.

3. List and describe some potential unobtrusive measures useful for assessing the musical achievement and attitudes of (a) elementary school general music students, (b) junior and senior high school performance groups, and (c) college-level applied music students.

4. Select three classroom behaviors to study, design a simple observation coding system for recording occurrences of the behaviors, and use the system to observe a music classroom. Tally and analyze the data from the observation instrument and discuss the conclusions that might be drawn from it.

5. Discuss the feasibility and potential problems of using the computer and various other electronic devices in measuring musical behaviors.

REFERENCES

Anderson, S.B., Ball, S., Murphy, R.T., & Associates. *Encyclopedia of educational evaluation*. San Francisco, Calif.: Jossey-Bass, 1975.

Bloom, B.S. (Ed.). *Developing talent in young people*. New York: Ballantine Books, 1985.

Campbell, D.P. *Manual for the Strong-Campbell Interest Inventory*. Stanford, Calif.: Stanford University Press, 1974.

Campbell, D.P., Crichton, L., Hansen, J.L., & Webber, P. A new edition of the SVIB: The Strong-Campbell Interest Inventory. *Measurement and Evaluation in Guidance*, 1974, 7, 92–95.

Dainow, E. Physical effects and motor responses to music. *Journal of Research in Music Education*, 1977, 25, 211–221.

Educational Testing Service *Graduate Record Examination, Subject Test—Music*. Princeton, N.J.: ETS., 1951–

Educational Testing Service *National Teacher Examinations, Specialty Area—Music Education*. Princeton, N.J.: ETS., 1979, 1985.

Erbes, R.L. The development of an observational system for the analysis of interaction in the rehearsal of musical organizations (Doctoral dissertation, University of Illinois, 1972). *Dissertation Abstracts International*, 1973, 34, 806A. (Order No. 73-17,197)

Ervin, C.L. Systematic observation and evaluation of conductor effectiveness (Doctoral dissertation, West Virginia University, 1975). *Dissertation Abstracts International*, 37, 1976, 7034A. (Order No. 76-11,878)

Finkelstein, B. Family studies. In H.E. Mitzel (Ed.), *Encyclopedia of educational research* (5th ed.) (Vol. 2). New York: Free Press, 1982.

Gipson, R.C. An observational analysis of wind instrument private lessons (Doctoral dissertation, The Pennsylvania State University, 1978). *Dissertation Abstracts International*, 1978, 39, 2118–2119A. (Order No. 78-18,757)

Grayson, L.P. New technologies in education. In H.E. Mitzel (Ed.), *Encyclopedia of educational research* (5th ed.) (Vol. 3). New York: Free Press, 1982.

Gronlund, N.E. *Measurement and evaluation in teaching* (4th ed.). New York: Macmillan, 1981.

Hedden, S.K. Prediction of music achievement in the elementary school. *Journal of Research in Music Education,* 1982, *30,* 61–68.

Hollien, H. Analog instrumentation for acoustic speech analysis. In J.K. Dorby, Jr., (Ed.), *Speech evaluation in psychiatry.* New York: Grune & Stratton, 1981.

Hollingshead, A.B., & Redlich, F.C. *Two-factor index of social position.* New Haven, Conn.: The authors, 1957.

Hopkins, K.D., & Stanley, J.C. *Educational and psychological measurement* (6th ed.). Englewood Cliffs, N.J.: Prentice-Hall, 1981.

Kuder, G.F. *Kuder Occupational Interest Survey: General manual.* Chicago: Science Research Associates, 1966.

Lehman, P.R. *Test and measurements in music.* Englewood Cliffs, N.J.: Prentice-Hall, 1968.

McCarthy, J.F. The pitch test. *Creative Computing,* 1984, *10*(3), 211–212; 216–217.

Madsen, C.H., Jr., & Madsen, C.K. *Teaching/discipline: A positive approach for educational development* (expanded 2nd ed.). Boston: Allyn and Bacon, 1974.

Madsen, C.K., & Yarbrough, C. *Competency-based music education.* Englewood Cliffs, N.J.: Prentice-Hall, 1980.

Medley, D.M. Systematic observation. In H.E. Mitzel (Ed.), *Encyclopedia of educational research* (5th ed.) (Vol. 4). New York: Free Press, 1982.

Medley, D.M., & Mitzel, H.E. Measuring classroom behavior by systematic observation. In N.L. Gage (Ed.), *Handbook of research on teaching.* Chicago: Rand McNally, 1963.

Peters, G.D. Feasibility of computer-assisted instruction for instrumental music education (Unpublished doctoral dissertation, University of Illinois at Urbana-Champaign, 1974). *Dissertation Abstracts International,* 1974, *35,* 1478–1479A. (Order No. 74-14,598)

Phillips, D. An investigation of the relationship between musicality and intelligence. *Psychology of Music,* 1976, *4* (2), 16–31.

Radocy, R.E., & Boyle, J.D. *Psychological foundations of musical behavior.* Springfield, Ill.: C.C. Thomas, 1979.

Rainbow, E.L. A pilot study to investigate the constructs of musical aptitude. *Journal of Research in Music Education,* 1965, *13,* 3–14.

Reynolds, K. Modification of the observational system for instructional analysis focusing on appraisal behaviors of music teachers in small performance classes (Unpublished doctoral dissertation, Ohio State University, 1974). *Dissertation Abstracts International,* 1974, *35,* 3040A. (Order No. 74-24,390)

Robinson, R.L. *Microcomputer adaptation of the Drake Musical Aptitude Tests.* Gainesville: University of Florida, 1985.

Sears, W.W. A study of some effects of music upon muscle tension as evidenced by electromyographic recordings (Doctoral dissertation, University of Kansas, 1960). *Dissertation Abstracts,* 1960, *21,* 208. (University Microfilms No. 60-2316).

Sergeant, D., & Thatcher, G. Intelligence, social status, musical abilities. *Psychology of Music,* 1974, *2* (2), 32–57.

Simon, A., & Boyer, E.G. (Eds.). *Mirrors for behavior: An anthology of observation instruments.* Philadelphia: Research for Better Schools, Inc., 1967; 1970.

Snapp, D.W. *A study of the accumulative musical and verbal behavior of teachers* and students in fifth grade instrumental music classes. Unpublished master's thesis, Ohio State University, 1967.

Stallings, J.A. *Learning to look: A handbook on classroom observation and teaching models.* Belmont, Calif.: Wadsworth, 1977.

Stern, R.M., Ray, W.J., & Davis, C.M. *Psychophysiological recording.* New York: Oxford University Press, 1980.

Wagner, M.J., Brainwaves and biofeedback, A brief history—Implications for music research. *Journal of Music Therapy,* 1975, *12*(2), 46–58.

Warner, W.L., Meeker, M., & Eells, K. *Social class in America.* Chicago: Science Research Associates, 1949.

Webb, E.J., Campbell, D.T., Schwartz, R.D., & Sechrest, L. *Unobtrusive measures: Nonreactive research in the social sciences.* Chicago: Rand McNally, 1966.

Whellams, F.S. The relative efficiency of aural–musical and non-musical tests as predictors of achievement in instrumental music. *Council for Research in Music Education,* 1970, *21*, 15–21.

Withall, J. The development of a technique for the measurement of social-emotional climate in classrooms. *Journal of Experimental Education,* 1949, *17*, 347–361.

11

Test Administration and Scoring

A carefully planned and meticulously constructed test may become a disappointment if it is not appropriately administered and scored. Improper administration and scoring increases the proportion of error variance in overall test variance and thereby reduces reliability. To a large extent test administration and scoring are a matter of common sense, but there is value in systematically reviewing certain steps that can make a difference between successful and unsuccessful testing. This chapter considers administering group tests and individual tests, including auditions. Test anxiety and motivation receive attention. Younger and exceptional children's testing needs are considered, as are requirements for different scoring schemes. While much of the chapter is based on the authors' experience, Clemans's (1971) comprehensive formal treatment of test administration is acknowledged.

ADMINISTERING GROUP TESTS

Virtually all paper-and-pencil measures commonly used in assessing musical behavior are intended for administration to groups rather than individuals. Common examples include classroom tests and standardized aptitude and achievement measures. Whether the testing group is an intact group that normally is together at the particular time and place or is a group especially comprised for the occasion, advance planning for administration is essential.

There should be a comfortable testing environment. While it may seem obvious, a comfortable environment includes adequate lighting, sufficient seating, freedom from background noise, comfortable temperature, and, for many music tests, a sound system of satisfactory quality. Given the zealous energy conservation efforts and inadequately insulated buildings of some educational institutions, there may be little the test administrator can do about creature comforts, but the available facilities should be used as advantageously as possible.

Adequate time, including time for distributing and receiving papers, must be allowed for the test. Many published standardized tests have rigid time allocations that, in the interest of adhering to conditions under which the test was standardized and intended for administration, should be observed. Teacher-made tests must allow a "reasonable" amount of time for a majority of the group to complete the test. Only the teacher can determine just what, based on the test content and the students' abilities, is "reasonable."

There is a distinction between speeded and power tests. A *speeded* test is intended to assess examinees' abilities to work rapidly; how much can be done in a given amount of time is important. Individual items are rather simple. Tests involving key signature recognition or construction, or writing intervals might exemplify speeded tests. A *power* test is intended to assess examinees' abilities to answer questions, provide information, and solve problems regardless (theoretically) of how much time is required.* Realistically, an element of "speededness" exists in any power test that must be completed within a designated amount of time, such as a class period. In music, a speeded test of notation skills might be appropriate at certain stages of students' development, but generally a power test is more appropriate in most assessments of musical achievement, so the expectation is that adequate time will be allowed. Within any test requiring listening there is the speededness inherent in the time required for hearing musical examples: Music is a time-based art form.

Test takers should have adequate room to write, place any

---

*In this context "power" has no connection with the "power" of an inferential statistical test of a null hypothesis, which is that test's ability to enable an experimenter to reject a null hypothesis when it is in fact false.

answer sheets or completed forms, and keep unessential materials out of the way. An "open book" test may require extra space for the authorized books and class notes. Students in wheelchairs may require extra space, and students who require the use of a reader or clerk due to some sensory or physical impairment need to be located so they can work without disturbing other students. Students ideally should be far enough from each other that they can resist temptation to look at other students' papers.

Cheating can be a problem at all educational levels. Flagrant copying of answers from another student's paper can occur, as can far more subtle forms of unauthorized references to answers, such as writing on shirt cuffs, bottoms of shoes, facial tissues, edges of papers protruding from notebooks, and so on. In addition to any moral and educational damage resulting from cheating, test reliability and score interpretation are affected. Active proctoring, that is, constant observation of the test takers may discourage cheating. This means walking quietly around the room, standing behind various groups of people for a while, and continually shifting attention around the room, *not* sitting at a desk and reading. Extra proctors should be employed for large groups.

The testing room should be free of any chalkboard writing or bulletin board displays that might provide clues for answering test questions. For example, in a general music class, a colorful poster of orchestral instruments might give extra help on a test requiring knowledge of symphonic instrumentation to those students who can view the poster!

Clear directions are essential. With young students, step-by-step details are necessary; this is discussed below. All examinees need detailed directions for particular item sections as well as general instructions. Standardized tests generally have instructions that are to be read verbatim. Among the things that examinees need to know are where to place their name and in what format, where to place any identification number or descriptive information, whether they are subject to any guessing formula, whether there is more than one "right" answer for any item, whether essay items should begin on new pages, what writing implements (pencil, black ink, blue ink) are acceptable, whether calculators are allowed (they are useful in musical acoustics and psychoacoustics), whether they may write on the test form, and what to do with the test form when they are finished.

When machine-scorable answer sheets are employed, special attention to what kind of pencil to use, the importance of erasing thoroughly any changed answer, the need to avoid stray marks on the answer sheet, and the proper placement of name and/or number, including blackening any required spaces, is necessary. It usually is wise to provide pencils.

Although paper shuffling may seem trivial, considerable time can be wasted in distributing test papers and/or answer sheets. Freshly printed or duplicated papers may stick together; advance shuffling and splitting of a stack of papers may save time.

Modern word-processing, microprocessor-controlled item file storage and retrieval, and xerography are valuable aids in test construction, but they also can lead to some embarrassing moments. It is always important to proofread test copy carefully, but there are subtle errors that may be easy to overlook when test items have been retrieved from a file: Particular intended items may be omitted and replaced by already printed items or unintended items from the file. Blank pages may appear in test forms in lieu of intended pages; identical pages may appear twice. It is well worth the administrator's time to inspect test materials, including original and duplicated copies, soon enough prior to testing time that necessary corrections can be made. Once the test has begun, it is difficult or impossible to help the students who discover that "We have no page three!".

Basically, then, smooth administration of a group test comes down to preparing necessary materials well in advance, having an adequate test site, making directions clear, and anticipating the unexpected. There are motivational considerations, which are discussed next within the context of administering individual tests.

ADMINISTERING INDIVIDUAL TESTS

An individual test in music usually means some type of performance measure. A student may be auditioning for an ensemble, taking a test for an applied music grade, demonstrating ability to clap, sing, or tap rhythms, or manipulating equipment, as in demonstrating skill in oiling valves or tuning a guitar. Some aspects of group administration apply; an appropriate physical environment is important. Making the individual test taker comfortable and able to cope with understandable anxiety becomes especially important, and the examiner should understand some aspects of test anxiety, motivation, and the potential importance or unimportance of the test to the test taker.

Text anxiety is a very real psychological phenomenon. It may arise during study or practice time prior to the test or performance and has both a cognitive and an emotional component (Krohne & Schaffner, 1983). People with test anxiety tend to focus on personal inadequacy and its consequences; they frequently expect failure. They view the potential outcome of an inadequate evaluation with alarm. They create extra information in the form of what Sarason (1983, p. 143) calls "maladaptive personal feedback" that interferes with processing relevant information. Self-centered thoughts negate concentration on the test or audition.

Evaluative cues (e.g., "This is important to you because . . .", "Be sure that you don't . . .", "You're doing all right so far . . .") may motivate persons who are low in test anxiety, but those identical cues may threaten those who are highly anxious. Low but significant correlations between test anxiety and grades have been reported. Reassurance that a negative evaluation will not be made may enable highly test-anxious people to perform as well as or better than people low in test anxiety. Focusing attention on the test task, being told not to worry, relaxation techniques, prior practice (with reward) in the test task, and information about study and test taking skills may help alleviate anxiety (Sarason, 1983). Helping a student distinguish between evaluation of himself or herself as a person and evaluation of his or her writing, conducting, musical performance, or test score may be difficult but is very useful at any level of music education.

Motivation is a critical aspect of learning, regardless of one's theoretical position, and if a student is to perform well in a test setting, adequate motivation is crucial. Yet excessive emphasis on the need to do well or "produce" can cause anxiety that will decrement the performance. Clemans (1971, p. 193) recommends motivating students without producing excessive anxiety by letting students know in advance of testing the purpose of the testing and advantages to the student of making a "sincere" effort.

The student's "sincere" effort will interact with the student's motivation. Walker (1980, pp. 476–479) identifies three types or sources of motivation that operate in human learning. In *autarkic* motivation, an individual is motivated to perform a task solely for the sake of the performance. The joy of making music is sufficient reason for striving to do well in an audition. Autarkic motivation may be considered as intrinsic motivation, as may *idiocratic* motivation, which is extrinsic to any particular task but nevertheless rises from an individual's personal characteristics. Some personal drive to succeed may impel a student to do well on his or her audition, not for the music but for the student's self-esteem.

Although extrinsic to the task, idiocratic motivation is intrinsic to the person. *Extraneous* motivation for performance occurs when an incentive to perform is present; it disappears when the incentive disappears. Realistically, many students at all levels of education strive to do well because of receiving grades, the possibility of completing an unpleasant task or requirement, or earning some privilege.

Thus the individual who has appeared for a test may be motivated by what is inherent in the test, by self-image, and/or by the opportunity for reward or punishment. Furthermore, the particular test may be viewed as a contingent or noncontingent step on what Raynor (1981) calls a psychological career path: It may be perceived as essential or non-essential to make further progress along a path toward a goal.* Raynor also notes that about 25 percent of students are *success-oriented*, about 25 percent are *failure-threatened*, and the remaining 50 percent have roughly equal predispositions. As the names suggest, success-oriented students look forward to accomplishment while failure-threatened students are motivated to avoid failure. Whereas Raynor recommends clear explication of standards and explanation of the importance of a present task (such as a test or audition) to an attractive future for success-oriented students, minimizing evaluation, emphasizing extrinsic gains, and not linking the student's future to the present task are recommended for failure-threatened students.

Motivation is more than a behavioral catalyst; it directly influences ability. As Atkinson (1983) clearly indicates, research shows a curvilinear relationship between the amount of motivation and efficiency of test performance. As motivation strength increases, performance increases to a certain point; after that, an increase in motivation causes a decrease in performance. There are separate curvilinear relations for separate ability levels: Higher ability levels result in steeper curves. Performance level on a test thus is a product of ability and the examinee's efficiency, which is enhanced by optimal motivation.

Thus the administrator of an individual test ideally should know something of each examinee's personal characteristics and prior testing experiences. When the administrator is the examinee's

---

*A psychological career is not necessarily occupational. Raynor identifies occupational, sexual, and family careers as characterizing most individuals' lives. Career is related to self-image.

teacher, that may be possible. In any case, it probably is wise at the moment of testing to be as nonthreatening yet businesslike as possible. *Certainly* a test should never be used as punishment, nor should it be given solely to fill time.

Students and testers should have readily available whatever is needed for the test procedure. Music stands, tapes, recorders, music, and any other necessary equipment and materials should be on hand so that once a student and the examiner are ready, the test can proceed. If a "blind rating" procedure is used in order to avoid a "halo effect" (see Chapter 5) or excessive attention to nonmusical visual aspects of a performance (see Chapter 8), an assistant must be employed to manage recording and submitting the necessary tapes or holding performances behind some barrier.

Individual test administration refers to one individual test taker. The traditional "jury" examination in which an individual plays or sings for a panel of judges, as often occurs in a conservatory or school of music, is a type of individual test. Clear specifications regarding what must or need not be accompanied, when and where a student is supposed to warm up, and what repertoire is expected may facilitate the flow of students through a jury procedure. As part of a relaxed-but-businesslike atmosphere as well as common courtesy, all jury members should appear interested in the student and listen intently while he or she is performing, regardless of the quality of performance or length of the jurors' day. Oral and written feedback to the student should dwell on the performance, not on the student as a person.

An individual test places the tested individual in a type of "spotlight." The test administrator needs to make that moment in the "spotlight" as organized and productive as possible.

SPECIAL PROBLEMS IN TESTING YOUNG AND EXCEPTIONAL CHILDREN

When group or individual tests are intended for children in the primary grades or preschool, certain administrative considerations arise due to the children's attention span, lack of reading ability, immaturity, and lack of test taking experience. Children with various physical, sensory, and emotional handicaps may require special consideration. Implementation of Public Law 94-142, passed by the U.S. Congress in 1975 as the Education of All Handicapped Children Act and interpreted through regulations issued by the U.S. Office of Education in 1977, means, among other things, that many exceptional children must be accommodated, instructed, and evaluated in music education settings.*

Young children may have difficulty with tasks that are so automatic to adults unaccustomed to working with children that no thought was given to those tasks in test preparation. Finding an answer on a crowded page might be difficult. Drawing a circle around a picture, symbol, or word might require a surprising amount of time. Instructions given prior to the actual test task may be forgotten. Children may be distracted easily by irrelevant aspects of the testing procedure, such as a "funny" teacher or musical example, or superfluous material on a test form. One strategy that the authors have employed effectively with kindergarten and first and second grade pupils is the "talk through" test.

The "talk through" test is administered as a tape-recorded narrative. The narrator relates the test directions and content in the style of a story while the children follow a test form that is appropriate to their perceptual abilities and the test content. The narration is pleasant and straightforward; it is not "childish" or filled with artificial excitement.

As an example of a "talk through" test, consider a situation in which first graders' sensitivity to phrase structure is tested.** The children have test forms containing rows of large numerals, 2 3 4, one row per page. The test tape, containing the narration and the musical examples, is played. The tape content might be:

> Hello, boys and girls. We are going to listen to some music. You will be drawing circles around numbers to tell something about the music.
>
> Listen to this short song. [A brief two-phrase piano excerpt is played.] That song had two parts to it. Each part is called a *phrase*. This is the *first* phrase. [Play first phrase.] This is the *second* phrase. [Play second phrase.] Now listen to the song, both phrases together. [Play song.] Now on your paper you see the numbers 2, 3, and 4. Draw a circle around the 2 because the song had two phrases. [Pause.] OK? Now turn the page. [Pause.]

---

*For a detailed description of what PL 94-142 requires and does not require and the opportunities and obstacles it poses for children, parents, teachers, and professional support personnel, see Paul's chapter (pp. 146–159) in the Lidz (1981) text.

**This example is based on one part of the Contemporary Music Project's Seminar on the Evaluation of Comprehensive Musicianship. The entire evaluation project is reported by Boyle and Radocy (1973).

> Listen to *this* song. [A four-phrase excerpt is played.] How many phrases did that song have? [Pause.] Well, here is one phrase. [Play first phrase.] Here's another. [Play second phrase.] Here's *another*, the third one. [Play third phrase.] And there's one more, the *fourth* phrase. [Play fourth phrase.] Listen to the four phrases together in this song. [Play song.] Now draw a circle around the 4, because there are four phrases in the song. [Pause.] All right, now turn the page. [Pause.]
>
> Listen to the song and count the phrases for yourself. [Play song.] Draw a circle around the number of phrases in the song—2, 3, or 4. [Pause.]

The test would continue for the desired number of items. The classroom teacher or some proctor would have to verify that the children were turning the pages and circling only one numeral. The initial "lesson" may be dispensed with if the children have been practicing counting phrases.

The "talk through" test format provides an opportunity to have the test takers practice their skills. The pace of completing administrative details as well as giving answers is determined by the rate of narration. The test form is keyed to the tape and vice versa. Naturally, some children will have difficulty with this or any other group testing format; they will require individual testing.

The pictographic scale represented by a continuum of smiling–frowning faces such as,

is used effectively in many children's tests, including the Gordon *Primary Measures of Music Audiation* (see Chapter 6). May (1983) used "faces" to assess young children's musical preferences; apparently children can relate visual strength of smile to some affective feeling.

Marking locations on a test form with drawings of familiar objects is possible if the test writer believes that numerals are confusing (the *PMMA* do this), but there is controversy regarding whether an array of drawings is less confusing than numbers.

As preschool programs develop and music education develops with them, testing preschool children's musical preferences, facts, and understandings may become increasingly important. Lidz (1981, pp. 101–102), citing Blank (1973), stresses the importance of not prematurely assuming ignorance in individual testing situations when a preschool child fails to give an immediate answer or quickly gives a wrong answer. Although written in the context of assessing learning difficulties, their suggestions have merit for any testing situation involving young "academically unsophisticated" children, so they are paraphrased here. (Some suggestions may be applicable to older children as well.)

If a child seems overly impulsive, that is, answers a question or performs some task immediately without any apparent thought for the task at hand, the impulsivity rather than lack of knowledge may be at fault. The child may be told to wait before responding; the delay conceivably provides an opportunity to "think."

Occasionally a child's attention may require focusing. Having the child repeat a question or what he or she is to do may be useful when the child responds in terms of a preformed habit, as in giving his or her name, rather than in terms of the current testing situation, as in naming a toy or instrument on request. Sometimes the test administrator may repeat the instructions.

Although rephrasing questions on a standardized test is a psychometric no-no, common sense indicates that paraphrasing instructions may alleviate errors due to unfamiliar vocabulary. "Leading" the child by partially completing an answer or task may also be helpful.

If a manipulative task seems too complex for a child, as in arranging bells or tone bars in a particular order, the task may be broken into smaller components or restructured, as in evaluating each bell or bar individually.

When the child can not answer an open-ended question, there may be value in offering several specific choices, as in showing a bell and asking if it is a bar, drum, whistle, or bell.

Effort to relate what is unknown to familiar objects and events in the child's environment may help a child to focus on relevant aspects of the test taking tasks.

Lidz (1981, p. 118), again writing in the context of assessing learning difficulties, notes that

> Assessing children ages three through five can be a very unpredictable experience. . . . Critical elements in the child's response to assessment are his degree of separation anxiety, ability and willingness to respond to a stranger, activity level, attention span, language development, and general attitude toward responding to requests.

She stresses the importance of testing at the child's pace, which probably means that one session is insufficient (p. 118). Free play with the test materials is recommended (p. 119), as is avoiding any statement that implies that the child is about to play a game—disappointment is inevitable if there is no "game" (p. 125). Lidz further cautions (p. 125) that children may have negative expectancies regarding a "doctor" (as whom the test administrator, if a stranger, may appear) or a classroom "test."

When dealing with children who are impaired in some way, the test administrator must modify the testing procedure. Although some modifications may be obvious, there is no general rule for modifying tests for special populations. Since there is considerable variability within special populations, any modification must suit the individual child (Lidz, 1981, pp. 112–113). Lidz (p. 118) cautions that "In general, any modification should be determined by the particular behavior the child manifests, rather than by the disability."

Lidz offers certain suggestions, based on her experience in school psychology and clinical assessment as well as reviews of literature, for accommodating various impairments.

Hearing-impaired children who can lip-read can benefit from a test administrator who speaks slowly and repeats (but does not add) information. Pantomiming and drawing pictures may help. (Musical stimuli that must be heard may not be practical. Some children may "hear" music through bone conduction or feeling vibration in the arms, feet, or chest. The viability of music education for the hearing-impaired depends on the nature and degree of impairment.)

Visual impairment may hinder verbal development. Obviously tests can be read to children who can not see if they can understand the aural input. Music notation in Braille is possible if the necessary expertise is available. Partially sighted children may employ enlarged materials, self-determined reading distances, extra bright lighting, and thick pencils in printed tasks. Contrast between print and paper is especially important; clear black type on white paper, as produced by high-quality typing, printing, or xerography, is vastly superior to purple dittoed copies.

Children who have a motor handicap that affects their speech can be exceedingly difficult to understand. The testing procedure may be modified to enable the child to provide a yes or no answer, possibly through saying facsimiles of the words, head movement, or blinking. Lidz (p. 115) suggests using pictures for which a child can indicate a yes or no in response to the tester's pointing.

Children who have cerebral palsy may require an explanation that a test is not a medical examination. A lengthy test could be spread over several sessions, and providing rewards may keep the cerebral-palsied child motivated. These children require a comfortable chair and, if making marks is expected, a pencil large enough to use. Distracting surroundings, including the attention-getting aspects of the tester's clothing, should be minimized. When practical, a parent can be a useful interpreter.

The child who is "learning-disabled" may present a particular problem because of the lack of an obvious visible handicap. Definitions of learning disability vary; one of the most comprehensive was stated by Kirk and Gallagher (1979, p. 285):

> A specific learning disability is a psychological or neurological impediment to spoken or written language or perceptual, cognitive, or motor behavior. The impediment (1) is manifested by discrepancies among specific behaviors and achievements or between evidenced ability and academic achievement, (2) is of such nature and extent that the child does not learn by the instructional methods and materials appropriate for the majority of children and requires specialized procedures for development, and (3) is not primarily due to severe mental retardation, sensory handicaps, emotional problems, or lack of opportunity to learn.

Weener and Senf (1982) note that a learning disability may be accompanied by reading disorders, minimal basic dysfunctions, hyperactivity, or hyperkinetic syndrome, but some learning-disabled children show none of those conditions. For testing purposes, once a learning-disabled child is identified, adjustments in format and allowable time may make a drastic difference in test performance.

Modifications of testing procedures may seem perplexing and time consuming, but they are necessary if children with special problems and needs are to be able to show their musical knowledge and skills. Merely excusing these children from testing implies that for them music education is no more than a pastime. While it is foolish to pretend that any child can do anything, it is unfair not to try adapting testing procedures to allow a child to show what he or she can do.

Music therapists use music and musical activity to help their clients reach therapeutic and educational goals. A staff music therapist, when available, is a valuable resource in any educational situation where music learning is expected because he or she may be familiar with the needs of particular children and ways to adapt music, musical instruments, and music evaluation for them. For example, different children with cerebral palsy react differently to identical music examples: What stimulates one child may sedate another. A music therapist may make recommendations regarding particular music that is being considered for use in testing a particular child. Consultation with other persons who work with a child and examining a child's IEP (individualized educational program, required by Public Law 94-142 for any child receiving special services under the law) may provide information regarding a child's strengths and weaknesses as they pertain to testing procedures.

Thus, the test administrator must use his or her imagination, guided by whatever relevant information is available, to test young and/or exceptional children at a pace and in a manner appropriate for them.

SCORING TESTS

Scoring a test must be in consistent accordance with pre-established rules. The procedure for virtually all cognitive tests that are collections of items is simply to sum the correct answers. With affective measures, a summative scoring model is also usually the rule; degrees of agreement are summed. It is possible to adjust a score by penalizing a wrong answer more than an omitted one (so called "guessing" formulas) or by differential weighting of particular items.* In certain settings, such as some "objectives-referenced" or "domain-referenced" tests, there may be no total score; the proportion of examinees who can provide an acceptable answer is noted for each item.

Many situations, such as rating musical performances and essay items, require assigning a particular score as a judgment rather than counting specific answer points. This could be conceived as categorization or a limited form of magnitude estimation (see Chapter 8). When such "judgment calls" are the basis for scoring, interscorer reliability or degree of agreement among judges becomes important.

---

*Differential weighting generally is awkward and not worthwhile. If certain areas are more important than others, more items related to those areas should appear (Mehrens & Lehmann, 1973, p. 324).

One procedure for interscorer reliability is simply to express the proportion of agreements contained in the total of agreements and disagreements. For example, if three judges read five essays, there are three potential agreements or disagreements among the judges per essay, for a total of 15 agreements plus disagreements. Suppose that the following results are obtained in reading essays for which a maximum assignment of 10 points is possible:

Essay	J1	J2	J3	Agreements	Disagreements
E1	10	10	9	1	2
E2	5	8	6	0	3
E3	9	9	9	3	0
E4	8	8	7	1	2
E5	3	4	3	1	2

Six of 15 pairings are agreements; $6 \div 15 = .40$, so the interscorer reliability is .40 when agreement is defined as assigning an equivalent score. This procedure makes no discrimination of *degree* of disagreement; if agreement in the above example were defined arbitrarily as ratings within ± 1 of each other, the total of agreements would be 13, resulting in an interscorer reliability of .87.

A better procedure would be to use coefficient alpha (see Chapter 3), with each judge considered an "item" and the sums of the scores for each essay considered the sources of overall score variance. Less foreboding mathematically (although that rarely is a consideration with modern computational aids) is the coefficient of concordance.

Kendall's coefficient of concordance (W) essentially is an extension of rank order correlation that estimates the divergence among a group of judges in performing a ranking task. The greater the W value, the less divergent and the more reliable the rankings. Since the procedure for computing W uses ordinal data, raw scores, if present, are converted to ranks. For the above data, the essay-by-judge matrix becomes:

Essay	J1	J2	J3	Sum of Ranks (R_j)
E1	1	1	1.5	3.5
E2	4	3.5	4	11.5
E3	2	2	1.5	5.5
E4	3	3.5	3	9.5
E5	5	5	5	15.0

The highest scoring essay is ranked 1, the lowest 5. Ties are expressed as the mean of the tied ranks, for example, E2 and E4 are tied for ranks 3 and 4 with J2, so each receives a $(3 + 4) \div 2 = 3.5$.

The formula for W (Siegel, 1956) is

$$W = \frac{s}{\frac{1}{12} k^2 (N^3 - N)},$$

where

k = number of judges,
N = number of phenomena ranked,
s = sum of squares of the observed deviations from the mean of the row sums (R_j), i.e.,

$$s = \left(\sum R_j - \frac{\Sigma R_j}{N} \right)^2$$

In the above example, each row's sum of ranks (R_j) is the sum of each judge's rankings for each essay, as indicated in the final column. The mean of the row sums is $45 \div 5 = 9$. The respective values, E1 through E5, for $(R_j - \Sigma R_j/N)$ thus are -5.5, 2.5, -3.5, 0.5, and 6.0. The respective *squared* values then are 30.25, 6.25, 12.25, 0.25, and 36.00. Their sum, s, equals 85. Plugging $k = 3$ judges, $N = 5$ essays, and $s = 85$ into the formula for W yields an interscorer reliability estimate of .94.

Simple correlation procedures will work when there are only two judges, but there is no three-way or greater product–moment correlation procedure. All possible pairwise correlations (e.g., 3 for 3 judges) may be averaged to provide an overall estimate of reliability. Multiple correlation requires designating one variable as a criterion and the others as predictors, although in a reliable scoring procedure any combination of judges minus one conceivably could predict the remaining judge's scores equally well.

When hand scoring of objective tests is employed, painstaking care is necessary to avoid mechanical errors. The scorer should have an answer key, preferably in the form of a completed test, that indicates the correct answers, and, for open-ended items, acceptable alternative answers. The number correct should be checked against the total of points possible minus the number wrong. The opportunity for personal feedback is excellent with hand scoring; the scorer can write an explanation of why a choice or statement is wrong or refer the student to a particular reference.

When machine scoring is used, a quick search through the answer sheets for names, filled in letter spaces, and extraneous marks is recommended. Despite careful directions and admonishments, even experienced test takers may omit names or doodle on the paper. The answer key for the scoring machine should be prepared in advance and be checked carefully for accuracy—a miskeyed answer is frustrating for test giver and test taker alike!

Most scoring services provide statistical information, including item analysis. This is one advantage of machine scoring, because while item analysis is easy in principle by hand it becomes rather time consuming. Care must be taken when a scoring service is used that the test administrator makes the necessary detailed requests and allows adequate time.

When scoring recorded musical examples, judges should have some idea of what they are listening for and on what to base evaluation (see Chapter 8). An evaluation form, even for simple procedures, is useful. There needs to be some identification of each taped performance, and if some coding system is employed to protect performer anonymity, someone must keep track of who in fact each performer is. Judges need ample opportunity to rest to avoid fatigue and careless rating.

SUMMARY

The major points in this chapter include:

1. Advance planning is necessary for smooth test administration and scoring.

2. A comfortable and secure environment is beneficial for group and individual tests.

3. Care must be taken that sufficient time and adequate and accurate materials are available.

4. Active proctoring, especially in large groups, may discourage cheating.

5. Examinees need clear directions regarding exactly what they are supposed to do.

6. An individual about to be tested or auditioned should be made as comfortable as possible under the circumstances.

7. Test anxiety may result in fear of consequences and self-deprecating information that hampers performance.

8. Test anxiety may be alleviated by reassuring the student and focusing evaluation on the performance rather than the individual.

9. There are internal and external sources of motivation that interact with a person's ability to affect the score.

10. Motivation influences an individual's efficiency in a curvilinear way; neither inadequate nor excessive motivation is desirable.

11. Some individuals are motivated to attain success; others are motivated to avoid failure.

12. Young children may require special testing formats to keep them on task and stay within the range of their abilities.

13. Children with disabilities require various individual modifications to enable them to be tested.

14. Modifying a test for a special child should be guided by the child's needs and behavior rather than psychometric theory or the nature of the disability.

15. Music therapists, other support personnel, and IEPs may be valuable in guiding test modification.

16. Scoring a test, whether by hand or machine, requires a painstaking concern for accuracy.

17. Interscorer reliability, estimated through coefficient alpha, a coefficient of concordance, or a proportion of agreements procedure, is important when more than one judge evaluates essays or musical performances.

18. Special care is necessary to keep judging of taped performances accurate.

Study Questions

1. What are some considerations in preparing for a group administration of a music test that includes listening? (Consider the test papers and the room.)

2. What are some steps you can take to avoid cheating by examinees in a group-testing situation?

3. How might the administration of a music recognition test to the first grade differ from administration of a music recognition test to the ninth grade?

4. What could you do to enhance performance and minimize undue anxiety in an individual audition procedure?

5. Consider a test of rudiments of notation appropriate for a fifth or sixth grade. What adjustments from a "typical" group administration procedure would you make for the following exceptionalities?

   A. a visually impaired child

   B. a hearing-impaired child

   C. a child with cerebral palsy who is unable to grasp a pencil

   D. a child with a learning disability that makes reading (of words) extremely difficult

6. Suppose that four judges rank order six student compositions in accordance with the following composition-by-judge matrix:

Composition	J1	J2	J3	J4
Ambivalence	1	1	5	2
Crystal Haze	4	5	3	4
Golf Ball Gavotte	2	3	4	1
Jogging Shoe Waltz	5	4	2	5
Pickle Polka	6	6	1	6
Refractions	3	2	6	3

   A. What procedure would you use to determine interscorer reliability? Why?

   B. What *is* the interscorer reliability?

   C. What happens to the interscorer reliability if Judge 3's rankings are eliminated?

REFERENCES

Atkinson, J.W. Motivational psychology and mental measurement. In S.B. Anderson & J.S. Helmick (Eds.), *On educational testing.* San Francisco, Calif.: Jossey-Bass, 1983.

Blank, M. The wrong response. In M. Blank (Ed.), *Teaching learning in the preschool: A dialogue approach.* Columbus, Ohio: Merrill, 1973.

Boyle, J.D., & Radocy, R.E. Evaluation of instructional objectives in comprehensive musicianship. *Council for Research in Music Education,* 1973, *32,* 2–21.

Clemans, W.V. Test administration. In R.L. Thorndike (Ed.), *Educational measurement* (2nd ed.). Washington, D.C.: American Council on Education, 1971.

Kirk, S.A., & Gallagher, J.J. *Educating exceptional children* (3rd ed.). Boston: Houghton Mifflin, 1979.

Krohne, H.W., & Schaffner, P. Anxiety, coping strategies, and performance. In S.B. Anderson & J.S. Helmick (Eds.), *On educational testing.* San Francisco, Calif.: Jossey-Bass, 1983.

Lidz, C.S. *Improving assessment of schoolchildren.* San Francisco, Calif.: Jossey-Bass, 1981.

May, W.V., Jr. Musical style preferences and aural discrimination skills of primary grade school children (Doctoral dissertation, University of Kansas, 1983). *Dissertation Abstracts International,* 1983, *44,* 1016A.

Mehrens, W.A., & Lehmann, I.J. *Measurement and evaluation in education and psychology.* New York: Holt, Rinehart, and Winston, 1973.

Raynor, J.O. Motivational determinants of music-related behavior: Psychological careers of student, teacher, performer, and listener. In R.G. Taylor (Ed.), *Documentary report of the Ann Arbor Symposium.* Reston, Va.: Music Educators National Conference, 1981.

Sarason, I.G. Understanding and modifying test anxiety. In S.B. Anderson & J.S. Helmick (Eds.), *On educational testing.* San Francisco, Calif.: Jossey-Bass, 1983.

Siegel, S. *Nonparametric statistics for the behavioral sciences.* New York: McGraw-Hill, 1956.

Walker, E.L. *Psychologial complexity and preference: A hedgehog theory of behavior.* Monterey, Calif.: Brooks/Cole, 1980.

Weener, P., & Senf, G.M. Learning disabilities. In H. E. Mitzel (Ed.), *Encyclopedia of educational research* (5th ed.) (Vol. 3). New York: Free Press, 1982.

12

Reporting Systems

Whether in the elementary school general music class, the secondary school performance class, or the college applied music studio, the assignment and reporting of grades has been a perplexing problem for music teachers. Some teachers do not appear to take the task of grade assignment very seriously; others may be serious about it, but when confronted with the reality of providing music grades for the several hundred elementary children they teach each week, they become overwhelmed at the prospect of providing meaningful grades and simply assign all students who are not "problems" a satisfactory grade. In many performance groups at both the secondary and collegiate levels, students are simply awarded grades on the basis of attendance, participation, and/or attitude. The resultant high grades often cause colleagues and administrators to criticize music teachers for lack of academic respectability and contributing to grade inflation. It is far more serious, however, that inappropriate grading and reporting of student progress reflect a weakness of the overall instructional program in meeting the needs of individual students. Educators are obligated to provide meaningful feedback to students and parents regarding students' progress in educational endeavors. Furthermore, grades often are bases for important decisions about individual students, both within and beyond the school setting, and for this reason alone warrant great care and consideration.

The overall process by which grades are determined variously is called a grading system, marking system, or reporting system, and references to the process tend to use the terms interchangeably. Grades, or marks, are the symbols, usually letters or numerals, used to summarize and characterize a student's performance in an educational endeavor. They typically are assigned at the conclusion of a set period of time, usually called a grading or marking period, and then reported to the student and/or parents. Traditionally they are single letters or numbers, supposedly reflecting achievement during the grading period, but in actuality reflecting a wide variety of assessments on several different dimensions. There is a convenience in reducing something as complex as response to instruction over an 18-week period to one simple letter or numeral, and many students, parents, teachers, and other persons interested in evaluation of educational achievement have become accustomed to the practice and appear to be satisfied with it. Others, most notably Kirschenbaum, Napier, and Simon (1971), have been much more vocal in opposition to traditional practices.

Claims that inadequate reporting systems (a) pervert the education process by narrowing the focus of education, (b) create undue anxiety, (c) are unreliable, (d) cause students to focus on extrinsic rewards rather than the intrinsic rewards of learning, (e) are disruptive to the overall education process, and (f) generally are ineffective at communicating students' achievement have been voiced by many critics. Milton and Edgerly (1976, p. 45) summarize the problem as follows:

> There is this paucity of detailed help for students because evaluation now tends to mean the assigning of letter symbols for record-keeping purposes. The subject of grading is laden with prejudices, dogmas, and unfounded opinions. . . .

While some might take issue with all of the criticisms, there is little question that the grading systems in many schools are less than adequate, even though they have long-standing traditions. From the authors' perspectives, it appears that grading practices in music, from primary school through graduate school, are particularly fraught with problems.

Reporting student progress is an integral and important part of any school instructional program and warrants far greater consideration than it usually has received from music teachers. The purpose of this chapter, therefore, is to review the uses of grades, discuss the different grading systems and bases for grading, and examine a number of issues involved in grading. Finally, some guidelines will be offered for establishing a grading system for use in music classes.

USES OF GRADES

Terwilliger (1971) states that "the purpose of grading systems is to provide a systematic and formal procedure for transmitting value judgments made by teachers to the student and to others most directly concerned with his welfare and development" (p. 7). Geisinger (1982) emphasizes that the overriding function of grades is effective communication of these judgments, and goes on to identify six uses of grades: (a) informational, (b) institutional, (c) sorting and selecting, (d) motivating students, (e) research, and (f) preparation for life. Following is a brief discussion of Geisinger's six uses.

The informational use of grades is intended primarily for students and their parents. Grades should provide feedback to students regarding their academic performance; such feedback should "permit students to judge their performance in detail; lead to modification of their behavior, where appropriate; differentiate strong and weak areas of their performance; and serve as reinforcement for jobs well done" (Geisinger, p. 1140). Geisinger questions whether traditional single symbol grading systems can provide adequate information for such purposes, although he does acknowledge that much information of this type may be provided to students as part of feedback from tests, written papers, and/or oral comments from the teacher throughout the grading period. Whether a single symbol grade provides parents with adequate information regarding their child's class performance is doubtful.

Institutional uses of grades are many and varied. Grades may be used as bases for decisions relative to student promotion, assignment to various academic tracks, admission to special courses and programs, awarding academic honors, and awarding of scholarships. Geisinger maintains that grades probably are valid data upon which to base these decisions in that grades indicate a student's status in the educational system. Any time that grades are a criterion upon which further educational opportunities are offered or denied their importance is increased.

Besides the uses within the institution that a student attends, there are many decisions regarding his or her educational opportunities beyond that institution for which grades are at least a partial basis. The most common use of this type is for admission for advanced education. Grade point average (GPA) is an important consideration for admissions to most institutions of higher education, and undergraduate GPA is a particularly important consideration for admission to graduate education. Geisinger states that "past grades are probably the best predictors of future grades, and the effectiveness of marks as predictors . . . has dictated their use in making selection and placement decisions" (p. 1140). Awards of scholarships, fellowships, and other academic honors often are based either partially or entirely on grades. Further, employers sometimes use high school, college, and professional school grades in making hiring decisions.

There is little question that grades are effective motivators for some students, but there is much controversy regarding the appropriateness of such use. Geisinger notes that high grades appear to serve as reinforcers for increasing student studying and learning behaviors. Critics of grading systems maintain that grades are extrinsic motivators, and that many students study simply to get the high grades and/or to avoid getting low grades. Furthermore, it is argued that if studying and learning is done purely to obtain high grades, this behavior will extinguish after education is completed; therefore, the over-dependence on extrinsic reinforcers, such as grades, actually may be detrimental to long-range educational goals. Another disadvantage of too much emphasis on grades as motivators is that students may feel "forced" to work for high grades under penalty of receiving low grades and consequently develop negative attitudes toward academic behavior.

The effect of grades as motivators will vary from student to student and from group to group. Geisinger notes that adult learners in continuing education courses rarely are influenced by course grades; in contrast, for younger students, many of whom are conditioned from infancy to be competitive, grades may be important motivators.

Geisinger notes that an often overlooked function of grades is the role they play in educational research. A particular use is in studies on student admission to selected programs or schools. Perhaps because of their ready availability, grades are the most consistently used criterion against which predictor variables are validated. Whether this should be is debatable, because grades reflect judgments, many of which are often based on questionable criteria.

A final use of grades relates to the extent to which they prepare students for adjusting to the real work-a-day world in which they are apt to receive evaluative feedback on a job. Most jobs require some type of training. With this training there usually is some type of evaluative feedback, and it has been argued that the ability to accept and learn from evaluative feedback is useful. A second use of grades in preparing one for life is in their role as feedback to be used in educational and vocational counseling. Grades, which become a part of a student's academic record, may reflect strengths and weaknesses that are useful in career decision making.

In conclusion, it is apparent that grades may serve many important functions regarding educational and career decisions for the individual student, and it is imperative that teachers make every effort to ensure that grades awarded in their classes be valid indicators of student performance.

GRADING SYSTEMS

By far the most common grading system uses letters as the communicative symbols. Other systems in use include (a) percentage grading, (b) pass–fail grading, (c) credit–no credit grading, (d) descriptive grading, (e) contract grading, (f) self-assessment, and (g) multi-dimensional grading. Brief discussions of the respective systems follow.

Gronlund (1981, p. 516) notes that a recent survey of grading practices revealed that 72 percent of the elementary teachers and 82 percent of the secondary teachers responding to the survey used letter grades as the method for reporting student progress to parents. The most commonly used letters are A, B, C, D, and F; however, some school districts use an E instead of an F for the lowest grade, presumably to avoid specific connotations of "failure." Plusses or minuses frequently are coupled with the symbols, in effect increasing the number of levels in the system. Other schools, particularly in higher education, do not include the plus or minus on the official grade that is recorded on a transcript. Advantages of the system are its convenience and apparent simplicity. Disadvantages are that (a) it is difficult to tell what the letter means (e.g., is it solely a reflection of achievement, or does it take into consideration such variables as effort, attitude, and/or good behavior?), (b) even if it reflects only achievement, it provides no indication of relative strengths and weaknesses, and (c) as typically used, letter grades seem to cause an undesirable emphasis on grades as ends in themselves. Variations in the letter system use different letters and/or numbers of letters, but most of these systems appear to have the same basic problems.

A grading system that was popular during the latter part of the nineteenth century and the early part of the twentieth century involves reporting progress in terms of percentages. A teacher simply assigns a student a number between 0 and 100, and this presumably reflects the percentage of the instructional material that the student has learned. In some ways this system is akin to the magnitude estimation technique discussed in Chapter 8, but there is only one person making the estimates—the teacher. In this instance, the teacher is working within a fixed framework; true magnitude estimation, even with a predesignated standard, does not place a limit on the potential range of estimates. Geisinger notes several problems in using this system, the most serious of which is that teachers generally are unable to make distinctions of less than 4 to 7 points. Also, the total 100-point scale is rarely used, thus compacting the ratings. Despite the difficulties in using the system, Geisinger reports that as recently as 1976, 16 percent of high schools were using percentage grading.

A grading system that appears to have increased in popularity in recent years is the pass–fail system. Sometimes called a satisfactory–unsatisfactory system, the rationales for use of the system seem to vary, but one view is that such a system is much more appropriate for use with criterion-referenced testing than is the traditional five-letter system. Basically criterion-referenced evaluation implies either meeting the criterion or not meeting the criterion. Students meeting the criterion would receive passing grades; those not meeting the criterion would receive failing grades. The five-letter system appears to be more suited to systems where grades are determined from a normative base, which shall be discussed later. A perceived advantage of the pass–fail system is that it takes away the incentive to work for high grades per se.

Many colleges and universities allow students to take a limited number of courses under a pass–fail or satisfactory–unsatisfactory option even though the institution's predominant grading system may be a five-letter system. The rationale for allowing this is that students will be able to explore courses out of their major without the risk of hurting their overall GPA, since pass–fail grades are not figured in the GPA. Usually, an instructor does not know which students are taking the course pass–fail; they simply turn in the letter grade for the student, and any A, B, C, or D is converted to a "pass." One problem with pass–fail grades in higher education, however, is that they create problems for admissions offices trying to figure GPAs. Kirschenbaum, Napier, and Simon (1971, p. 305) criticize pass–fail systems as being a type of "blanket" system for grading, thus allowing teachers to avoid the responsibility of evaluation and failing to distinguish between students of different abilities. Even with criterion-referenced measurement there still may be obvious differences between students who merely meet criteria and those who excel. A variation of the system is to add an "honors pass," in effect taking a step toward becoming more like the five-letter grading system. Still another variation of the pass–fail system is what Geisinger calls a nonpunitive grading system. If a student passes a course, it is so indicated on his or her school records; if he or she does not pass the course, no entry related to the course is entered on the student's school record. The argument for this is that students should not be "punished" by having a record of their inadequate performance entered on their permanent school record. Closely related to this variation is the rather common practice in higher education of allowing students who are doing poorly in a course to "withdraw" from the course; the only entry on their transcript is a "W" to indicate the withdrawal. There is no negative effect on the student's GPA.

Descriptive grading essentially involves having the teacher prepare a written statement assessing the student's progress in the classroom. A particular advantage of this system is that it allows the teacher to focus on both *how* a student learns and *how much* a student learns. Descriptive grading allows much more emphasis on the qualitative aspects of learning than the traditional single symbol grading systems. A recent variation of the descriptive grading system is to use computerized checklists of descriptive statements from which the teacher then selects the appropriate ones for each child, thus alleviating the need to write individual narratives for each student.

While a descriptive grading system appears to offer many advantages over the single symbol systems, it has been criticized from three perspectives: (a) the extensive documentation needed to differentiate among students with noncomparable records, (b) the validity of the descriptions, and (c) the amount of time and effort needed to prepare them. The computerized checklist overcomes some of the concern about labor in preparation of the reports; however, for it to be effective, the statements must reflect closely the instructional objectives for the course for which students are being evaluated. Criticisms regarding the validity of the descriptions appear to reflect the concern that the descriptions tend to focus too much on the student's stylistic and personality qualities rather than on achievement and potential for future learning. At best, comparisons of students on the basis of descriptive grading systems will remain cumbersome. Geisinger (1982, p. 1143) suggests that perhaps the most effective use of descriptive grading would be in conjunction with some type of letter or numeral system.

Contract grading essentially is a grading system that allows for individualized grading, that is, all students are not graded according to the same criteria. The teacher and each student agree and stipulate in writing the work to be accomplished by the student during the grading period, and the grade for that grading period is based on the teacher's assessment of that work. Typically, the grades used for contract grading are the traditional five-letter system. Proponents of the system claim that contract grading individualizes learning and, to a certain, extent eliminates the subjectivity from grading; critics, however, maintain that contract grading tends to focus on quantity rather than quality of work, and, hence, that the quality of student work in many contract systems tends to suffer.

Self-assessment grading systems essentially involve two stages: self-assessment, in which a student formally discusses his or her progress in a descriptive manner, and self-grading, the determination of his or her own grade on the basis of the self-assessment. The chief advantage of the system is that it forces the student to evaluate carefully his or her own performance. However, the disadvantages of the system appear to outweigh the advantages. When a student evaluates his or her own performance, the perspective of comparability that a teacher has is lost. The system also rewards those students who overestimate their work and punishes the modest, and because of the apparent pressure for high grades in many schools, the system creates situations that undermine values related to honesty. Geisinger notes that self-grading systems have not achieved wide use.

Gronlund (1981, pp. 516–520) argues that rather than limiting reporting to a single letter grade, it would be more appropriate to use a multiple grading and reporting system. The typical multiple reporting system retains a traditional grading system, usually letters, and supplements it with checklists of objectives. Terwilliger (1971, pp. 119–123) argues that provisions should be made for reporting nonachievement outcomes of learning efforts, and essentially multiple grading systems allow grades to reflect these, as well as other attributes of performance besides achievement. He suggests that rating scales and checklists are the two most common procedures for reporting such information. For example, for such variables as work habits, cooperation, and attentiveness a simple three-step scale such as "superior," "average," or "below average" could, with minimal effort by the teacher, provide much additional information to the student and his or her parents. Checklists typically present either a list of desired behaviors or undesired behaviors against which the teacher then checks the appropriate behaviors for that student. Terwilliger maintains that it is better to use the positive list so that a check in effect becomes a reinforcer. A variation of the checklist is to list the behaviors in neither a positive nor neutral context and then to provide a rating scale from positive to negative on which the teacher rates the child for each behavior. A slightly more cumbersome procedure, it allows the teacher to present more information. Terwilliger, however, cautions against making rating scales and checklists too complex. There appears to be a point of diminishing returns with completeness and complexity of information.

Each grading system appears to have some merit. Tradition, efficiency in record keeping, and the simplicity of the single symbol letter or numeral systems undoubtedly will cause them to continue to be much used. School systems and teachers concerned with more effective communication of student progress, however, are using, and will continue to explore the further use of, multiple reporting systems. Because of the diverse nature of the outcomes of instructional programs in music, whether at the elementary, secondary, or collegiate levels, it appears that multiple reporting systems will greatly facilitate both quality and accuracy in reporting student progress in music learning.

BASES FOR GRADING

Even though some teachers consciously or subconsciously may allow other variables to enter into assigning grades, grades ostensibly reflect achievement. Assuming that achievement is the primary consideration in student grades, the question remains: Achievement in relation to what? An absolute standard, ability, growth or improvement, effort expended, or achievement of other students? Geisinger (1982, p. 1144) follows the lead of Thorndike and Hagen (1977), who consolidated the above possible bases into three, and examines them under the headings of perfection, peers, and potential. The present discussion examines them under the same three bases.

When students are graded according to perfection, each student's work is compared with some preset, absolute standard. Essentially the individual student is compared with the standard irrespective of the achievement of other students. Many music teachers have their own ideal performance standards against which students' performances are evaluated; if their standard for "in tune" allows no room for deviation from equal-tempered pitch, then any student who does not perform absolutely in tune would be graded low with respect to pitch performance.

A problem with absolute standards is that they may be set so high that no students perform as the teacher expects; on the other hand, the teacher's standards might be set so low that all students appear to perform well, although they may in fact be performing at a standard that other evaluators might consider low. Obviously a teacher must have some understanding of the performance realities for his or her students in order to set appropriate standards.

Geisinger maintains that preset standards are appropriate for use in instructional programs featuring mastery testing and criterion-referenced testing. Also, they appear to be appropriate in areas such as mathematics, typing, foreign languages, and some aspects of music where the subject matter appears to follow natural units of performance or a hierarchical structure.

Teachers who "grade on the curve" are using *peer* performance as the basis for evaluating the achievement of the individual student. Standardized achievement tests by definition provide representative national norms against which students' scores may be compared, but teachers who calculate means and standard deviations for their own test score distributions are involved in peer- or norm-referenced evaluation. Also, teachers who subjectively compare a student's performance behaviors with those of his or her peers are using a norm-referenced basis.

The other broad base for assessing achievement is in relation to the individual being evaluated, his or her growth or improvement in performance, his or her achievement with respect to ability, and the apparent effort he or she demonstrates during the learning process. Referred to as *potential,* this grading base will award high grades to the student who improves his or her performance greatly, appears to "work up to his or her ability," and appears to be expending much effort toward learning. With this as a base, a clarinet player near the end of the section who has demonstrated some or all of these behaviors, yet still does not play the clarinet as well as students seated higher in the section, may receive the higher grade if the others do not reflect similar behaviors. An underlying assumption of this base is that the evaluator is capable of estimating a student's potential ability.

Each of the three bases for evaluating achievement for grading purposes has its shortcomings. The perfection basis is at the mercy of whoever sets the standards. If too high, everyone fails; if too low, everyone is graded highly. The peer basis puts unfair pressure on students who either by chance or design have been placed in a class with students whose achievement rates are higher than theirs; on the other hand, a strong student may be graded too highly if he or she is in a class with weaker students, while not achieving anywhere near his or her own potential. Grading in terms of potential may be particularly appropriate in some situations, but totally inappropriate in others, depending primarily on the educational setting. Generally people would prefer that brain surgeons be evaluated on some absolute standard for mastery rather than on someone's estimate of their potential. Similarly, we prefer to listen to professional symphonies that hire their musicians on the basis of demonstrated performance skills rather than potential.

The base on which a teacher chooses to assess achievement could depend on a number of variables, and a teacher should consider strongly the merits of the various bases relative to the function the grades are going to serve, the nature and purposes of the instruction, and, perhaps most of all, the potential effects of the grades on individual students. Sometimes information relative to more than one base may be of interest, and using a multiple reporting system allows this. For example, in classrooms where instruction is in relation to specific behavioral objectives, the basis for grading achievement should be in relation to the behavioral objectives. However, a teacher may also wish to convey his or her views regarding a student's work in relation to his or her peers and/or potential. Additional rating scales could be added to the reporting form so that separate estimates of achievement in relation to peers or potential might be shown without creating any ambiguity regarding what the original grading symbol means.

OTHER VARIABLES INFLUENCING GRADING

Besides the bases selected by the teacher for grading and the considerations mentioned in the previous section, a number of other variables may influence the grades a teacher assigns. Certainly the limitations and expectations of the educational institution within which the instruction and evaluation occur have an influence. Teachers usually are expected to conform to the system their school district or other institution uses. If the system is a single letter five-category system, the teacher must use it, even if it appears inadequate. However, a teacher concerned with providing additional feedback to students and parents in the form of other rating scales, checklists, or descriptive reports can usually do so with the blessing of his or her administrators, but this should be done only after consulting with one's supervisor or administrator regarding the purpose, intent, and nature of the additional information.

Even though grades may be based primarily on objective measures of achievement, there usually is some judgment involved in determining the final grade for each student. With judgments there may be other contaminating effects (Anderson et al., 1975, p. 186). Anderson notes that personality factors and teachers' responses to such, either consciously or subconsciously, may influence grades. The "teacher pleaser" student actually may be attempting to manipulate teachers' grading responses. Furthermore, teachers may be susceptible to the "halo" effect and tend to award grades during one grading period somewhat similarly to what they had assigned students in a previous grading period.

Whether grades should be used as punishment for disruptive behavior or as reward for attendance and good attitude is questionable. Such practices are common, particularly in music classes and performance situations, but they undermine the entire concept of grades as reflections of progress or achievement. While their uses in these manners may appear to be effective for motivation and other short-term goals, such use appears to be a misuse of grades, and teachers who depend solely on grades for maintaining good attendance and/or alleviating disruptive behavior should reexamine their strategies for motivation.

GENERAL ISSUES IN GRADING

Several issues regarding grading are apparent beyond those related to uses of grades, the chosen grading system, and the bases for grading. These include (a) reporting the affective component of student behavior, (b) grade inflation, (c) the effects of student ratings, (d) the effects of differential standards, (e) fairness, and (f) by-products of grading.

Reporting Affective Behaviors

Combining assessments of attitude, effort, motivation, and/or work habits, each of which appears to reflect a large measure of affect, with assessments of cognitive and/or psychomotor achievement into a single symbol grade usually results in grades with unclear meaning to anyone. Furthermore, some teachers may be interested in reporting their assessments of such traits as dependability, cooperativeness, interpersonal behaviors, or other non-achievement-oriented traits. Few would argue that affective behaviors are not important aspects of school experiences, but combining them with achievement, while common, is unsatisfactory and not recommended. Teachers concerned with reporting affective assessments should use some type of multiple reporting system that clearly distinguishes achievement from affective assessment.

Grade Inflation

Virtually every university and most elementary and secondary schools have at one time or another been concerned with grade inflation. Rarely is a "C" an average grade in most schools today. Teachers of music classes, and performance groups in particular, appear to be some of the worst offenders, although by no means the only offenders. Reasons for grade inflation appear to be many and varied. Some explanations attribute grade inflation to changing expectations of students, teachers, institutions, and society in general. Other explanations attribute it variously to changes from norm- to criterion-referenced measurement and evaluation, the use of pass–fail systems, and, particularly in higher education, the declining student population and increased competition for students. Whatever the causes, grade inflation has created other concerns. For example, when grades are used as a basis for student selection, the differences between individual students' GPAs are decreased. Many universities have raised their GPA standards for the honors awards given at graduation. One institution has even set differential standards for graduation honors for students from schools or colleges that appear to be the worst offenders regarding grade inflation.

For those uses of grades that involve sorting and/or selecting among students, the compacting of grades toward the upper end of a grading scale has created some problems, but perhaps the more serious concern is the possible misconception that inflated grades may give a student and his or her parents about the student's achievement. The awarding of unwarranted high grades, for whatever reasons, reflects either unethical or irresponsible teacher behavior. Teachers concerned with motivation through high grades at the expense of honest, responsible evaluation are doing both the student and the educational system a disservice.

Nevertheless, it is a fact of life that teachers of elective courses, such as many music courses, must consider the rigor of evaluation and grading and the potential effect on enrollment. Students will not remain in elective courses if they continually receive low grades. The balance between grades and attrition is delicate and a reality with which teachers must cope.

Effects of Student Ratings

Student ratings of instructional and teacher effectiveness are standard practice in higher education and receive limited use in secondary education. Claims have been made that student ratings are a contributing factor to grade inflation. The charge is that teachers may be concerned with receiving good ratings for their classes and consequently will tend to grade students more highly than they might otherwise. Correlations between grades and students' ratings of teachers, however, do not corroborate the charges; generally the correlations are low or negligible (Geisinger & Rabinowitz, 1980). Nevertheless, the concern remains that some effects, undetected by correlation studies, persist. Teachers may subconsciously tend to grade students higher when they know that they are to be rated by students, particularly when teacher ratings are used as a criterion for promotion and tenure considerations. With decisions of such a critical nature (to the teacher) as promotion and tenure depending at least partially on student ratings, there is the danger that grades and ratings will become political tools for both students and teachers. This could become a serious issue in higher education, and research is needed to defuse a potentially serious political problem related to the interaction of two important aspects of educational evaluation.

Differential Standards

An overall grade-point average used as a basis for student selection for awarding honors and/or admission to special programs or institutions is a composite of assessments made by different teachers who may use different bases for assigning grades. The final grade for each student in each course reflects a convenient and simple-to-use reduction of much varied evaluative data. Besides using different evaluative bases in assigning grades, teachers may vary considerably in the extent to which they allow nonachievement variables to influence the summative mark for a subject or course. Further, even when teachers use the same evaluative bases, there may be widely varying levels of stringency in applying them. Some teachers tend to be "tough" graders; others tend to be "easy" graders.

Because of this, questions have been raised regarding the efficacy of using GPA as a basis for critical selection/admission decisions, especially with students from different schools that themselves may have different standards and practices for grading. There is much truth to these arguments, particularly when attempts are made to use GPAs from different schools or even departments within a school. Geisinger recommends that GPAs from different schools *not* be used for selection decisions; rather, the more appropriate measures are "rank in class" or "percentile rank." These measures indicate an individual's standing relative to his peers in the same school.* Relative standing in a class, based on GPAs, has proven to be an effective and much used predictor of future academic success.

Fairness

Fairness in assigning grades is a long-standing and continuing issue that does not appear to be going away. If anything, the

---

*Of course, class rank says nothing about the distances between adjacent ranks. Furthermore, someone who ranks fifth in a graduating class from an "easy" high school may in fact have less academic ability than someone who ranks twenty-fifth in a graduating class from a "difficult" high school.

increased social and political concerns regarding evaluation magnify the problem. Grading systems that compare an individual's achievement with that of other students are a particular concern. Critics claim that such systems are unfair to minorities and other educationally and socioeconomically disadvantaged students. Another criticism is that grades tend to reward students who by virtue of background, conditioning, and/or personality find working toward grades particularly rewarding. In essence, grades tend to reward competitive individuals more than others.

There is little doubt of the validity of these charges in some instances, particularly regarding advantages to competitive individuals in situations where undue emphasis is placed on grades as motivators. In certain instances where minorities and other disadvantaged students would be in unfair competition with other students, norm-referenced bases should *not* be used.

Other charges of unfairness are varied and generally are related to either of two matters: (a) validity of the grades for the instruction and evaluation procedures and (b) bias. Charges of invalidity of grades most often come in instances where a single symbol is used to report student progress and the teacher attempts to reflect more than instructional achievement in the grade. Part of the difficulty is the inappropriateness of the reporting system for doing this, with the resultant effect being either perceived invalidity of the grade or confusion regarding its meaning. Teachers must ensure that grades indeed reflect student progress. The use of carefully structured multiple-reporting procedures probably will alleviate most charges of grade invalidity, but if a teacher must use a single symbol system, the grading bases and criteria should be well-defined and communicated to students and parents.

Another factor contributing to charges of grade invalidity is that some teachers assign grades with little or no evaluative basis and/or on inappropriate bases. For instance, in many elementary general music situations, music teachers are required to provide grades for some 500 to 600 students every six or nine weeks, yet because of their heavy teaching schedules, possible inappropriate use of instructional time, and various other reasons, they actually have little information on which to base individual students' grades. Or, in some performance classes at the secondary level, teachers may spend a majority of the instructional time preparing for a public performance, yet base a large proportion of the students' grades on some sight-reading test or a paper-and-pencil test of music fundamentals. In such cases, grade validity and fairness clearly are questionable, especially since students who take private music lessons outside of school may tend to score much better on tests devised for the latter instance.

Charges of bias in grade assignment no doubt will continue to be leveled against teachers, because even with great care taken to ensure that objective bases are used for grading, grades still include a judgmental component. However, teachers who develop valid, objective bases for grading and communicate these bases to students and parents will do much to alleviate appearances of bias, and hence, charges of bias.

By-products of Grading

There appear to be several by-products of grading, chief of which include an affective component, concepts about ability, and confusion. These effects vary greatly from one individual to another, but they nevertheless are real in many instances.

Affect may either be positive or negative, depending largely on whether the assigned grade was higher or lower than expected, and this affective reaction may influence subsequent effort and learning. Some students receiving grades that were lower than expected may generalize the affect to the teacher and class content, consequently creating attitudinal problems influencing their learning. Other students receiving grades higher than expected may respond to the grades as a reward or incentive for learning and respond accordingly. The resultant differential response may magnify motivational differences among students in a class, tempting the naive teacher to consider inflating grades for all students in an effort to motivate all students more. The temptation should be avoided.

Students' and parents' interpretations of the meanings of grades undoubtedly run the gamut. A problem is that unwarranted high grades may lead to misconceptions regarding a student's ability. This problem is particularly acute in applied music courses at the collegiate level where grades may reflect a strong "effort" or "improvement" component. Students and parents may interpret four years of "A" to mean that the student is far above average on his or her instrument, excels most other students, and/or is progressing well toward becoming a professional musician. However, an audition or two with a professional symphony or an opera company may suggest otherwise. At the secondary school level, consistently high grades in music, in addition to the many other reinforcements a music student receives, may encourage some students to pursue music as a career, when in fact the student's performance level is marginal for such a career. While all students should have an opportunity to pursue musical training to the extent that they desire, teachers have a responsibility to ensure that enough accurate information is conveyed to students and parents via grades and/or other means so that they have a realistic perspective regarding ability and potential, thus facilitating appropriate career decisions.

The third by-product is confusion regarding what the grade means. As previously mentioned, the meaning of the single symbol grade often is unclear, with both students and parents being unsure of its basis. This is especially apparent in music classes where all students get high grades, regardless of apparent effort or achievement. The net result may be that the value of grades as reports of student progress is greatly diminished, even to the point that they are not taken seriously. This is unfortunate because reporting should be an integral and important part of a school's evaluation program.

SPECIAL PROBLEMS IN MUSIC GRADING

There is little question that music teachers are confronted with a number of particular problems in grading. The problems vary for different instructional levels and types of courses; however, they do exist, and some understanding of them may alleviate a teacher's frustrations and/or inappropriate grading practices. Three particular problem areas are elementary general music, secondary and collegiate performing groups, and applied music at the collegiate level.

As mentioned previously, expecting an elementary music teacher who meets from 500 to 600 students each week to provide meaningful grades every six or nine weeks is unrealistic, especially when a single symbol grade must be used. Evaluating each student in relation to each objective conceivably could require an inordinate proportion of the instructional time, which usually is about one hour per week. Solutions to this dilemma are not simple, but teachers should nevertheless have some valid bases for grades assigned to students. Multiple reporting systems will facilitate reporting at this level and allow the teacher to rate students on attributes of performance that may be determined from group evaluation, for example, willingness to participate, apparent effort, and attending behaviors. The grade for achievement, however, should be in relation to instructional objectives, and evaluation of such is a part of the instructional process. Because of large numbers of students and limited instructional time, however, teachers may have to rely on fewer samples of achievement behavior than desired.*

Grading in secondary school and collegiate performing groups is a particular problem. Many teacher/conductors appear to be reluctant to take instructional/rehearsal time for evaluation of individual students' achievement. Often grades are rewards for "good attitude," participation, effort, or attendance. Attendance appears to be the predominant grading basis in collegiate performing groups. In many performance groups, teachers must deal with large numbers of students, thus compounding the problems.

It would be inappropriate to expect that all performing groups have the same grading basis, but total disregard for evaluation of student achievement is unwarranted. As for grading in the elementary music classroom, there is no simple solution for grading in performing groups, but an important first step is to clarify the instructional objectives for the group and base grades on achievement in relation to those objectives. Instructors who desire to provide feedback regarding effort, attitude, attendance, or other behaviors should consider using multiple reporting systems. Also, music teachers/conductors should reconsider the appropriateness of grades in some collegiate performing groups.

Grading in applied music at the collegiate level also has its problems. The close interpersonal working relationship between teacher and student may lead the teacher to use grades for encouragement or as rewards for improvement or effort expended. Many schools also base applied music grades partly on jury performance, thus compounding the issue. Perhaps there never will be consensus regarding the extent to which applied music grades should depend on a teacher's assessments or a jury's assessments. Certainly the teacher has a better perspective on growth or improvement during the grading period, but the jury provides an external viewpoint that may reflect a different grading basis.

---

*Occasionally it is possible to group students into small subgroups, perhaps in the form of small ensembles, in which each student has a prominent performing role that is supported by other students yet conspicuous enough to allow meaningful individual evaluation.

Besides these particular problems, grading music instruction is fraught with all of the other problems of grading, and there is no apparent simple, quick, and easy way of resolving them. However, the following section offers some guidelines that may be helpful in resolving some of the grading problems.

GUIDELINES FOR MUSIC GRADING

Numbers of students, the diversified nature of music instruction, limitations regarding instructional time, and the nature of the grading systems imposed on music teachers make grading a continuing and challenging responsibility for music teachers. Nevertheless, grading is an important aspect of the instructional process, and while it is a less-than-perfect procedure for reporting student progress, it does serve several important educational functions. Because of this teachers should undertake to provide the best possible reporting to students and parents that can be accomplished, given the limitations and other restraints of their respective teaching situations. The following guidelines, based in part on some recommendations by Gronlund (1981, pp. 518–519), may be helpful.

1. The meaning of a grade should be unambiguous; students and parents should be informed of the bases for the grade.

2. Whenever possible a multiple reporting system should be used. Even when a school uses a single symbol reporting system, it should be supplemented with other rating scales or descriptive information that will convey clearly the various other types of information that a teacher desires to communicate to students and parents.

3. The development of the grading and reporting system should be guided by the functions to be served.

4. Parents and students should have input into the development of the grading and reporting system.

5. Grades should be based on achievement in relation to clear statements of instructional objectives.

6. Grades should have an adequate (i.e., sufficient samples of relevant behaviors) evaluation basis.

7. The reporting system should be detailed enough to be informative and yet compact enough to be practical.

SUMMARY

Grades are used to summarize and characterize a student's performance in an educational endeavor. Their overriding function is to convey information, but they also serve other functions for schools and individuals.

The most common grading system is the single symbol system, usually letters with five levels or categories. Other grading systems include pass–fail, percentages, descriptive grading, self-assessment, and multiple reporting systems.

Grades should reflect achievement, and a student's grade may be based on achievement in relation to an absolute standard, the student's peers, or the student's potential, including effort and/or growth. Teachers interested in reporting additional dimensions of a student's behavior related to performance during the grading period should use a multiple reporting system.

Particular issues related to grading include (a) reporting the affective dimension of student behavior, (b) grade inflation, (c) the effects of student ratings, (d) differential standards, (e) fairness, and (f) by-products of grading.

Study Questions

1. For the elementary schools, secondary schools, and colleges with which you are familiar, discuss the uses that are made of grades. Compare these with the uses discussed in Chapter 12.

2. Discuss and compare the relative merits of the various bases for grades for (a) general music classes and (b) performance classes.

3. Discuss the general issues in grading that are most relevant to grading in music classes.

4. Suggest ways for resolving some of the special problems in music grading.

5. Design multiple reporting systems for (a) elementary general music and (b) secondary band, orchestra, or choir.

REFERENCES

Anderson, S.B., Ball, S., Murphy, R.T., & Associates. *Encyclopedia of educational evaluation.* San Francisco, Calif.: Jossey-Bass, 1975.

Geisinger, K.F. Marking systems. In H.E. Mitzel (Ed.), *Encyclopedia of educational research* (Vol. 3). New York: Free Press, 1982.

Geisinger, K.F., & Rabinowitz, W. Individual differences among college faculty in grading. *Journal of Instructional Psychology,* 1980, *1,* 20–27.

Gronlund, N.E. *Measurement and evaluation in teaching.* New York: Macmillan, 1981.

Kirschenbaum, H., Napier, R., & Simon, S.B. *Wad-ja-get? The grading game in American education.* New York: Hart, 1971.

Milton, O., & Edgerly, J.W. *The testing and grading of students.* New Rochelle, N.Y.: Change Magazine and Educational Change, 1976.

Terwilliger, J.S. *Assigning grades to students.* Glenview, Ill.: Scott, Foresman, 1971.

Thorndike, R.L., & Hagen, E.P. *Measurement and evaluation in psychology and education* (4th ed.). New York: Wiley, 1977.

13

Program Evaluation

Measurement and evaluation of musical behaviors traditionally imply assessment and evaluation of *individuals*, and much of this book reflects that focus. However, since the accountability movement began in the 1960s, all areas of education have had need for more and better *program evaluation*. As critics of education call for increased emphasis on the "basics," the need for program evaluation in the arts has become increasingly important. Changing emphases in schools' social and political climates dictate that arts programs not only must provide evidence of accountability, but also must have sound bases for curriculum development and revision if they are to survive. The thesis of this book, and particularly this chapter, is that evaluative feedback is an essential and critical aspect of the music curriculum, and should be an integral part of a school music program, thus providing an important basis for curriculum development and revision.

The purview of program evaluation in music traditionally has been limited, not only in scope, but also in quality and applications. The educational, sociological, and political realities of the 1980s, coupled with expectations of continuing changes in the decades ahead, however, suggest an urgent need for music teachers, supervisors, and administrators to develop better understandings of the functions of, approaches to, and applications of program evaluation. The purpose of this chapter, therefore, is to provide an overview of program evaluation, including its definitions, functions, and methodological issues. The chapter concludes with a discussion of the applications of program evaluation to music education.

A PERSPECTIVE ON PROGRAM EVALUATION

"Program evaluation, as a field of scholarly study and as an applied professional endeavor, has undergone enormous changes over the past decade" (Talmadge, 1982, p. 593). The proliferation of books, journals, and "models" concerned with evaluation of educational programs supports Talmadge's claim. A cursory review of the literature reveals a core of professionals whose work and writing pervade the literature, and readers interested in developing expertise in program evaluation must examine particularly the writings of Cronbach (1982), Cronbach et al. (1980), Madaus, Scriven, and Stufflebeam (1983), Scriven (1967), Stake (1975), Stufflebeam et al. (1971), and Talmadge (1982).

Many of these professionals have developed "models" for program evaluation (see, for example, the "CIPP" model, the "discrepancy" model, the "responsive" model, and the "goal-free" model), although Nevo (1983), following the lead of Stake (1981), suggests that the models really are more appropriately termed "approaches" or "persuasions." Regardless of how they are labeled, the "models" appear to have enough distinctive features for classification according to various criteria, such as goals, methodology, underlying assumptions, or outcomes. Talmadge (1982) and House (1983) offer two particularly useful classification schemes. Talmadge classifies approaches to educational evaluation under four headings: experimental, eclectic, descriptive, and cost-benefit analytic. She compares them on several bases, including philosophical base, discipline base, methodology, participants' and evaluators' roles, political pressures, and the focus of the evaluation report. House's taxonomy of major evaluation models illustrates the breadth and diversity of approaches that have evolved as program evaluation has developed as a field of study. House's taxonomy relates the models to the ethics, epistemology, and political implications inherent in the philosophy of liberalism, and recognizes eight categories of models: systems, behavioral objective, decision making, goal-free, criticism, accreditation, adversary, and transaction.

A cursory examination of the two classification schemes reveals that various approaches appear to have different purposes, be based on different assumptions, use different methodologies, and serve various clientele. Each also appears to have a particular philosophical basis and subsequently to have varying educational, social, and/or political implications. Just as experimental designs provide a point of departure for designing an experiment, the evaluation models provide a point of departure for planning program evaluation; however, many factors must be considered prior to formulating an evaluation plan, and Nevo (1983), following the lead of Stufflebeam (1974), argues that program evaluation can be conceptualized better by addressing ten underlying dimensions representing the major issues that the most prominent educational evaluation approaches address. Brief discussions of Nevo's ten dimensions follow.

How Is Evaluation Defined?

Perhaps the best known definition of program evaluation is the traditional view espoused by Tyler (1950, p. 69), who states that evaluation is "the process of determining to what extent the educational objectives are actually being realized." Another definition suggests that program evaluation should provide feedback for educational decision making: *"Evaluation is the process of delineating, obtaining, and providing useful information for judging decision alternatives"* (Stufflebeam et al., 1971, p. xxv). More recently, however, Nevo (1983, p. 118) notes that "considerable consensus has been reached among evaluators regarding the definition of evaluation as the *assessment of merit or worth"* [emphasis added]. Reflecting this consensus, a joint committee on standards for evaluation, representing 12 organizations concerned with educational evaluation, defined evaluation as "the systematic investigation of the worth or merit of some object" (Joint Committee, 1981, p. 12). However, Cronbach et al. (1980) reject the idea that the evaluator should be the one to judge the merit or worth of a program.

The definition issue appears to hinge on whether evaluation should "provide feedback for decision making" or "involve judgment of merit or worth" of a program and its various aspects. Clearly, program evaluation must provide information for decision making, but the extent to which external evaluators' judgments should be the basis for policy and program decisions depends on a number of factors. Suffice it to say here that their judgments should be rendered and considered, but the ultimate decisions regarding policy and program changes must rest with the individuals accountable for planning and managing the program.

What Are the Functions of Evaluation?

Nevo recognizes four functions of evaluation: (a) formative, (b) summative, (c) psychological or sociopolitical, and (d) administrative. Scriven (1967) appears to have been one of the first to distinguish between formative and summative evaluation. *Formative* evaluation is concerned with program *improvement* and essentially involves examining program planning and processes. *Summative* evaluation examines outcomes and products of an educational program and primarily serves an *accountability* function. The *psychological* or *sociopolitical* function essentially refers to using evaluation to promote professional, political, and public *awareness* of a program, its goals, activities, and outcomes. Whether programs should serve a psychological or sociopolitical function may be debatable, but such a function appears to be increasingly prevalent in many evaluation endeavors. Nevo's fourth function (*administrative*) involves the unpopular practice of using evaluation as an exercise of authority, that is, where administrators use evaluation to demonstrate and reinforce their authority over individuals subordinate to them in an educational program.

While employing the authority function is of dubious value both ethically and as evaluation, the other three functions are legitimate uses of educational evaluation data. The particular function(s) to be emphasized will necessarily vary, depending on the scope, nature, and objectives of both the program and the evaluation itself. For most program evaluation, whether for ongoing programs or new or experimental intervention programs in schools, comprehensive formative evaluation is essential. Summative evaluation appears to be less critical than in the past two decades, but the sociopolitical function seems to be increasingly recognized as an important and legitimate evaluation function. Decisions regarding which to emphasize must be made jointly by individuals involved in managing the evaluation, those managing the program, and those to whom they are accountable.

What Are the Objects of Evaluation?

Traditionally students and teachers have been the primary objects of program evaluation. Nevo maintains that nearly all measurement and evaluation literature up to the mid-1960s focused on evaluation in terms of student achievement, but he attributes change and broadening of emphasis in program evaluation to the many developments in American education that resulted from federally funded projects and legislation such as the Elementary and Secondary Education Act of 1965.

On the basis of his review of contemporary evaluation literature, Nevo (1983, p. 120) draws two major conclusions regarding the objects of evaluation: "(a) Almost everything can be an object of evaluation, and evaluation should not be limited to the evaluation of students and school personnel; and (b) the clear identification of the evaluation object is an important part of the development of any evaluation design." He argues that determining the objects of evaluation is essential in the design of any program evaluation, because it provides a focus for the evaluation and helps to clarify and resolve conflicts and potential threat among stakeholders and others likely to be affected by the evaluation.

What Kinds of Information Should Be Collected Regarding Each Object?

The current trend is clearly toward using a broad information base in program evaluation. For example, Stufflebeam's well known CIPP evaluation model involves collection of information about four aspects of an educational program: context, input, process, and product. These four types of information provide, respectively, bases for (a) planning decisions regarding selection of goals and objectives, (b) structuring decisions to facilitate strategy selection and procedural designs for achieving program objectives, (c) implementing decisions relative to carrying out and improving the selected strategies and designs, and (d) recycling decisions, that is, decisions whether to continue, change, or terminate a program. The scope of information required for such decisions obviously is broad.

The evaluation model for Project IMPACT, *Interdisciplinary Model Program in the Arts for Children and Teachers* (Arts IMPACT, 1973), also was designed to elicit a broad base of information. Besides information regarding student products and performance in the arts, the model was designed to elicit information about performances in non-arts areas, as well as descriptive and attitudinal data from a variety of sources, both internal and external to the project, regarding project planning, conduct, and administration in each of its five sites. Particular effort was made to elicit information about the project's interactions with broader goals of the respective schools, communities, and arts organizations.

Stake's (1975) responsive approach to arts education also emphasizes the importance of a broad information base. He identifies 13 types of data that may be needed to evaluate an educational program, and divides them into two broad categories: descriptive and judgmental. He also maintains that there should be differential emphasis on antecedent, transaction, and outcome information when describing and making program judgments. Essentially, his model focuses on describing a program, its setting, and issues, and engaging in responsive dialogue with the appropriate audiences regarding issues and values.

To summarize, contemporary evaluation requires a broad information base, clearly involving more than examination of achievement or other program outcomes. However, evaluation priorities and/or practical constraints will necessarily help to delimit the range of information sought and provide focus to the evaluation. Above all, program evaluation must elicit information relative to the function(s) that the evaluation is to serve.

What Criteria Should Be Used to Judge the Merit or Worth of an Evaluation Object?

Evaluators who view evaluation merely as collection of data to serve others (i.e., the "relevant decision makers") do not concern themselves with this issue. Also, evaluators who limit the focus of evaluation to assessment of outcomes in relation to program objectives essentially make the decision to evaluate on the basis of "achievement in relation to goals and objectives," somewhat akin to one of the bases for grading in the classroom. Certainly both of these approaches have validity. In the former case, the argument is that the relevant decision makers are in a better position to make important policy and planning decisions. In the latter case, achievement in relation to goals and objectives may be the most appropriate criterion if summative evaluation for accountability is the primary function of the evaluation.

The overriding factors in selection of evaluative criteria must be the specific context and function(s) of the evaluation. Nevo also suggests several alternative bases for evaluative criteria: (a) identified needs of clients, (b) ideals or social values, (d) standards set by experts or other relevant groups, and (d) the quality of alternative programs. Whatever criteria are to be used for judging the worth or merit of a program, they must be identified early in planning evaluation so that adequate data are collected for making the judgments.

Who Should Be Served by an Evaluation?

Those who view evaluation primarily as providing information for decision making apparently view other "relevant decision makers" as the individuals to be served by an evaluation. These might include program directors, supervisors, and managers, as well as other individuals who have been involved in planning and shaping program policy. Cronbach et al. (1980) argue particularly that program evaluation should serve the policy-shaping community rather than just managerial decision makers. The clientele or audience served by an evaluation may be broad and, in many cases, diverse. Nevo (1983, p. 122) has identified three "propositions" regarding who should be served by an evaluation: "(a) An evaluation can have more than one client or audience; (b) different evaluation audiences might have different evaluation needs; and (c) the specific audiences for an evaluation and their evaluation needs must be clearly identified at the early stages of planning an evaluation."

The needs of different groups will influence the type of information sought, the level of data analysis, and the nature of the evaluation reports. Furthermore, clear and early identification of the persons to be served by the evaluation not only will facilitate, but will force evaluators to establish priorities in selecting the types of information sought.

What Is the Process of Doing an Evaluation?

An evaluation process necessarily reflects the theoretical basis of an evaluation approach. The traditional evaluation model in which goals and objectives form the basis for evaluation might involve a relatively straightforward process such as (a) identifying goals and stating them in behavioral terms, (b) developing measuring instruments, (c) collecting data, (d) interpreting results, and (e) making recommendations.

Stake's (1975) responsive model, however, might have an evaluation process involving (a) describing a program, (b) reporting the description to relevant audiences, and (c) engaging the evaluator(s) in responsive dialogue with the relevant audiences regarding their judgments of the program.

Proponents of program evaluation as gathering data to serve other relevant decision makers (Stufflebeam et al., 1971) suggest a process that (a) delineates information requirements through interaction with the decision-making audiences, (b) obtains the needed information through formal data collection and analysis procedures, and (c) provides the information to decision makers in a communicable format.

While these and other variations in process reflected in other evaluation models suggest a lack of consensus among evaluation experts regarding the "best" process to follow in conducting an evaluation, most agree that "all evaluations should include a certain amount of interaction between evaluators and their audiences at the outset of the evaluation to identify evaluation needs, and at its conclusion to communicate its findings. Evaluation cannot be limited to the technical activities of data collection and analysis" (Nevo, 1983, p. 122).

What Methods of Inquiry Should Be Used in Evaluation?

Traditional approaches to program evaluation were patterned after experimental and quasi-experimental research designs, thus considering the program and its various attributes as independent variables and student achievement, attitudes, and other outcomes as dependent variables. A cursory examination of the various models or approaches to evaluation that are advocated today, however, suggests that many other methods of inquiry are also appropriate and useful for program evaluation, for example, descriptive methods, naturalistic methods, quantitative methods, qualitative methods, and so on. While such methodologies are not necessarily discrete, they each reflect particular theoretical and/or philosophical bases and subsequently different emphases.

Nevo suggests that, given the present state of the art of program evaluation, the best move might be to take an eclectic approach to evaluation methodology and incorporate quantitative-scientific-summative methodology and qualitative-naturalistic-descriptive methodology as appropriate for given evaluation needs and functions. It is doubtful that there is a "best method" for all program evaluation purposes.

Who Should Do Evaluation?

Nevo (1983, p. 123) maintains that

> to be a competent and trustworthy evaluator one needs to have a combination of a wide variety of characteristics. These include technical competence in the area of measurement and research methods, understanding the social context and the substance of the evaluation object, human relations skills, personal integrity, and objectivity, as well as characteristics related to organizational authority and responsibility.

He further argues that the realities of finding such individuals are slight and consequently recommends that program evaluation be conducted by teams of individuals. He also recognizes two important distinctions that must be taken into account when selecting program evaluators: (a) internal versus external evaluators, and (b) amateur versus professional evaluators.

Internal evaluators usually are employed by the program and report directly to its management, thus perhaps having less credibility than external evaluators who are not directly employed by the program and hence appear to have a greater degree of autonomy. Professional evaluators are those individuals who have extensive training in program evaluation and whose primary job is to conduct evaluation; amateur evaluators, however, usually have their major professional training in other areas and, while they may be highly knowledgeable and competent evaluators, usually have other professional responsibilities. In many instances an amateur evaluator may be more appropriate than a professional because of his or her understanding of a program's unique qualities and needs.

Decisions regarding whether to use internal or external evaluators need not be "either–or"; to the contrary, each may make particular contributions that the other might be unable to make. Regardless of membership, the evaluation team must maintain frequent and effective communication with the program management from the initial planning stages throughout the evaluation. Furthermore, the evaluation team must include individuals who possess (a) competence in research methodology and data analysis techniques, (b) understanding of the program's social context and unique character, (c) the ability to develop and maintain good rapport with other individuals and groups involved in the evaluation, and (d) sufficient perspective to integrate all of these characteristics.

By What Standards Should Evaluation Be Judged?

With the changing functions, theoretical underpinnings, methodologies, and approaches to evaluation that have occurred in recent years have come questions related to evaluating the evaluations of educational programs. It no longer is enough to just have an evaluation program; the evaluation must provide the necessary information for the policy-making and managerial decisions essential to developing and maintaining quality education programs, both for ongoing programs and intervention programs.

Various professional evaluators have defined standards against which program evaluation might be judged, but most sets of standards reflect a particular theoretical and/or philosophical base that renders them inappropriate for judging all evaluation models. Talmadge (1982), however, notes that the standards developed by the Joint Committee for Standards on Education Evaluation (1981) appear to be useful for evaluating most program evaluation models. Developed by representatives of 12 professional organizations concerned with educational evaluation, the 30 standards are grouped under four broad attributes that are considered necessary and sufficient for program evaluation: *utility, feasibility, propriety,* and *accuracy.* Utility refers to the extent to which the evaluation is responsive to the needs of the client group and includes such standards as audience identification, evaluator credibility, report clarity, and timeliness. Feasibility standards are concerned with the practicality, cost effectiveness, and political viability of the evaluation design for the setting in which it must be conducted. Standards for propriety are concerned with the rights of the persons affected by the evaluation, and the 11 standards for accuracy reflect concern for clear object identification and description, valid and reliable measurement, systematic data analysis, justified conclusions, and objective reporting.

While the standards are conceived as guidelines and generally are viewed as a major positive contribution to the field, they have created a certain amount of professional controversy. Talmadge (1982, p. 607) expresses concern:

> The key issues revolve around whether or not program evaluation needs an external set of guidelines for conducting evaluation, the negative effects of externally imposed standards on a scholarly field of study, and whether or not standards improve the quality of evaluations. If standards become more than guidelines, is certification far behind?

GUIDELINES FOR EVALUATING MUSIC PROGRAMS

As noted above, early approaches to program evaluation were patterned after experimental research designs. The "program" was considered the independent or treatment variable (i.e., the variable being manipulated) and the summative results of the evaluation, usually student achievement or attitudes, were considered the dependent variables, that is, the outcome or effect presumably dependent on the independent variable.

Readers who have undertaken experimental research in education or other social sciences are quite aware of the difficulties in designing an experiment in such a way that (a) the treatment variable is so carefully defined that there is no question regarding its specific attributes and (b) the results or outcomes can unequivocally be attributed to the treatment variable. The latter essentially reflects the concern for the study's internal validity, that is, that no "plausible rival hypotheses" persist for explaining the results of an experiment.

Program evaluation presents even more control problems. A "program" in a school often is difficult to clearly delimit and/or define, particularly since educational programs may involve many people in their planning and implementation, include a wide variety of curriculum materials and strategies, be either ongoing programs or new intervention programs, and be implemented in widely varying educational, sociological, and political contexts. However, much of the literature on program evaluation implicitly treats programs as if they were experimental treatments with clearly definable and finite attributes. In reality, most education programs, whether ongoing or interventive, are dynamic in the sense that change, albeit slow at times, is an integral aspect of the "treatment." Consequently, evaluation of most educational programs, in terms of the program as an experimental treatment and the outcomes as the dependent variables, often is inappropriate.

Program evaluations that continue to follow the experimental research model usually focus on summative evaluation, thus reflecting a concern for accountability. The position taken here, however, is that program evaluation's primary function should be to facilitate planning and policy making regarding *present* and *future* directions for a music program. While summative evaluation is an important aspect of program evaluation, it should not be the primary focus for most evaluations of music programs, because it reflects a *backward* outlook, seeking to provide accountability for the time, effort, and expense of a program. Certainly summative data are useful, particularly when decisions are to be made regarding whether to terminate or continue a program, but such data rarely provide the information needed for *improving* an educational program. Curriculum or program development most often is a gradual, ongoing process, and formative evaluation data appear to be more useful than summative for facilitating change and improvement in a program. Therefore, formative evaluation should comprise a major focus of program evaluation unless specific goals for the evaluation dictate otherwise.

The key to effective program evaluation is careful planning. Ideally, each of the dimensions discussed in the first part of this chapter should be considered and dealt with. The realities of the resources for program evaluation, however, may limit the breadth and depth of an evaluation plan, thus forcing the planners of the program and the evaluation to make critical decisions early on regarding the nature of the evaluation. Many variables must be considered when making these early decisions because they ultimately will affect the nature and usefulness of the evaluation. Evaluations that merely serve the sociopolitical function, to the neglect of providing a basis for improving a program, are of dubious value. The balance of this chapter, therefore, offers some guidelines for planning and conducting program evaluation in music. The guidelines are offered in response to several basic questions that must be answered during the process of planning and conducted a program evaluation.

Why Initiate a Music Program Evaluation?

The functions of program evaluation were discussed in Chapter 1. Essentially, program evaluation today is thought of as a forward-looking activity: planning for the future, particularly with respect to improving the program to better meet the instructional needs of the students it is intended to serve. Other specific functions of program evaluation that were identified in Chapter 1 include (a) accountability, (b) instructional effectiveness, (c) teacher effectiveness, (d) policy making and management, and (e) research or project evaluation. While the accountability function is important for developing and maintaining program standards, it is usually summative in nature and lacks the broad base for facilitating future program development. *The primary reason for initiating a music program evaluation is to facilitate future policy-making, management, and implementation decisions.* Evaluation data will be useful both internally to the program policy-makers, managers, and implementers, as well as to those administrators and other individuals who by virtue of their position in a school district or on a school board must make decisions that have fiscal implications for music programs vis-à-vis other programs in a school. Programs that have strong evaluation data, assuming other variables to be equal, are more likely to receive favorable consideration when difficult decisions must be made.

Who Should Initiate a Music Program Evaluation?

While many program evaluations are mandated by state or other accrediting agencies on a regular basis, many times there is a need for a different type of evaluation and for more frequent evaluation than may be mandated. Furthermore, many ongoing so-called evaluation programs really do not serve any primary function of evaluation—planning for the future. Rather, they are often ritualistic self-reports in the form of year-end summaries of activities, which in effect are a type of "show-and-tell" for the respective program leadership. The traditional reliance on public musical performance to demonstrate quality and accountability also reflects a very limited mode of program evaluation.

Anytime a program does not have an ongoing broad-based evaluation plan, the leadership or those accountable for the program are responsible for initiating such an evaluation. Others, however, also might take the initiative in bringing about an evaluation of the program. Teachers might discuss some of their concerns with the administrators of the music program; school boards, and/or school administrators not directly involved with the music program but who are responsible for the total school program, may take the first steps to get an evaluation program under way; or interested parents and other members of the community may exercise their influence in initiating an evaluation of a music program.

Because any evaluation is potentially threatening to those being evaluated, it is critical that the initial steps be presented and recognized as a collaborative concern and effort toward improving a music program rather than as assessing blame for any perceived shortcomings of a program. Human nature being what it is, this is a difficult task, but also a critical one if an evaluation program is to be effective. Once discussions are under way regarding the possibility of establishing an evaluation plan for a music program, there are several steps that must be taken to ensure at least acceptance of the idea to all concerned.

What Are the Initial Steps in Planning a Music Program Evaluation?

The first step in planning an evaluation for a music program is to establish clearly the need for the evaluation, or, in more traditional language, to conduct a needs assessment. In everyday language, the potential value of the evaluation must be established. Factors both internal and external to the program might be needs, for example, changing school populations, changing value systems regarding school music, external pressures such as the "back to basics" movement that may affect a music curriculum, changing personnel, philosophy, and goals of teachers and administrators, perceived curricular imbalance both within and between various courses, and so on. Other needs might be less obvious but equally important. Sometimes even "good" programs stagnate and need some impetus for change. The process of evaluation in and of itself often can provide a stimulus for rejuvenation of a program.

After the need for program evaluation is established, the second step involves planning the evaluation, perhaps the most critical aspect of the entire process. The specific steps may be different for ongoing programs and for new intervention programs being implemented in a school, but essentially the same types of decisions must be made. Planning should involve teachers, managers, policy makers, and other appropriate individuals, both internal and external to the program, including at least one professional evaluator. The planners must answer (or get answers to) several basic questions in order that they may make some critical decisions regarding the evaluation. Specifically, the planners must determine the (a) functions that the evaluation is to serve, (b) resources that are available for the evaluation, (c) general time frame for the evaluation, and (d) leadership of the evaluation effort and the responsibilities of the evaluation leadership to the program leadership.

The planners may not have complete autonomy in making the decisions relative to the above steps; sometimes functions of evalutions are mandated from accrediting agencies or a higher level administration within a school district, and resources obviously are limited. Also, there may be certain time constraints that must be adhered to, and finally planners do not always have free reign in selecting the evaluators for a program—some school districts may specify that the evaluation be conducted through their own research and evaluation office or that the evaluation be conducted in cooperation with a particular outside agency. Decisions relative to use of external evaluators necessarily have fiscal implications.

Underlying the planning of a program evaluation is the development of a budget, the need to gain approval of the budget from the appropriate authorities, and the establishment of an evaluation team. A rule of thumb that the U.S. Office of Education has used to determine a budget for an evaluation was 10 percent of the total program budget. However, total program budgets in ongoing programs often are difficult to ascertain because of the different ways in which programs are funded, but a planning committee has the responsibility to determine the budget needs for an evaluation and to ensure that the budget is adequate for the functions that the evaluation is to serve. Should resources clearly be inadequate for conducting the needed evaluation, then the planners must reconsider the scope of the evaluation.

To summarize, the initial steps in planning program evaluation may be grouped into three broad steps: (a) establishing the need for the program evaluation, (b) planning in terms of functions, resources, time frame, and leadership of the evaluation, and (c) securing the necessary budget and leadership for the evaluation team. Implicit in all of this planning phase is the need to establish good rapport and understanding among all of the individuals involved in the program regarding roles, intent of the evaluation, and responsibilities.

Carrying Out a Music Program Evaluation

Some of the decisions made during the planning phase of the evaluation necessarily dictate procedures and strategies to be followed in carrying out a music program evaluation. For example, if some of the needs of the evaluation were to examine a music program in relation to how well it incorporated new philosophies and trends in music education, the evaluation would not only have to be designed to elicit information relative to this need, but also provide some basis for planning changes to implement such, should the data reveal discrepancies between practice and the new philosophies or trends.

Other planning decisions that have particular implications for the conduct of the study concern selecting the leadership of the evaluation. Will the leadership be external to the program, and, if so, how much autonomy will it have? What kind of balance will there be between internal and external members of an evaluation team? Will the evaluation team be data gatherers who provide information for decisions to be made by the program leadership, or will the evaluators be asked (or allowed) to render judgments regarding various aspects of the program?

What will be the relative emphases on descriptive-formative-qualitative evaluation and objective-summative-quantitative evaluation? The better these questions are answered during the planning phase of a program, the more effective and efficient the evaluation will be.

Particular responsibilities of the evaluation team are to provide information relative to the functions of the evaluation. This may include a wide variety of information with varying emphasis on different types depending on the functions emphasized. To avoid reactive effects, the evaluation team should gather relevant information with as little intrusion into the program as possible. Judicious sampling will reduce the sheer amount of information to be processed, although care should be taken to avoid exclusion of relevant data.

The relative emphasis on testing, observations, and audio or video recording of musical performances must be weighed in light of the uses to be made of such data. Some data may be particularly valuable for a sociopolitical function but of little use for facilitating planning for improvement of a program. All data gathered must be for some specific purpose. It is a waste of everyone's time and energy to gather unneeded data.

Throughout the conduct of an evaluation, evaluators must not lose sight of the purpose of the evaluation. While many of their decisions regarding procedures and data focus are indicated by the planning phase of the evaluation, evaluators have the autonomy and responsibility to make decisions that will influence the efficacy of the conduct of the evaluation. Judicious decisions regarding many of these matters may influence the adequacy with which an evaluation serves the functions intended and ultimately the impact it may have on the program.

What Should Be the Nature of the Evaluation Report?

The major decision here is whether information should be provided continuously throughout an evaluation or at the conclusion of the evaluation. Again, what is "right" seems to be related to the function of the evaluation. If it is to provide formative data for improving a program, continuous evaluative feedback clearly is essential. If it is to evaluate the instructional effectiveness of a new experimental program of study systematically, perhaps summative data are all that are necessary. However, if the evaluation also is to serve some sociopolitical function, then perhaps appropriate continuous reporting is necessary throughout the project.

A particular concern in reporting the results of an evaluation is that they be reported expeditiously and to the appropriate individuals. Evaluation essentially is a service to the program leadership or some governing or policy-making agency, and evaluators should leave it to those individuals to make public any evaluative data unless they are specifically instructed to do so.

The bottom line in reporting the results of an evaluation is that appropriate data relevant to the function(s) of the evaluation be reported clearly to the appropriate authorities. Objective and subjective data should be clearly delineated so that there is no question about which is which. Reporting should be as objective as possible, and even when judgments are rendered, they should be void of possible biasing language.

What Are Some Pitfalls to Avoid?

Because of its complexity, its educational, sociological, and political implications—and its expense, program evaluation appears to be fraught with potential weaknesses. A problem that appears to affect the entire profession of program evaluation is that as evaluators attempt to design evaluation plans to account for all of the complexities of a program, the evaluation designs are becoming so complex, multi-faceted, and expensive that many practitioners are apt to dispense with them altogether and continue with minimal subjective bases for program planning and evaluation. Music has several unique dimensions that add to the complexity. Furthermore, values of music education philosophers and practitioners tend to differ, with the result that the types of data sought and the functions to be served by the data are not clearly agreed upon. As a result of the complexity of program evaluation and the diversity of opinion about what the data should be used for, program evaluation has yet to become an important aspect of most music programs. Music educators should not allow the sheer magnitude of the task or diversity of opinion to deter them from undertaking the increasingly important task of program evaluation.

Another pitfall essentially is related to the human element in evaluation. Sometimes evaluators are viewed as threats by program managers and teachers. The leadership of both the program and the evaluation must make every effort to diffuse any potential negative feelings toward the evaluation and the evaluators. Defensiveness and hostility undermine the purpose of evaluation, and the evaluation should be couched in a positive light, reflecting a concern for helping everyone involved.

SUMMARY

The nature and scope of program evaluation have changed greatly over the past two decades, and a variety of evaluation "models" or approaches have been devised, including the "CIPP" model, the "discrepancy" model, the "responsive" model, and the "goal-free" model.

A perspective on program evaluation can be gained by examining it in terms of 10 underlying dimensions: (a) the definitions of evaluation, (b) its functions, (c) the objects of evaluation, (d) the kinds of data to be gathered regarding each object, (e) the criteria for judging the merit or worth of an evaluation object, (f) who should be served by evaluation, (g) the evaluation process, (h) the methods of inquiry, (i) who should evaluate, and (j) the standards for judging evaluation.

Guidelines for evaluating music programs focus on the following: (a) why a music program evaluation should be initiated, (b) who should initiate a music program evaluation, (c) initial steps in planning a music program evaluation, (d) carrying out a music program evaluation, (e) the nature of the evaluation report, and (f) some pitfalls to avoid.

Study Questions

1. To what extent do program evaluation and student evaluation overlap? To what extent are they different?

2. What factors should be considered in determining the nature and scope of an evaluation program?

3. Discuss the pros and cons of evaluation programs designed primarily to provide data to program administrators (who then use the data in making decisions regarding the program) and evaluation programs in which the outside evaluators are involved in the "assessment of merit or worth" and hence make some decisions regarding the program.

4. Describe in your own words how program evaluation may be used in planning and policy making regarding music programs.

5. Outline the design of an evaluation program for a school music program with which you are familiar. Briefly describe the program and include information regarding (a) the functions of the evaluation, (b) the types of data to be sought, (c) the individuals who will be involved in the evaluation, (d) the steps, sequence, and calendar for the evaluation, and (e) the type of evaluation report projected.

REFERENCES

Arts IMPACT Evaluation Team. *Arts IMPACT: Curriculum for change, A summary report.* University Park, PA.: Pennsylvania State University (for the U.S. Office of Education), 1973.

Cronbach, L.J. *Designing evaluations of educational and social programs.* San Francisco, Calif.: Jossey-Bass, 1982.

Cronbach, L.J. et al. *Toward reform of program evaluation.* San Francisco, Calif.: Jossey-Bass, 1980.

House, E.R. Assumptions underlying evaluation models. In G.P. Madaus, M.S. Scriven, & D.L. Stufflebeam (Eds.), *Evaluation models: Viewpoints on educational and human services evaluation.* Boston: Kluwer-Nijhoff, 1983.

Joint Committee on Standards for Educational Evaluation. *Standards for evaluation of educational programs, projects, and materials.* New York: McGraw-Hill, 1981.

Madaus, G.P., Scriven, M.S., & Stufflebeam, D.L. (Eds.). *Evaluation models: Viewpoints on educational and human services evaluation.* Boston: Kluwer-Nijhoff, 1983.

Nevo, D. The conceptualization of educational evaluation: An analytical review of the literature. *Review of Educational Research,* 1983, *53,* 117–128.

Scriven, M. The methodology of evaluation. In R.E. Stake (Ed.), *AERA monograph series on curriculum evaluation* (No. 1). Chicago: Rand McNally, 1967.

Stake, R.E. *Evaluating the arts in education: A responsive approach.* Columbus, Ohio: Charles E. Merrill, 1975.

Stake, R.E. Setting standards for educational evaluation. *Evaluation News,* 1981, *2*(2), 148–152.

Stufflebeam, D.L. et al. *Educational evaluation and decision-making.* Itasca, Ill.: F.E. Peacock, 1971.

Stufflebeam, D.L. *Meta-evaluation* (Occasional Paper No. 3). Kalamazoo, Mich.: Western Michigan University, Dec. 1974.

Talmadge, H. Evaluation of program. In H.E. Mitzel (Ed.), *Encyclopedia of Educational Research* (5th ed.) (Vol. 2). New York: Free Press, 1982.

Tyler, R.W. *Basic principles of curriculum and instruction.* Chicago: University of Chicago Press, 1950.

14

Future Concerns

No mortal can predict the future with anything approaching total accuracy. The remaining years of the 1980s and the 1990s undoubtedly will see changes due to technological advances and changing concepts of education, but the precise substance of those changes and how they may influence measurement is hard to specify. This chapter offers speculation regarding accountability and competency testing, potential reactions against testing, cultural bias considerations, an aesthetics versus achievement issue, and a few technological considerations. It concludes by stating some guiding principles that probably will not change.

ACCOUNTABILITY AND COMPETENCY TESTING

Education experiences many trends, counter-trends, and would-be trends that excite theoreticians and generate many articles. Sometimes the general public becomes enamored of a trend, and legislators, corporate executives, and various education-minded activists direct attention to schools in accordance with the trend. After a time, the trend dissipates and attention turns elsewhere, with or without any enduring changes.

In the early 1970s there was a hue and cry regarding *accountability,* as inspection of journals and books from that time indicates. The concept that educational institutions and educators should be accountable for their professional actions was manifested in various ways. In one view, accountability meant showing how resources were expended and for what benefits. In another, accountability meant holding teachers accountable for their students' test performances. In yet another, accountability meant a good faith effort to meet the best standards of professional pedagogical practice, whatever they might be. Despite the earlier concern for accountability, the editors of the fifth edition of the *Encyclopedia of Educational Research* (Mitzel, 1982) did not include an article on accountability in that very comprehensive survey of educational theory, thought, practice, opinion, and research. Remaining results of the accountability movement evidently have been channeled into other areas.

Accountability was and is of concern to music educators for several reasons. Ensemble directors, in school as well as college settings, who work in highly performance-oriented environments often experience a very direct form of accountability through their general public's reactions to contest-festival ratings, shows, concerts, and recitals. For them, accountability might be merely an explicit formalization of existing implicit procedures. For other music educators, accountability might mean a new concern not only for performance quality but also for what their students specifically are learning about music. Another reason for concern is that in their desire to make their schools accountable for "academic" skills, which usually mean reading, writing, and arithmetic and perhaps science and social studies, administrators and policy makers might place less emphasis on and direct fewer resources toward music and the other arts.

Nash (1979) expressed other general reasons for concern about accountability. He was wary that a concern for short-term goals would reduce the integrative aspects of education. Furthermore, just who is accountable for what? Nash expresses the belief (p. 328) that

> To hold the teacher accountable not only for what she [sic] does but also for what students learn is in conflict with certain humanistic assumptions about the freedom of people to respond as they will to others' inputs. Making the teacher accountable for precise student learnings may merely serve to increase the dependence of the student on the teacher.

There is considerable question regarding how much control teachers have over students' lives. How are they any more accountable than peers, parents, "media," and others who influence students? Who ultimately makes decisions about goals and measures of performance? Are they the same individuals who are responsible for reaching the goals?

Despite such criticisms, accountability is not a bad thing if it is used to structure education in a positive way. Teachers *should* use their best skills to enhance the learning of all students, and evaluation of their efforts can be useful. Bunda (1979) distinguishes between evaluation and accountability by noting that evaluation is aimed at overall programs while accountability assumes personal responsibility of teachers. Whereas accountability assumes goals with self-evident value and implies causation, evaluation requires research for validating goals and establishing causation.

While interest in accountability as such may now have waned or be expressed differently, interest in competency testing, which may be conceived as a metamorphosis of accountability, assuredly has not waned. Music educators may have to solve important measurement problems related to the establishment and testing of competencies. As McKenna (1982) notes, the major responsibility for competency has been shifted to students! This represents a change from the demands for competency-based teacher education (CBTE) that were strong in the early and mid-1970s; in many cases CBTE programs were developed from an advocacy rather than a research base and proved too difficult to implement in many teacher education settings. Competency testing of students represents, for some, a change in social policy from society providing a minimum of educational services to the individual being responsible for meeting minimal educational standards set by society (Cohen & Haney, 1980). Competency testing, as it now is generally understood, usually means testing for minimum competencies in secondary school students prior to graduation; it did not result from educators' activities (Tittle, 1982).

According to Blau (1980), some researchers, legislators, employers, university officials, and "back-to-basics" advocates favor competency testing, usually because of a wish to motivate students and/or use test results to improve teaching and curricula. Some educators and parents oppose competency testing because of what they perceive as unfairness to minorities, a lack of validity and reliability in the tests, the danger that teachers will "teach to the test," a possibility that all schools will pursue mediocrity, and negative consequences of "labeling" children.

Blau believes, on the basis of his psychological work with school-children, that students do not like competency tests because the tests are perceived as a waste of time and/or just another way in which adults and "society" may harass them.

As Tittle describes them, most competency tests are in a multiple-choice format. Sometimes they are developed by the state or a contractor thereof; sometimes they are adapted commercial tests. Competencies must be validated in terms of school curricula or life skills that they supposedly represent: Opportunity to learn or develop the competencies is critical. If expert judgments are the basis for validation, documentation of those judgments is critical. Reliability should be the consistency with which competent and noncompetent people are classified correctly. Item bias and material offensive to minorities and women may be a problem. Grise (1980) notes that flexible scheduling and test settings, recording answers, mechanical aids, and revised test formats (including opportunities for large print and tactile reading, sign language, and auditory presentations) are possible to accommodate the needs of some handicapped students.

Given the reality of competency testing, there are several issues with implications for the measurement of musical behavior. One is recognition of any need for competency testing in music. Competencies usually are considered of prime importance in academic areas. If music education is perceived as an educational frill or as a strictly extracurricular activity, there is little if any need for statement or testing of musical competencies. If there is little need for musical competencies, perhaps there is little need for education to develop those competencies, especially given increasing costs and potential national priorities for mathematics, science, foreign language, and computer literacy. While failure to recognize any need for competency testing in music might save a lot of work in objective and test development, it might also place music education exclusively in the sphere of private lessons for the talented few. Justifying music education is beyond the scope of this book, but ability to prepare satisfactory measures of musical competencies may be important in showing that music is a viable and rigorous part of a comprehensive education.

A Nation at Risk (National Commission on Excellence in Education, 1983), which attracted considerable attention in the general public as well as the education community with statements such as "If an unfriendly foreign power had attempted to impose on America the mediocre educational performance that exists today, we might well have viewed it as an act of war" (p. 5) and "In effect, we have a cafeteria-style curriculum in which the appetizers and desserts can easily be mistaken for the main courses" (p. 18), recommended that the so-called "Five New Basics" (i.e., four years of English, three years of mathematics, three years of science, three years of social studies, one-half year of computer science) be the "foundation" for secondary curricula (p. 24). This recommendation, along with recommendations for foreign language proficiency (p. 26), increased emphasis on grades (p. 27), more rigorous college admission standards (p. 27), a more effective or longer school day or lengthened school year (p. 29), and "far more homework" (p. 29), could be interpreted as a threat to the arts and any curricular area that appears to lack rigor and means for students to demonstrate excellence. The report does contain statements that allow for the arts if they are sufficiently rigorous and serious, for example, "A high level of shared education in these Basics, together with work in the *fine and performing arts* [emphasis added] and foreign language, constitutes the mind and spirit of our culture" (pp. 24–25).

> The high school curriculum should also provide students with programs requiring rigorous effort in subjects that advance students' personal, educational, and occupational goals, such as the fine and performing arts and vocational education. These areas complement the New Basics, and *they should demand the same level of performance* as the Basics [emphasis added], (p. 26)

> The curriculum in the crucial eight grades leading to the high school years should be specifically designed to provide a sound base for study in those and later years in such areas as English language development and writing, computational and problem solving skills, science, social studies, foreign language, and the arts. (pp. 26–27)

Thus, rightly or wrongly, there may be considerable pressure for the arts, including music, to show over and over again that they are viable curricular areas that hold students to standards of excellence and develop competencies.

If competency testing is accepted as vital for music, questions arise regarding what the competencies should be. One popular dictionary (Woolf, 1974, p. 155) simply defines "competency" as "competence," which in turn is defined as "adequate means of subsistence" or "fitness, ability." Tittle (1982), as mentioned earlier, said that competencies must be validated in terms of the curriculum or life skills. What are musical life skills? What in the curriculum is really important for people to know and be able to do musically?* While numerous curriculum guides, articles, and beliefs about goals, objectives, and would-be competencies exist, development of competency tests must be preceded by documented construction of competency statements that are related to the curriculum that those who will be tested will undergo. Simply accepting what a curriculum guide or some "blue ribbon" committee of music educators says will not be sufficient.

Given competency statements, appropriate measures are necessary. As this book has demonstrated, there are ample ways to measure musical knowledge, performance, and attitudes. Competency implies meeting a standard, though, and where does one set a standard? One older procedure for multiple-choice tests (Nedelsky, 1954) involves systematically eliminating (through educated guesses) in order responses that the lowest D, C, B, and A students "should" be able to answer correctly. The reciprocals of the remaining responses (e.g., one quarter in an item where 1 of 5 responses has been eliminated, one half where 3 of 5 have been eliminated) are added together to form, along with an addition of an estimated standard deviation multiplied by a constant, criterion scores for various grade levels. Ebel (1972, pp. 492–496) discusses five approaches for setting minimum scores on tests where certification is an issue. One is to require passing the test with a perfect score, which is unrealistic because no test is perfect. Another is to set an arbitrary percentage of items, which may be modified by setting a minimum passing score halfway between the "ideal" percentage and the chance score percentage or by taking into account relevance and difficulty of particular items. A third approach is essentially a norm-referenced one in which a passing score is set with consideration for how many people "should" pass in accordance with some policy decision. A fourth approach sets an arbitrary percentage of items to be answered correctly but allows for modification if too many or too few people pass. Ebel's fifth approach suggests administering the test to a large sample of practitioners and setting the passing criterion

---

*Ironically, competencies in curricular areas other than language and mathematics may be more prone to legal challenge than competencies in those "basic" areas because other areas lack the relative racial and ethnic neutrality of basic language and mathematical skills (Tractenberg, 1980).

in accordance with those practitioners' scores: If increased standards are desired, the score earned by only the upper 10 or 15 percent of practitioners could be the passing score for would-be practitioners. Extended to tests of musical competency, this approach suggests that test scores of some identified musically literate adults should be the basis for establishing passing scores on musical competency examinations. There is no easy way to set justifiable standards, and someone with authority will have to make any final decisions.

However and wherever standards are set, one must consider what, if anything, will be done with students who are assessed as musically "incompetent." Is remedial education in order? Does musical "incompetence" really matter? Why?

Time will indicate what becomes of the possibility of and need for competency testing in music. The history of education suggests that any strongly voiced advocacy eventually meets opposition. Nevertheless, competency testing seems to have the general public's approval, so it may be advantageous to explore competency testing in music.

REACTIONS AGAINST TESTING

Reactions against testing are nothing new, and it is inevitable that there will be negative criticisms of how tests are constructed, used, and interpreted. Music tests, while generally not having the "visibility" of tests of "academic" areas or intelligence, are no exception. Burns (1979), in a book that is sharply critical of educational testing, expressed a belief that tests are abused, with too much blame for the abuse placed on test users rather than developers (p. 3). Among conditions leading to abuse are (a) the misleading nature of percentile ranks, due to uncertainty regarding the norm group and the fact that a small difference in score could make a large difference in percentile rank (pp. 23–27), (b) the likely departure of a distribution of test scores from normality that causes misleading interpretations of standard scores and deviations (p. 41), and (c) the nonequal distribution of grade equivalent scores among raw scores (pp. 64–65).

Any test score is an estimate of what someone appears to know or be able to do, in accordance with stated or implied objectives as they are represented by particular items. It is not perfect, and it is not unchangeable. While test scores can help a general music teacher make a decision about grades, a private studio teacher make a decision about whether or not someone should study an instrument, or a college professor decide whether a music major knows "enough" music history, test scores in and of themselves are only imperfect pieces of evidence. Just as it is unethical to classify someone as mentally retarded because of one test score, it is unethical to classify someone as unmusical or a musical failure because of one test score.

As the next few years unfold, complaints about music testing may occur. Complaints about auditions and rated music festivals certainly are nothing new. It will behoove those who are responsible for measuring musical behavior to ensure that their measures be carefully planned, administered, and interpreted in as consistently fair a way as possible. A test should not be a threat: It should be an opportunity.

CULTURAL BIAS CONSIDERATIONS

Cultural differences abound in society. Differences that exist from a particular vantage point may be intrinsic, as in language or religion, or extrinsic, as in dress or speech patterns. Differences may be the basis for a subculture's "peoplehood." Cultural diversity, resulting from culturally different groups zealously transmitting and guarding their identities, and cultural pluralism, a potentially desired state of affairs building on existing cultural diversity, are contemporary concerns (Pratte, 1982). The possibility of bias for or against one culture or another means that test takers must consider cultural fairness, representation, and stereotyping.

Validity is the extent to which a test measures what it is supposed to measure; culturally "unfair" test results conceivably are a validity problem. Invalid tests, that is, tests inappropriate to a particular purpose, will yield invalid results. Is invalidity as a function of cultural bias inherent in tests? Regarding validity, Wolf (1982) indicates that bias probably is more of a philosophical than a psychometric issue. Values must be attached to various possible outcomes of testing; such attachment generally is a matter for public policy makers rather than measurement specialists. The American Psychological Association (1974, p. 2), in setting forth its standards for constructing and using tests, says

> Some unfairness may be built into a test, for example, requiring an inordinately high level of verbal ability to comprehend the instructions of a non-verbal test. Many of the social ills at-

tributed to tests, however, seem more a result of the ways in which tests have been used than of characteristics of the tests themselves; for example, errors in administration, failure to consider the appropriateness of normative data, failure to choose an appropriate test, use of incorrect assumptions about the causes of a low or deviant test score, or administrative rigidity in using test scores for making decisions.

Any test should be written and administered in a way that affords test takers a fair chance to understand it. This means language adjustments when the student's language is not English; it means adjustments in test format for students with various handicapping conditions.

Racist and sexist stereotypes should be avoided in constructing test items. Names that would portray any particular identifiable ethnic group in a negative manner should be avoided in test items that describe characteristics of particular individuals. A hypothetical person should not be referred to exclusively as a "he" or a "she" when in fact that person could be of either gender, as in "A teacher wishes to . . . she. . . ." or "A student practices . . . he. . . ."*
If a person in a particular role could be a "he" *or* a "she," the pronoun representation should, accordingly, be "he or she."

Using varied musical styles and excerpts within styles for testing purposes might alleviate musical cultural biases. While the curriculum determines the content of achievement tests, test material need not be limited to the teacher's favorites. Concepts of form can be tested (and taught) through popular music and folk music of various cultures as well as art music. Many musical works, including contemporary works, can be the basis for essay items requiring descriptions of musical characteristics. Poland's (1970) study of music history and theory texts, eminence rankings, and available recordings suggested that the core of "serious" music study is built around Bach, Beethoven, Brahms, Haydn, and Mozart. Radocy and Boyle (1979, pp. 229–231) described an increasing preference among children and adolescents for rock music as they move to higher grade levels. Perhaps emphasizing varied styles in music tests could place more importance on

---

*The rule that masculine pronouns function generically and are understood to mean either gender would be fine except for glaring inconsistencies: In much educational and therapeutic writing a student, client, administrator, or member of the general public is a "he" but somehow a teacher or therapist is a "she"! There are female students and male teachers.

expanded listening and musical awareness, if not expanded preferences. Again, time will tell if musical biases are a future concern.

AESTHETICS VERSUS ACHIEVEMENT

Aesthetics "versus" achievement might be a non-issue, but it is possible that aesthetic education advocates may view extensive testing, whether of a "competency" nature or otherwise, as somehow hampering music education's aesthetic qualities due to excessive concentration on musical achievement, both in cognitive knowledge about music and in performance. Since a test elicits a sample of behavior, which may be anything observable, testing is not incompatible with any experience, including the aesthetic. Eisner (1982) notes that aesthetics deals with feelings, which are aroused by already existing art works. In the case of music, the artwork "unfolds" as it is created or recreated during the listening experiences; contemplation of the music supposedly involves feelings. Observing and obtaining information about a person's feelings need not degrade or debase those feelings, especially if the person understands that there are no "right" answers. Of course, if one believes that some aesthetic experiences aroused by "good" music "ought" to happen in a certain way there may be "right" answers.

Eisner (1982) also notes that aesthetic education varies in its conception and curricular approaches. One approach calls for in depth separate programs in each of the fine arts. Another is an "integrated" arts approach in which all art forms basically comprise one curricular area. Yet another attempts to stress "well-made forms" in all curricular areas; this is an arts *in* education approach. Test (and course) content in music might differ from what is customary in music classes in an integrated arts approach; it might differ radically in an arts in education approach. Yet the principles of good test construction and program evaluation need not be altered drastically.

Perhaps "aesthetics versus achievement," if it arises as an issue, will be especially important in performance-oriented programs. Program evaluation based on what students know about music in general and the music they perform as well as how they feel about it may help maintain a balanced program that can articulate with all the curricular viewpoints.

TECHNOLOGICAL CONSIDERATIONS

Existing and imminent technological developments may facilitate some aspects of measurement of musical behavior. Analyses of test data, administration, and performance evaluation may become more sophisticated, which will bring new challenges to test makers and evaluators.

There is no shortage of computer facilities and programs for very sophisticated analyses of test data. Huge numbers of test papers can be scored and summarized in various ways. Ever-increasing numbers of programs will become practical for microcomputers ("personal" computers) so that much analytical work can be done without the services of large, sometimes distant computer centers and examination services. Naive faith in any computer or program is useless, of course; the famous GIGO (garbage in, garbage out) principle will continue to apply, and one always needs to understand what the output means.

One intriguing idea that may become more practical and commonplace is sequential, incremental, or tailored testing. Experimented with in the early days of computer-assisted instruction (Hansen, 1968; Radocy, 1971) and conjectured as an impact on testing of technological development in the 1970s (Thorndike, 1971), the technique may be more versatile when it can be programmed into personal computers, although there are some sequencing problems for musical application. Essentially, sequential or incremental testing says that not every person needs to answer every item in a test if certain assumptions can be made about whether or not a person would have answered a non-administered item correctly. The individual test taker begins at a point in a test determined arbitrarily or possibly on the basis of his or her response history in previous tests. For example, in a 50-item test of increasing difficulty, a student might begin with item 25. If he or she answers correctly, he or she might branch ahead to item 30 (an "increment" of 5). A miss on item 30 might branch the student back to item 27. The student will move through the test in a sequence determined by success or failure on particular items; a criterion number of successive misses will end the test. Some students would complete the test by answering relatively few items because they have a good deal or very little of the necessary information. Problems include constructing an item sequence that is in a reliable difficulty order and assuming that a partial test is equivalent to a complete test. Unless a Guttman scale could be obtained (see Chapter 9), which is nearly impossible for most achievement tests where there is no one hierarchy of difficulty, it is unlikely that items can be ordered reliably. Yet, from the standpoint of the individual learner, a formative evaluation in a sequential testing format that stresses the particular student's needs, as indicated by his or her response history, still could be useful. Problems of test equivalence could be assessed via the little known but rigorous Medley (1957) method, which uses analysis of variance procedures to see if two tests rank the students in the same order and have equivalent variances of measurement errors, obtained scores, and means. Angoff (1971, pp. 568–586) discuss other complex methods for equating test forms in various combinations of random and non-random groupings of examinees.

If physical aspects of desired musical performances can be correlated with favorable subjective performance judgments, it is conceivable that a machine could evaluate at least individual tones and simple melodic excerpts. Modern spectral analysis equipment enables analysis of tones into frequency and intensity information as they change across milliseconds of time. There are so many concerns and subtleties in performance, though, that it is unlikely that much progress regarding complete evaluation of "real" performances will be made in the near future.

SUMMARY: SOME THINGS STAY THE SAME

Regardless of technological advances, philosophical arguments, attempts to eliminate inappropriate uses of tests, or the spread of competency testing, measurement of musical behavior should continue to be guided by certain principles. This book has made all the following points at one time or another, and they provide a fitting closure:

1. Musical knowledge, skills, and attitudes are evaluated through behaviors and/or products resulting from such knowledge, skills, and attitudes.

2. Anything that exists can be measured in terms of what is acceptable as evidence of its existence and amount thereof.

3. Music is human behavior, so the measurement of musical behavior may employ techniques from any discipline dealing with human behavior.

4. Systematic measures provide enhanced sources of information for making decisions about what a person's musical behavior indicates.

5. Any measure is developed in relation to stated or implied objectives.

6. Measures, regardless of format, must have some consistency in their application and interpretation.

7. Measures, regardless of format, must provide information that is related rationally and empirically to the underlying objectives.

8. Measures are evaluated in terms of their conceptual logic, practicality, and utility.

9. Care and concern in all phases of test construction and administration are essential.

10. While some measurement techniques may be relatively more objective than others, subjectivity is inherent in evaluating musical behaviors.

11. A test score or audition result is only an estimate of someone's status: It is neither infallible nor immutable.

12. Probing people's musical knowledge, skills, and attitudes does not alter music's stature as an art or craft.

Study Questions

1. Consider potential difficulties regarding competency testing, cultural bias, and testing's influence on aesthetic experiences. How should the education of a prospective music educator or therapist address those difficulties?

2. Make a list of some designated "competencies" that you believe a beginning music educator or therapist should have.

3. Should experienced music teachers and/or therapists have to pass competency tests as do beginning teachers and/or therapists? Why or why not?

4. Should minimum passing scores on competency tests be adjusted for members of particular ethnic groups? for military veterans? for men? for women? for people willing to work in "difficult" schools or other institutions? Why or why not?

5. As a result of reading this book, how will you react differently to taking tests than you have before?

6. As a result of reading this book, how will you write tests or construct other evaluation procedures differently than you might have before?

REFERENCES

American Psychological Association. *Standards for educational and psychological tests.* Washington, D.C.: American Psychological Association, 1974.

Angoff, W.H. Scales, norms, and equivalent scores. In R.L. Thorndike (Ed.), *Educational measurement* (2nd ed.). Washington, D.C.: American Council on Education, 1971.

Blau, T.H. Minimum competency testing: Psychological implications for students. In R.M. Jaeger & C.K. Tittle (Eds.), *Minimum competency achievement testing.* Berkeley, Calif.: McCutchan, 1980.

Bunda, M.A. Accountability and evaluation. *Theory into Practice,* 1979, *18,* 357–362.

Burns, E. *The development, use, and abuse of educational tests.* Springfield, Ill.: Charles C Thomas, 1979.

Cohen, D.K., & Haney, W. Minimums, competency testing, and social policy. In R.M. Jaeger & C.K. Tittle (Eds.), *Minimum competency achievement testing.* Berkeley, Calif.: McCutchan, 1980.

Ebel, R.L. *Essentials of educational measurement.* Englewood Cliffs, N.J.: Prentice-Hall, 1972.

Eisner, E.W. Aesthetic education. In H.E. Mitzel (Ed.), *Encyclopedia of educational research* (5th ed.) (Vol. 1). New York: Free Press, 1982.

Grise, P.J. Florida's minimum competency testing program for handicapped students. *Exceptional Children,* 1980, *47,* 186–191.

Hansen, D.N. An investigation of computer-based science testing. In D.N. Hansen, W. Dick, & H.T. Lippert (Prep.), *Semiannual progress report* (FSU CAI Center report No. 6). Tallahassee: Florida State University Computer-Assisted Instruction Center, 1968.

McKenna, B. Competency-based teacher education. In H.E. Mitzel (Ed.), *Encyclopedia of educational research* (5th ed.) (Vol. 1). New York: Free Press, 1982.

Medley, D.M. *A general procedure for testing the equivalence of two tests.* Paper presented at the meeting of the National Council on Measurement Usage in Education, New York, February 1957.

Mitzel, H.E. (Ed.). *Encyclopedia of educational research* (5th ed.) (Vols. 1–4). New York: Free Press, 1982.

Nash, P.A. A humanistic perspective. *Theory into Practice,* 1979, *18,* 323–329.

National Commission on Excellence in Education. *A nation at risk: The imperative for educational reform* (Stock No. 065-000-00177-2). Washington, D.C.: U.S. Government Printing Office, 1983.

Nedelsky, L. Absolute grading standards for objective tests. *Educational and Psychological Measurement*, 1954, *14*, 3–19.

Poland, W. The content of graduate studies in music education: Music history and music theory. In H.L. Cady (Ed.), *Graduate studies in music education*. Columbus: Ohio State University School of Music, 1970.

Pratte, R. Culture and education policy. In H.E. Mitzel (Ed.), *Encyclopedia of educational research* (5th ed.) (Vol. 1). New York: Free Press, 1982.

Radocy, R.E. *Development of a test for the nonperformance aspects of music education* (Grant No. OEG-2-700018 [509]). Washington, D.C.: U.S. Office of Education, 1971.

Radocy, R.E., & Boyle, J.D. *Psychological foundations of musical behavior.* Springfield, Ill.: Charles C Thomas, 1979.

Thorndike, R.L. Educational measurement for the seventies. In R.L. Thorndike (Ed.), *Educational measurement*. Washington, D.C.: American Council on Education, 1971.

Tittle, C.K. Competency testing. In H.E. Mitzel (Ed.), *Encyclopedia of educational research* (5th ed.) (Vol. 1). New York: Free Press, 1982.

Tractenberg, P.L. Testing for minimum competency: A legal analysis. In R.M. Jaeger & C.K. Tittle (Eds.), *Minimum competency achievement testing.* Berkeley, Calif.: McCutchan, 1980.

Wolf R.M. Validity of tests. In H.E. Mitzel (Ed.), *Encyclopedia of educational research* (5th ed.) (Vol. 4). New York: Free Press, 1982.

Woolf, H.B. (Ed.). *The Merriam-Webster dictionary.* New York: Pocket Books, 1974.

Appendix

Selected Published Music Tests

Bentley, A. (1966). *Measures of Musical Abilities*. London: George G. Harrap & Co. Ltd. (Educational Department, P.O. Box 70, 182–184 High Holborn, London WC1V 7BR, England)

Colwell, R. (1969–1970). *Music Achievement Tests*. Urbana, Ill.: MAT. (406 W. Michigan, Urbana, Ill. 61801)

Colwell, R. (1979). *Music Competency Tests*. Morristown, N.J.: Silver Burdett. (250 James Street, Morristown, N.J. 17960)

Drake, R. M. (1957). *Drake Musical Aptitude Tests*. Sarasota, Fla.: Raleigh M. Drake. (711 Beach Road, # 106, Sarasota, Fla. 34242)

Farnum, S. E. (1969). *Farnum Music Test*. Riverside, R.I.: Bond Publishing Co. (787 Willitt Avenue, Riverside, R.I. 02915)

Farnum, S. E. (1969). *The Farnum String Scale: A Performance Scale for all String Instruments*. Winona, Minn.: Hal Leonard. (8112 W. Bluemound Rd., P.O. Box 13819, Milwaukee, Wis. 53213)

Gordon, E. (1971). *Iowa Tests of Music Literacy*. Iowa City: The University of Iowa. (Publications Order Department, Iowa City, Iowa 52242)

Gordon, E. (1982). *Intermediate Measures of Music Audiation*. Chicago: G.I.A. Publications. (7404 S. Mason, Chicago, Ill. 60638)

Gordon, E. (1965). *Musical Aptitude Profile*. Boston: Houghton Mifflin. (Riverside Publishing, 8420 Bryn Mawr Ave., Chicago, Ill. 60631)

Gordon, E. (1978). *Primary Measures of Music Audiation*. Chicago: G.I.A. Publications. (7404 S. Mason, Chicago, Ill. 60638)

Long, N. H. (1970). *Indiana-Oregon Music Discrimination Test*. Bloomington, Ind.: Midwest Music Tests. (1304 E. University, Bloomington, Ind. 47401)

Seashore, C. E., Lewis, D., & Saetveit, J. (1939, 1960). *Seashore Measures of Musical Talents*. New York: The Psychological Corporation. (757 Third Avenue, New York, N.Y. 10017)

Simons, G. M. (1974). *Simons Measurements of Music Listening Skills.* Chicago: Stoelting Company. (1350 S. Kostner Avenue, Chicago, Ill. 60623)

Watkins, J. G., & Farnum, S. E. (1954, 1962). *Watkins:Farnum Performance Scale.* Winona, Minn.: Hal Leonard. (8112 W. Bluemound Rd., P.O. Box 13819, Milwaukee, Wis. 53213)

Wing, H. D. (1961). *Wing Standardised Tests of Musical Intelligence.* Windsor, England: NFER Publishing Company. (Darville House, 2 Oxford Road East, Windsor SL4 1DF England)

Author Index

Citations to jointly authored works are listed by the first author only.

Subject Index

327